REINTERPRETING RUSSIA

Edited by

GEOFFREY HOSKING

Professor of Russian History, School of Slavonic and East European Studies, University of London

and

ROBERT SERVICE

Fellow of St Antony's College, University of Oxford

ARNOLD

A member of the Hodder Headline Group
LONDON • SYDNEY • AUCKLAND
Co-published in the USA by Oxford University Press, Inc., New York

First published in Great Britain in 1999 by
Arnold, a member of the Hodder Headline Group
338 Euston Road, London NW1 3BH

http://www.arnoldpublishers.com

Co-published in the United States of America by
Oxford University Press Inc.
198 Madison Avenue, New York, NY 10016

British Library Cataloguing in Publication Data
A catalogue entry for this book is available from the British Library

Library of Congress Cataloging-in-Publication Data
A catalog record for this book is available from the Library of Congress

Production Editor: Julie Delf
Production Controller: Iain McWilliams
Cover Design: Terry Griffiths

ISBN 0 340 73134 6 (hb)
ISBN 0 340 73135 4 (pb)

1 2 3 4 5 6 7 8 9 10

Typeset by J&L Composition Ltd, Filey, North Yorkshire
Printed and bound in Great Britain by
MPG Books, Bodmin, Cornwall

What do you think about this book? Or any other Arnold title?
Please send your comments to feedback.arnold@hodder.co.uk.

Contents

Contributors

Roger Bartlett
School of Slavonic and East European Studies, University of London, UK
Human Capital. The Settlement of Foreigners in Russia 1762–1804 (1979);
Editor, *Land Commune and Peasant Community in Russia (1990)*; Editor
with E. Donnert, *Johann Georg Eisen (1717–1779). Ausgewählte Schriften.
Deutsche Volksaufklärung und Leibeigenschaft im Russischen Reich* (1998)

Simon Dixon
Department of History, University of Glasgow, UK
'The Orthodox Church and the Workers of St Petersburg, 1880–1914', in
H. McLeod (ed.) *European Religion in the Age of Great Cities 1830–1930*
(1995); Editor, *Britain and Russia in the Age of Peter the Great: Historical
Documents* (1998); *The Modernisation of Russia, 1676–1825* (1999)

Peter Gatrell
Professor of Economic History, University of Manchester, UK
The Tsarist Economy, 1850–1917 (1986); *Government, Industry and Re-
armament in Russia, 1900–1914: The Last Argument of Tsarism* (1994); *A
Whole Empire Walking: Refugees in the Russian Empire during the First
World War* (1999)

Geoffrey Hosking
Professor of Russian History, School of Slavonic and East European
Studies, University of London, UK
The Awakening of the Soviet Union, (2nd edition, 1991); *A History of the
Soviet Union* (3rd edition, 1992); *Russia: People and Empire, 1552–1917*
(1997); Editor, with Robert Service, *Russian Nationalism Past and Present*
(1995); Editor, with G. Schöpflin, *Myths and Nationhood* (1997)

Lindsey Hughes
School of Slavonic and East European Studies, University of London, UK
Sophia Regent of Russia 1657–1704 (1990); 'Peter the Great's Two Weddings: Changing Images of Women in a Transitional Age', in R. Marsh (ed.) *Women in Russia and Ukraine* (1996); *Russia in the Age of Peter the Great* (1998)

Catriona Kelly
Reader in Russian, New College, University of Oxford, UK
Petrushka, the Russian Carnival Puppet Theatre (1990); *A History of Russian Women's Writing, 1820–1992* (1994); Editor, with David Shepherd, *Constructing Russian Culture in the Age of Revolution* (1998); *An Introduction to Russian Cultural Studies* (1998); Editor, *Utopias: Russian Modernist Texts 1905–1940* (1999)

John Klier
Department of Hebrew and Jewish Studies, University College London, UK
Russia Gathers Her Jews: The Origins of the Jewish Question in Russia, 1772–1825 (1986); Editor, with S. Lambroza, *Pogroms: Anti-Jewish Violence in Modern Russian History* (1991); *Imperial Russia's Jewish Question, 1855–1881* (1995)

Dominic Lieven
London School of Economics
Russia and the Origins of the First World War (1983); *Russia's Rulers Under the Old Regime* (1989); *The Aristocracy in Europe, 1815–1914* (1992); *Nicholas II, Emperor of All the Russias* (1993)

David Moon
Department of History, University of Newcastle upon Tyne, UK
Russian Peasants and the Tsarist Legislation on the Eve of Reform, 1825–1855 (1992); 'Peasant Migration and the Settlement of Russia's Frontiers, 1551–1897' *Historical Journal*, 40, 1997; *The Russian Peasantry, 1600–1930: The World the Peasants Made* (1999)

Thomas C. Owen
Professor of History, Louisiana State University, USA
The Corporation under Russian Law, 1800–1917 (1991); *Russian Corporate Capitalism from Peter the Great to Perestroika* (1995); 'Autocracy and the Rule of Law in Russian Economic History', in J. Sachs and K. Pistor (eds) *The Rule of Law and Economic Reform in Russia* (1997)

Maureen Perrie
Reader in Russian History, Centre for Russian and East European Studies, University of Birmingham, UK
The Agrarian Policy of the Russian Socialist-Revolutionary Party (1976); *The Image of Ivan the Terrible in Russian Folklore* (1987); *Pretenders and Popular Monarchism in Early Modern Russia* (1995)

David Saunders
Reader in the History of the Russian Empire, University of Newcastle upon Tyne, UK
The Ukrainian Impact on Russian Culture 1750–1850 (1985); *Russia in the Age of Reaction and Reform, 1880–1881* (1992)

Robert Service
St Antony's College, University of Oxford, UK
The Bolshevik Party in Revolution. A Study in Organisational Change (1979); *Lenin: A Political Life*, Vols 1–3 (1985–1995); *The Russian Revolution, 1900–1927* (1986; 3rd edition, 1999); *A History of Twentieth-Century Russia* (1997)

Steve A. Smith
Professor of History, University of Essex, UK
Red Petrograd: Revolution in the Factories, 1917–1918 (1983)

Introduction

ROBERT SERVICE

There is something comforting for travellers, as they look at foreign countries, in concluding that things have always been the same. The delight of visiting alien cities and villages comes to a large extent from the *frisson* of feeling submerged in 'history'. There is always some degree of pleasure in believing that whereas one's own country is vibrant and changeable, other countries have a strong traditional essence. It helps us to reconcile ourselves to change itself. And also, let it be admitted, to give us a sense of superiority. No traveller observes with an unconditioned eye.

No country has been subjected to such treatment as intensely as Russia. For centuries Russia has had a static image – eternal Russia – characterized by barbarous rulers and an uncultured society. Russia has been depicted as the most uncivilized member of Europe's family of nations. Indeed, Russia is virtually a metaphor for non-Europeanness; and Russia and 'the West' are placed at opposite ends of a range of historical experience. This is not, however, a polarity shared exclusively by foreigners. Practically all Russian writers from the early nineteenth century onward took it as their premise that Russia was fundamentally different from countries to the west. Among these writers, furthermore, many suggested that the difference was greatly to Russia's disfavour. They became known as the Westernizers (*zapadniki*). They did not have the arena of public debate to themselves. In particular, they faced opponents – the so-called Slavophiles (*slavyanofily*), who took a more positive view of Russia and proposed that Russian traditions were superior to those of the rest of the world. Be that as it may, the Westernizers and the Slavophiles agreed that Russia for most of its history had been a very static society. The Westernizers wanted rapid future change on a 'Western' model; the Slavophiles aimed at avoiding 'Westernization' and hoped to build on existing religious and social traditions. But about the longevity of contemporary trends they had no dispute with each other.

Even after the October Revolution of 1917 there were writers in Russia who sought to demonstrate that the Soviet leadership had transformed the country less than had been claimed. Indeed the philosopher Nikolai Berdyaev, deported to Berlin in 1922, reflected that the ideological and social roots of Russian communism were to be found not in Marxism but in tsarism. Lenin and the early communists militantly repudiated this contention. But by the 1930s Iosif Stalin, who won the struggle for the political succession after Lenin's death in 1924, was himself urging that pride should be taken, albeit selective pride, in the traditions of the Russian state and people. This standpoint has not lost its appeal. In our own day it is occupied both by the Russian Communist Party of Gennadi Zyuganov and the Liberal-Democratic Party of Vladimir Zhirinovskii. Thus the case has continued to be put, by a wide variety of commentators and politicians, that several basic features of Russian history have persisted and flourished from time immemorial and these would be almost impossible to eliminate in a short period of rule.

But others have objected to the determinism of images of Eternal Russia. From Peter the Great onwards, several rulers and thinkers have proposed that Russian history has been capable of just as much plasticity as other countries and that the overlay of traditionalism can be removed by decisive political action. The Westernizers in the nineteenth century, while recognizing that life had been little changed over centuries, were confident that a massive transformation was feasible. This self-assurance was emulated by Lenin's communist generation in the early twentieth century. It was also the basic notion in the programme of Yegor Gaidar and the liberal economic reformers who supported President Boris Yeltsin at the start of the 1990s.

Both Lenin and Yeltsin represented the Soviet era not as a continuation but as a rupture with the Russia of tsarism. Of course, the consensus between the two leaders is not complete. Far from it: Yeltsin has asserted that the entire stretch of communist party rule was a totalitarian nightmare that chewed up everything beneficent in Russian political and social life. This was an analysis inaugurated by defeated Russian politicians, émigré writers and Western scholars. They noted the persistent features in Russia's distant and recent past; but they insisted that the creation of the communist one-party state was an event of genuinely new and universal importance. Communism broke the chain of Russian history. Prerevolutionary Russia may have been Europe's exotic plant, but it was still part of the same biological genus. The October Revolution marked it off from the rest of the garden. Such was the mainstay of Western writing on Russian history after the Second World War. Tsarism and totalitarianism were counterpoised – and the same contrast has been a feature of Russian debates after communism's fall.

It was the contemporary historians and social scientists who urged this case. Scholars who studied earlier centuries than the twentieth century tended to ignore them. Russian mediaevalists took no interest in Brezhnev;

students of Brezhnevite politics and economy were unmoved by the career of Ivan the Terrible. Moreover, there was a trend towards compartmentalization within specific periods. Political history became separated from economic history, and economic history separated from social and cultural history. Historians spake not unto literary critics and their silence was not unwelcome to those critics. Gradually, with extremely few exceptions, the academic community gave up paying attention to questions of *la longue durée*. We each of us had our little bits of Russia to keep us busy, and were content with what we had.

This myopia was rendered nonsensical by the onset of glasnost and perestroika under Mikhail Gorbachëv from the mid-1980s. The official Soviet establishment declared, with increasing stridency, that Russian national traditions from before 1917 should be accorded fair and positive scrutiny. The tone was set by Raisa Gorbachëv, who helped to lead the Soviet Cultural Foundation and protected Russian cultural heritage. Mikhail Gorbachëv himself walked the no man's land between Marxism-Leninism and Western social democracy, and issued a plea for support from all elements in society willing to support the gradual reform of the one-party regime. As his audacity increased and his difficulties mounted, he allowed nationalist critics of Marxism-Leninism to stand alongside him on his platform: the anti-communist Valentin Rasputin joined the Presidential Council. By the late 1980s it had become respectable for communist reformers to eulogize rural traditions, the peasantry and ancient Christian values and to include them on the agenda for the country's transformation.

The most vociferous advocate of Russian traditions was Boris Yeltsin, who reacted to his extrusion from the Soviet communist party central leadership in October 1987 by building up a political support-base in the Russian Soviet Federal Socialist Republic (RSFSR). From this vantage point Yeltsin could and did embarrass Gorbachëv politically, and in June 1991 he was elected RSFSR President. The communist opponents of Gorbachëv also used Russia as a base: in 1990 they formed a communist party for the RSFSR. While remaining formally subordinate to the USSR communist party, they opposed its reformist party policies. Both Yeltsin and Zyuganov in their different ways promoted Russian national interests. Then came the collapse of the USSR in December 1991. The very fact of Russia's state independence laid upon politicians and commentators the duty of explaining policies in the light of long-term interests. Even the Russian Communist Party, which had opposed the disintegration of the USSR, looked back fondly to many of the traditions of tsarist period and to the creation of an empire which only came to an end in 1991. Such was the popular disrepute of Marxism-Leninism that Zyuganov scarcely tried to defend Lenin and instead praised the Russian Orthodox Church as a historic protector of collectivist values.

Of course, in the political sense 'Russia' was a confusing term. There had been the Russian Empire, and then there was – within the Soviet

Union – the RSFSR, which was an 'historically contingent' phenomenon. The territory occupied by the RSFSR changed several times between 1917 and 1991, and was never referred to unambiguously as 'Russia'. With the collapse of the USSR, the RSFSR was redesignated the Russian Federation. In the new 1993 Constitution, moreover, the Russian Federation was mentioned interchangeably as Russia. Thus the state presently recognized as the largest successor state of the USSR is the first political entity to be known as Russia for three centuries, and all this has led to a massive wish – and indeed a massive need – to examine the historical origins of this Russia.

There is a struggle among Russian commentators about their versions of the country's history, and their contributions are conditioned by recent political events, for the commentators themselves have inevitably been influenced especially by their experience of the Soviet one-party state. First among the versions comes the old idea, resuscitated for the 1990s, that Russia has a permanent, ineradicable essence. Russian communist leader Gennadi Zyuganov explicitly holds this opinion. Russia, for him, is eternal in its basic features and has to have its eternity actively protected. A second version is that there are indeed essential features to Russia but that these features were cut off from their living sustenance by the October 1917 Revolution. It is this version that is proposed by Boris Yeltsin, who has maintained – since the late 1980s – that the Soviet dictatorship brutally interrupted a natural sequence of development. Even Yeltsin, however, admits that there was a nastiness about the tsarist rule. For others, this is an intolerable attack on the country's heritage. And so the third version, embodied by Alexander Solzhenitsyn's writings since the 1970s, is that tsarism was working for a better Russia and that only ill-luck and mis-judgement prevented the Russian Empire from evolving into something not only desirable for Russians but also a model for the rest of the world. Russia, according to Solzhenitsyn, had virtues that Europe would have done well to emulate.

Most commentators support one of these three versions. A fourth version, which contends that the Soviet one-party state was a great improvement on the Russian Empire and genuinely had the potential for constructing a humane state and society in Russia, has few supporters. Perhaps its greatest surviving exponent is the reformist communist Roy Medvedev. For him, the communist experiment remains an inspiration. Medvedev argues that Lenin had basically the right ideas and that only the onset of the Stalinist despotism diverted the country from the path of righteousness. Even Medvedev, however, has moderated his adulation of Lenin since the early 1990s.

Yet perhaps Medvedev has more sympathizers than do proponents of the fifth version of Russian history, who postulate that Russia can easily rid itself of its political, economic and cultural traditions, which are seen as amenable to rapid transformation. This was Peter the Great's contention.

It was also Lenin's. And in the 1990s it has been the argument of Yegor Gaidar. Under Gaidar, who was Yeltsin's prime minister in 1992, the guiding principle of governance was that the traditions of both tsarism and communism could be eliminated. Without delay Russia was to become a market economy and a political democracy. By 1993 Gaidar was out of government and his ideas were rejected by most politicians and commentators – along the range from the political left to the right – who urged that the new Russia had to be constructed with due respect for the country's traditions. Somehow, they declared, Russia had to remain 'true' to itself – whether that be its tsarist self, its communist self or both at the same time – if it was to maintain stability and enhance the conditions for social justice and popular material well-being.

These five versions of Russian history lie implicitly at the basis of the current attempts to make sense of the country. For Zyuganov there is Eternal Russia. For Yeltsin there is Russia Regained, a Russia successfully snatched back from the clutches of an inhuman alien ideology. For Solzhenitsyn, Russia remains the Lost Russia of the Tsar and Peasant. He asserts that national regeneration can occur only through a reversion to values that predate the twentieth century. In opposition to him there is the Soviet Russia of Medvedev. It is not a Russia that has ever existed since it largely excludes mention of the horrors of the Lenin years. Finally, there is the New Russia of Gaidar, a Russia that emulates the West – a Russia that has yet to be created and gives little sign of coming into existence. Truly, the Russian question involves a contest of extremely contradictory ideas.

It is worth pondering these ideas if only to remind ourselves that the writing of history is conditioned by the environment in which it is written. The polemics of Moscow are fuelled not only by a desire to comprehend the past but also by a desire to prescribe the future and dominate the present. Not for nothing do politicians such as Yeltsin, Zyuganov, Zhirinovskii and Gaidar let it be known what they think about Ivan the Terrible, Peter the Great, Lenin and Stalin. The oddity of all this is worth noting. No British prime minister since the First World War – with the exception of Winston Churchill, who wrote historical works as a means of earning a living – has provided a considered judgement on Alfred the Great, William the Conqueror or Oliver Cromwell. No French president has written at length about Louis XIV, Napoleon or de Gaulle. Russian leaders expatiate on history for two main reasons. The first is that there is a recent tradition, inherited by the communists from the nineteenth-century radical intelligentsia, of treating History as an inalienable element of any plausible world-view (*mirovozzrenie, Weltanschauung*) of politics, economics and culture. The second is that Russia, ever more openly since the mid-1980s, has been a country in search of an identity. To an even greater extent than Britain, Russia is a country that has lost an empire and not yet gained a role. Indeed Russia has not merely lost an empire. It has lost an ideology, a state structure and a whole way of life. History is an important instrumentality whereby political, economic, social and cultural change can be managed.

The lesson for historians – both in Russia and elsewhere – is to avoid becoming excessively influenced by the present conjuncture of Russian politics. Now that the USSR is no more, it is tempting to accept the continuities in Russian history as a permanent and unalterable fact. The commonplaces of recent Western journalism have begun again to resemble what appeared in the newspapers of the West at the start of the twentieth century. Then it was that the European and North American press treated Russia as a country that had always been exotic and barbaric.

The time is ripe to try to reinterpret Russia and its history. More is nowadays knowable about the Russian past than it was reasonable to hope would be possible. The communist and tsarist archives have for some years been more accessible than ever before. New documentary publications are appearing. Local and oral history is starting to be attempted. Fresh ideas, sometimes borrowed from the West, are being explored. Discussions have never been freer – and the classics of pre-revolutionary historiography are no longer banned. Western historians, furthermore, have been able to take their own measure of the past by visiting the country and conducting research without most of the old obstacles. Time was when scholars had to disguise their intentions in order to get a research-trip visa – and it was not unknown for notes to be taken away from scholars at the Soviet customs points.

Altogether, then, the moment has arrived to ask whether the conventional assumptions about Russian history in all their contradictory variety can withstand critical scrutiny. How is the turbulent, harrowing, inspiring Russian past to be understood? In setting about compiling this book, Geoffrey Hosking and I asked our contributors to range over the tsarist, communist and post-communist periods. The underlying questions in each chapter are the same: to what extent are deep continuities descernible in the history of Russia, and what explains the persistence of such continuities as are discernible? We had few preconceptions about the kind of book that might result from these questions, but we were sure that they should be asked.

The contributors came to a variety of conclusions. But it will be seen that nearly all of them find that continuity counts for more than discontinuity in Russian history, from tsars to presidents. Thus the visual arts, as Lindsey Hughes shows, retained a fascination with religious imagery throughout the three periods to a greater extent than is generally supposed. Cultural persistence is a key theme of the volume. It was the intention of the communists to suppress those aspects of continuity at variance with Marxism–Leninism, but they succeeded less than was thought at the time, and Stalin and Brezhnev found themselves identifying themselves with the Russian traditions that might consolidate their power. The consequence was that Russia, politically and economically as well as culturally, never underwent complete transformation. Dominic Lieven suggests that the primary cause was the geopolitical situation of the Russian Empire and its successor states, and this approach is paralleled by Peter Gatrell, Thomas Owen and Steve Smith in relation to economic organization and to attitudes to the market and entrepreneurialism.

Many assumptions about the discontinuities in Russian history, as David Saunders and David Moon affirm, derive from an overstatement of the rebelliousness of Russians. In fact the revolts have been the exception. Russia has been a surprisingly quiet and acquiescent country even in the raging twentieth century. Of course, the rulers have done much to keep Russia tranquil by maintaining a repressive state machinery and a highly hierarchical social structure. Roger Bartlett shows how the peasantry have always been kept poor, subordinate and separate. What makes this situation unpropitious for present-day reformers in town and countryside, as Geoffrey Hosking demonstrates, is the persistence of that nexus of little groupings, held together by both tradition and pressing material need, which repel unwanted interference by higher official authorities.

Their persistence over the centuries is caused by several factors. Russia, as Simon Dixon indicates, is a multireligious society; its rulers at their peril take a simplistic approach to problems of the variety of the people's beliefs. Similarly, John Klier stresses that Russia has always been a multi-ethnic society which could not be governed – even by Stalin at his most brutal – as if it were inhabited only by Russians. Religious and ethnic diversity puts limits on the scope of governance from above. What rulers wanted, needless to say, has changed a lot from tsar to tsar, from tsar to commissar, from commissar to commissar and from commissar to president. Maureen Perrie indicates how this is reflected, among the rulers and the ruled, in the changing image of Ivan the Terrible. Furthermore, Catriona Kelly reveals that the recurrent official campaigns to refine popular manners have been underpinned by changing cultural purposes. The activity has been constant, the purposes markedly different. Often the results have been very unsatisfactory for rulers. This is a question I deal with, concluding that the continuity in the political methods of Nicholas II, Lenin, Stalin and Yeltsin stemmed to a large extent from the need to use whatever resources were available to them at the time. Sometimes the continuity, moreover, disguises not only different purposes but also different sources of inspiration, including foreign ones.

And so however much the various contributors highlight continuity more generally in Russian history they draw attention simultaneously to the tensions within that continuity. The Russian past is not so overdetermined that what Russia was, Russia always will be. Such a caveat deserves emphasis at a time when the euphoric welcome given in Russia and elsewhere to the collapse of communism has been followed by widespread despair at the bandit capitalism of Yeltsin's Russia. Nothing in our chapters is meant to suggest that the present economic mess, political corruption and pervasive lawlessness will endure forever. The burden of the past is heavy; and when Russian reformers have endeavoured to introduce novelty, they have often employed the instruments of custom. The efforts by Peter the Great, Lenin, Stalin and even Yeltsin have had the effect of hardening traditions into a diamond-like strength. Here we discover the paradox of Russian history. The more the Russians try to change, the more they have stayed the same. The pessimistic Sicilian novelist Giuseppe di Lampedusa famously declared that if things are to stay the same, they have to change. In some ways it seems that Russian history shows that if things have to change, they are bound to stay the same. Thus it has been so far. But this is not how things must always be.

1

Russia as empire: a comparative perspective

DOMINIC LIEVEN

Comparative history is seldom easy to write. A great deal of ground has to be covered by the historian, much of it unfamiliar. The comparative historian depends on experts in the many areas covered by his or her study, and is inevitably hard pressed when these experts disagree. Laws, institutions and economies are often much easier to compare than the mentalities and cultures that lie behind them. Partly for that reason, comparison can often be superficial. National traditions in the writing of history exert a strong influence, as do the approaches and subjects fashionable among historians of specific schools and generations. The comparative historian of empire can end up comparing less empires themselves than, for instance, a Russo-Soviet marxist obsession with economies and historical stages, contemporary US concerns with language and 'history from below' and an older tradition of interest among British historians in imperial power, territory and constitutional forms.

Empires are particularly hard to compare. In the first place there is no clear and generally agreed definition of what an empire is. The dividing line between empire, multiethnic polity and nation-state is very blurred. How a state is defined depends greatly on the political bias of those who are doing the defining. It also depends on whether a specific era regards empire in favourable or hostile light. For much of Western history, to call a state an empire has been a compliment. In medieval Europe, for instance, the word often evoked an image of peace, stability and solidarity within the Christian world and its princes.[1] In the late nineteenth century empire had connotations of grandeur, civilization, progress and leadership among the world's nations. Every Western people wanted to found an empire. Today, by contrast, empire is a dirty word. It has connotations of imposed authoritarian rule, of inequality and of the devastation of Third World wealth and culture by Western exploiters. By most historical measures, for example, the contemporary People's Republic of China is an empire.[2] It is huge, powerful, authoritarian and rules without consent over vast non-Han territories which were acquired well after Europeans first arrived in the Americas. But the rulers in Beijing will be swift to deny that their state is an empire, for in contemporary parlance such an admission would lead to the conclusion that their state was illegitimate and doomed to destruction at the hands of the supposedly unstoppable forces of democracy and nationalism. Nowadays one can only safely call a state an empire once it is dead. That is one reason why studies of the Soviet Union as empire have recently become so fashionable.

Most great empires survive for centuries. They therefore change over time. They also differ hugely from territory to territory. The largely self-governing British white dominions of the late nineteenth century were very different from the Indian autocracy over which Lord Curzon presided. Neither had much similarity to the hugely profitable slave-based sugar colonies in the seventeenth-century and eighteenth-century West Indies. What connects these territories and eras is common subordination to the British crown and a common contribution to Britain's power, wealth and prestige.[3] Indeed power, wealth and prestige are always core elements of empire.

Certainly this was true in the Russian case. The determination to become and remain a European great power was the overriding goal of the tsarist state and was central to the self-esteem and legitimacy of its rulers. To them empire meant, more than anything else, a power and status equal to those of any other European monarch.

In the West, the Russian empire was generally seen as the land of autocracy and centralization. Like most cliches, this one contains much truth. Centralization was indeed a key distinction between a Russian empire founded largely on conquest and a Habsburg one built on the inheritance through marriage of long-established kingdoms whose ancient constitutions and identities the Habsburgs were in general unable or unwilling to destroy. There is a very great contrast for instance between tsarist homogenization and assimilation of Ukraine on the one hand, and the survival of strong separate identities and institutions in Habsburg Hungary on the other. Ivan III's ruthless uprooting of institutions and elites in late-fifteenth-century Novgorod was crucial to the later creation of a centralized, authoritarian empire. It has considerable similarities to the efforts of China's first emperor to weld his newly conquered kingdoms into a single homogeneous state. By the standards of Ivan III or the Emperor Shih-huang, Habsburg efforts to uproot disloyal elements in seventeenth-century Bohemia seem barely half-hearted, the survival of distinct regional identities and institutions obvious.[4]

The contrast between English and Russian empire also tells one a good deal about the heritage of autocracy and centralization. English colonists carried overseas legal and constitutional traditions originating in their homeland. By the eighteenth century the belief that the Englishman by definition was entitled to the rule of law and representative government was deeply rooted. Increasingly, it was part of a British identity and a feature which set Britain and its empire above all other past and present imperial traditions in the eyes of most Englishmen. Undoubtedly, British legal and political traditions, which flourished in a colonial frontier environment far from the centre of British metropolitan power, contributed to the ultimate spread of democracy worldwide. But self-governing institutions also contributed to the creation of separate colonial identities in Britain's White colonies and to the ultimate break-up of the British Empire.

In eighteenth-century Russia, Cossack and Siberian frontier communities were vastly different from the aristocratic, serf-owning 'Muscovite' core of the empire. Given freedom and representative institutions, they could very easily have sustained separate identities and established, in time, independent nation-states. Tsarist policies of autocracy and centralization made certain that this did not happen. One result of this is that Russia has absorbed and assimilated into the 'motherland' the jewel in its imperial crown, namely Siberia. That is one reason why, quite possibly, contemporary Russia can shed its empire and still remain a great power – unlike the English, Dutch, French and Spanish, whose loss of all their White overseas colonies inevitably relegated them to second-class status in international affairs. On the other hand, the Russian people has paid a heavy price for this tradition of autocracy and centralization, which was undoubtedly strengthened by the state's determination to control and integrate the huge territory and multiethnic population of a great empire.

To reduce the whole of Russian imperial history to a story of autocracy and centralization would, however, be nonsense. In the three and one half centuries between the conquest of the Kazan Khanate and the revolution of 1917 the empire changed greatly. For most of the eighteenth and nineteenth centuries important regions, above all the Baltic provinces and Finland, enjoyed a high degree of autonomy. Although the Russian Empire was not perhaps quite as diverse as the British Empire, it nevertheless contained a wide range of peoples of differing cultures and levels of development whom it would have been inconceivable to rule in uniform fashion.

Russian relations with the peoples of the Trans-Caucasus and Central Asia are most easily comparable to the history of the European maritime empires. Russian elites in general saw themselves as European, and as part of a civilizing European mission; in Central Asia they created cotton economies and 'protected' princely states along distinctly European lines. Quite unlike the English, Dutch or French empires, however, the Russian Empire also contained large European territories whose populations were economically and culturally more advanced than were the Russians themselves. In the nineteenth century tsarist policy in the Western Borderlands was increasingly driven by the sense that the imperial people – in other words the Russians – were in need of protection from the more enterprising, educated and cultured Poles, Germans and Jews. It is hard to find parallels to this in European imperial history. It is also important to remember that the non-Russian territories on the Empire's western borders were much more important to Russia's rulers than its more obviously 'colonial' possessions in Asia.[5]

Of all the borderlands, Ukraine and Belorussia were most crucial to the empire. They lay across the main invasion routes from the West, where Imperial Russia's most powerful and dangerous enemies lurked. They shielded the empire's capitals and its political and economic heartland. From the 1790s to 1917 Ukraine was the empire's breadbasket. By 1900 it was also its main metallurgical and mining centre. In addition, these two regions were crucial in demographic terms. By the end of the nineteenth century Great Russians constituted roughly 45 per cent of the overall population, Ukrainians and Belorussians an additional 20 per cent. If the Ukrainians and Belorussians were in fact separate nations then less than half the Empire's population belonged to its core nationality. The percentage of Russians in the tsar's Empire was no greater than that of Austrian-Germans and Hungarians in the Habsburg Monarchy. Increasing discord and weakness in the Habsburg realm arising from conflict between the nationalities provided dire warnings of possible future developments in Russia. In general, in an increasingly nationalist era a multiethnic polyglot empire appeared fragile and vulnerable. Great powers built around a single predominant national core looked far more stable. This was the logic behind British efforts at imperial federation in the late nineteenth and twentieth centuries: a 'Greater Britain' would turn the 'motherland' and the overseas White colonies into a single world-nation-empire.[6] A similar logic ruled St Petersburg's determination that separate national identities must not be allowed to develop in Ukraine or Belorussia.[7]

Russia's rulers in fact quite honestly believed that Ukrainians and Belorussians were Russians, albeit Russians with somewhat strange regional dialects and folklore. The annexation of these areas by Russia was perceived not as any form of colonial conquest but rather as the regathering of lands once ruled by the grand prince of Kiev, ruler of all the Rus', and inhabited by East Slav, Orthodox peoples whose language, culture, race and religion identified them firmly as Russian. From the perspective of 1998 this Russian view no doubt seems self-serving and incorrect, but at the time it was not unreasonable. Most so-called nation-states which are seated today in the United Nations are the product more of historical accident than of long-established ethnic-national identity. Many have absorbed over time peoples much further removed in language, religion and ethnicity from their ethnic core than are Ukrainians and Belorussians from Russians. In the 1860s most Europeans would certainly have believed that Ukrainians were much closer to Russians than Bavarians were to Prussians.

In most European empires at that time the borderline between the core metropolitan people and some other nationalities subject to its power was not a clear one. Since 1801, for example, Ireland was part of the United Kingdom. Its history has therefore usually been studied in the context of metropolitan rather than imperial politics. At the time it mattered enormously that Ireland was defined as part of the metropolis and not of the empire. By the 1870s it was accepted in London that White colonies, should they so desire, must be allowed independence. No such right was allowed to Ireland. In the period 1911–14 some British politicians were prepared to take the United Kingdom to the brink of civil war to avoid Irish home rule. Yet in comparative imperial perspective Ireland clearly was a colony, not part of the English-dominated British metropolis. Among other things it was after all in Tudor Ireland that most of the ideological underpinnings of English imperialism – the doctrines of civilizing mission and *terra nullius* to name but two – were first born.

The complexity and variety of empire over time and space makes comparisons between empires difficult therefore. Which British Empire and which Russian Empire is being compared? There may be interesting parallels between Ukraine and Scotland, for instance, but which British colony approximated to the position in the Russian Empire of Poland, the Baltic provinces or Finland? On the other hand, the political system of post-1857 British India assumed that the masses' backwardness and propensity for anarchy made necessary the benevolent paternalism of the bureaucratic state, while often romanticizing the sterling qualities of the simple peasant and the courageous warrior; the parallels with Russian elites' attitudes to their own peasantry are obvious.

But if comparing empires is difficult it is also important, and never more so than in contemporary Russia. Having just shed an empire, Russia in the 1990s is forced to come to terms with being for almost the first time a mere nation. A proper understanding of the imperial past is an essential part of this process, which must include the preservation of self-esteem and of a balanced but nevertheless real appreciation of past achievements as well as sins. On this in part hangs political stability in Russia, mutually beneficial integration into the world economy and society, and the legitimization of the existing state frontiers in contemporary Northern Eurasia. Empire is a politically very sensitive word in today's Russia. It can imply the legitimacy of Russian desires to reverse the territorial settlement of 1991. Applied to the Soviet Union, the term 'imperial' or empire suggests that the USSR was always illegitimate and that its demise was both inevitable and justified. To many Russians this is unacceptable, partly because it suggests that the lives, sufferings and ideals of the older Russian generation were valueless and indeed morally tainted. Since most Russians were educated to think of empire in rather crude Marxist–Leninist terms the insult is all the greater. In this context a cool, detached but not unsympathetic comparison of Russia's experience of empire with that of other imperial peoples has many uses.

Nor are these uses purely practical and non-academic: in fact, quite the contrary. Like other scholars, historians of Russia have a tendency to become very narrow and self-obsessed. The issues and methodologies fashionable in the field at the time attract a quite disproportionate amount of attention and, quite often, conflict and biliousness. In the 1960s–80s scholars of Imperial Russia were obsessed by the claims of 'history from below'. It is no criticism of the excellent scholarship often displayed in these decades to suggest gently that broader, comparative perspectives and a grasp of the international context in which Russia existed are useful to an understanding of Russian history and indeed of the 1917 Revolution itself. Nor are historians of empire and imperialism immune from similar types of criticism. Just as the spectre of the Cold War hung over the writing of Russian history after 1945, so scholarship on empire and imperialism is written against a background of economic, cultural and political conflict between races and between the First and Third World. Debates on imperialism or 'orientalism' can very quickly become as narrow, self-obsessed and political as battles between 'liberals' and revisionists over the 1917 Revolution. Into these debates the Russianist armed with his or her very different traditions and obsessions can bring fresh perspectives, wider horizons and different questions.

The Russianist also has something both to contribute and to learn from the old debate on the rise and fall of empires. The weakening hold of communist ideology and the growth of corruption were important elements in the decay and collapse of the Soviet regime. Edward Gibbon's work on the decline and fall of the Roman Empire is still worthwhile reading for the Russianist, as are contemporary classical scholars who stress the role of corruption in destroying public commitment to the polity and undermining the rulers' control over peripheral elites and administrative organs.

Comparison of imperial strategies to channel and combat nationalism is also deeply worthwhile. Through the millet system the Ottomans allowed great religious, cultural and educational autonomy to their non-Moslem minorities.[8] Austro-Marxist thinkers in the late Habsburg Empire developed theories which were in many ways a secularized, modernized variation on the Ottoman theme. Citizens had the right to choose to which national–cultural group they wished to belong and the state devolved the maximum possible autonomy to these groups with regard to educational and cultural matters. Within the Austrian monarchy were developed most of the concepts (for example, consociational democracy) and most of the practices (for example, communal rights to separate schools, the management by consensus not majority vote of contentious linguistic issues) now used by multiethnic democracies to combat nationalist conflicts.[9] The Ottomans and the Austro-Marxists vigorously rejected the linking of ethnic–cultural identity to regional, territorial institutions. In opting for a federal solution to the problem of ethnicity in the USSR the Soviet regime rejected both the late-tsarist example of edging the Empire towards becoming a Russian nation-state and the Ottoman and Austro-Marxist models. Its federal solution exploded in the face of the Soviet regime in 1988–91 and played a big part in the Soviet Union's collapse. The causes and consequences of the adoption of Soviet federalism are both enormously important and best understood with some sense of the comparative context.

Arguably, the single most fatal blow dealt by Stalin to the Russo-Soviet empire was his annexation of the Baltic republics, Western Ukraine and Moldova in 1944–45. In the 1985–91 period it was in these regions (and the Trans-Caucasus) that nationalism was strongest. The Balts provided a model, a degree of leadership and some practical support for all the other nationalist movements which contributed to the Soviet Union's collapse. Because of Ukraine's size, wealth and ethnocultural closeness to Russia, the survival of some form of Soviet multiethnic empire above all depended on what happened in Kiev. Many factors influenced Kiev's decision to secede in 1991, but without the impetus provided to Ukrainian nationalism from the regions of West Ukraine annexed by Stalin it is hard to imagine that secession could have occurred.

In the context of empire, however, it is easy to understand Stalin's decision. The German threat had overhung Russia for generations: now was the time to end it by using victory over Hitler to establish a glacis well to the west of the Soviet heartland. Galicia was the home of Ukrainian nationalism: better to bring it within the empire, where its troublesome people could be 'disciplined' by Stalin's police, than to leave it to pursue a possible independent irredentist future. Indeed, so long as the Soviet Union remained an authoritarian, repressive police state the Galicians were not a major threat. For any empire which absorbs a potential irredenta, however, democratization is an unaffordable luxury. In the 1899–1902 period the British invaded and annexed the Boer Republics of southern Africa. In London's view, the huge economic potential of these republics would draw the Boer population of the Cape and thereby all southern Africa into their orbit, undermining Britain's imperial power in a key strategic and economic area. The next British Liberal government, however, quickly conceded self-government to White South Africans. The result of this was in the end to hand all South Africa, Natal and Cape Colony included, over to the radical Boer nationalists whom Britain had conquered and annexed in 1902. In this imperial context it is also easier to understand the Habsburgs' dilemma in 1914 with regard to Serbia. The latter was a dangerous irredenta but, if the Serbian Kingdom was annexed, would not millions of additional Serbs within the Monarchy contribute to domestic political instability and weaken the ability of Austro-German and Hungarian elites to retain their position of dominance? Hungarian leaders thought so, blocked Vienna's plans to annex Serbia and were unenthusiastic about Austria's strategy in the wake of the Archduke Franz Ferdinand's assassination at Sarajevo.[10]

In contemporary Western academia two rather different conceptions of empire coexist. The first draws its inspiration from a tradition of empire stretching back to antiquity. Best embodied by the French political scientist, Maurice Duverger,[11] it sees power, rule over great territories and many subject nationalities and, often, autocratic monarchy linked to some major religion as being key hallmarks of empire. Duverger argues that the term 'empire' was applied inappropriately by analogy to the non-European possessions of the nineteenth-century British, French and Dutch.

The other concept of empire, more fashionable in the social sciences, precisely takes the modern maritime European empires as its model. Above all it sees the political domination and, often, economic exploitation of peripheral territories by an alien metropolitan centre as the essence of empire. The best known exponent of this definition of empire is the US political scientist Michael Doyle.[12] This concept of empire is more widely used than Duverger's because it appears more relevant to the contemporary world and more easily utilized in current political polemics. Assyria and ancient Rome are remote, but the disparities in power and wealth between the First and Third World which originated in the era of Western maritime imperialism still exist, and indeed dominate current political debate. Post-war changes in the Third World and, even more, ethnic and cultural conflicts in the West (especially the USA) make aspects of cultural imperialism a hotter issue now than they were in the age of formal empire, if only perhaps because the subjects of empire have gained a voice and acquired powerful allies in the West.

Of these two models, Duverger's is more obviously appropriate to Russia. Tsarist Russia was a huge and multiethnic land empire, a centralized monarchical autocracy linked closely to one of the world's great religions, and a formidable military power. The comparisons with a host of empires, ancient and modern, are obvious. Of course, the Russian Empire had its own very characteristic features. It was quite unlike ancient Rome, in which (at least before the third century AD) an extremely small central apparatus left almost all the business of government to the myriad of municipal self-governing authorities of which the empire was constituted.[13] Nor, at least until the nineteenth century, did Russia bear much resemblance to the Chinese tradition of empire, in which a large and minutely regulated civilian bureaucracy dominated not only the polity but also the cultural and intellectual world. For most of its history Imperial Russia was dominated by an hereditary, military and landowning aristocracy, albeit an aristocracy which in some respects differed considerably from the English model of aristocracy which Anglo-American scholars are too inclined to see as the European norm. Like many others of its type, the eighteenth-century and nineteenth-century Russian Empire was more an aristocratic–dynastic polity than a Russian national one. The rather cosmopolitan ruling aristocracy was far removed in culture and sympathy from the mass of the Russian population, most of whom were its serfs, but the aristocracy were usually willing to accommodate and assimilate the elites of the non-Russian territories absorbed into the empire. Only in the last decades of Imperial Russia was a consistent effort made to identify the empire and the tsarist regime with the culture, values and interests of the mass of the Russian people.

In this respect, as in a number of others, tsarist Russia differed considerably from the British, French and Dutch nineteenth-century empires. In all three states democracy ruled by the 1880s, at least formally. Few contemporaries doubted the existence of British, French and Dutch metropolitan nations or the sharp line which ran between them and the non-White peoples of their overseas colonies. The distinction between the metropolitan people's possession of political rights and their absence in the non-White periphery was fundamental. So too were the differences between trans-oceanic empire, on the one hand, and a consolidated landmass extending over the centuries from the initial imperial core, on the other. Not merely was this imperial landmass easier to defend, but the Russian colonist's sense of having abandoned his or her homeland was much weaker than that of a European emigrant who had made a perilous sea voyage to a distant land with a bizarrely new stock of animals and vegetation.[14]

Nevertheless, important parallels did exist between tsarist Russia and the European maritime empires. The expansion and contraction of Russia – both territorial and demographic – occurred at roughly the same time as that of the other European empires. Viewed from Dresden or Prague, let alone London, Russia may sometimes be seen disparagingly as 'Asiatic'. Viewed from Tokyo, Tehran or Beijing it is all too depressingly European. Russia expanded in Asia by employing European techniques and technologies. In the period 1550–1850 the rise of Russia and the decline of the Ottoman Empire owed much to the fact that Christian Russia was closer to European Christian civilization than it was to Islamic Ottoman Society and was more willing to welcome and employ European ideas and cadres in the cause of modernization. In many ways Khrushchev's Virgin Lands scheme of the 1950s in Kazakhstan can be seen as the last example of European territorial expansion at the expense of non-European, Moslem or pagan, and very often nomadic, peoples.

In the era of High Imperialism (*c.* 1850–1917) lower-class Russians – in other words, peasants and soldiers – seem to have been less arrogant and less racially conscious than was generally the case with their West European equivalents.[15] Apart from anything else, the economic and cultural gap between Russian peasant and non-European subject of the Tsar was less wide than the divide between a working-class English person and an Indian native. Among educated Russians a minority to some extent identified with Asiatics as fellow sufferers from European arrogance and pressure, though the motives for such identification probably had much more to do with resentment of Europe than any real empathy with Islamic or oriental people. Certainly, the nineteenth-century perception, shared by much of educated Russia, that Russia was a backward society – a failure in war, economic development and political modernization – did much to weaken the identification of elite society, both Russian and non-Russian, with the tsarist state. Europe always looked over Russia's shoulder. Even after the flowering of the Russian intelligentsia in the nineteenth century, Russian high culture could never exercise the same magnetic pull and domination over non-Russian elites as Chinese high culture had managed over the centuries in East Asia. Consolidation of the empire was therefore that much more difficult. Nevertheless, the core of empire is power, and between 1750 and 1917 Russia was unequivocally a European great power, alongside not only France and Britain but also Austria, another land-based empire which does not perfectly fit the imperial model advanced by Michael Doyle.

Comparison of the tsarist regime with other empires is not particularly contentious. Tsarist Russia called itself an empire and rejoiced in the word's connotations. The Soviet Union by contrast claimed to be the leader of the anti-imperialist camp. It called its Western foes imperialists: they responded by naming the Soviet Union an empire. One way to escape these polemics is to remember that empire was not always a dirty word. During much of history empires provided their subjects with considerable peace and prosperity, sustained most of the world's great civilizations and monuments and spread its most influential religions and philosophies across the globe. Also important to remember is the fact that no single word or even concept can express the vast sum of experience contained in the history of empire. The Soviet Union was undoubtedly a very great power, with a huge impact on the international relations of an era. It ruled without overt consent over huge territories and the many peoples who lived in them. It created and propagated a universal ideology which was designed to transform most aspects of human existence fundamentally and forever. This makes it worthy of the title of empire, at least as that concept is conceived by Maurice Duverger.[16] Of course, mere common sense will qualify this statement by acknowledging that a twentieth-century, secular, socialist land-based polity is bound to differ fundamentally both from ancient and early modern empires and from the overseas colonial regimes of the British, French and Dutch.

In the Soviet case, probably the most interesting imperial comparison is the one made long ago by Arnold Toynbee:[17] namely, the parallel with early Islamic empire. Marxism–Leninism was in the tradition of dogmatic, Judaic monotheism. Its gospel was universal and even as applied in the Soviet Union, in other words briefly and imperfectly, it created a society in which people lived, thought and worked in ways radically different both from their ancestors and from their peers in the contemporary West. As with other universalist, monotheistic religions-cum-empires in Late Antiquity[18] the communist world showed a tendency to split among regional centres of power (Beijing, Belgrade), whose rulers espoused different variations of the doctrine and denounced each other as heretics. In the Islamic context the obvious points to note about the Soviet Union are that it collapsed within a lifetime and produced no revolts from elite or mass in the name of a truer or purer version of the official faith. By 1991 the ideology really did appear to be dead. In part that may well have been because of its all too rational and secular twentieth-century nature. The ideology probably failed to meet a number of ineradicable human religious and emotional needs. More certainly, by promising material achievements as the proof of communism the ideology was all too easily disproved by the evidence of any eye that was relatively well educated and to some extent aware of comparisons with the outside world. Increasingly, sections of the Soviet elite could make intelligent comparisons, and their growing loss of faith was crucial to the regime's demise.

The most interesting, though not necessarily the most weighty, comparisons between Soviet and modern Western empire also revolve around ideology. In the 1820s and 1830s Thomas Macauley and his fellow liberal thinkers had no doubt that the British both should and could Anglicize India. On the one hand, they were contemptuous of traditional Indian culture. On the other, they shared none of the later racialist conceptions about the inherent inferiority of Indians or their inability to educate themselves. This was Victorian liberalism in all its pristine energy, optimism and self-confidence.[19] The Soviet regime lived in this tradition, which is not at all surprising since Marxism was liberalism's child – sharing its belief in unilinear progress, its materialism and its faith in rationality. In the British Empire the voice of metropolitan liberalism was challenged by Romantics, racialists and many others as well: it was also, of course, tempered by political realities and the pragmatism of cautious colonial bureaucrats. In the Soviet Union, a pragmatic, *de facto quieta non movere* principle did begin to inform nationalities policy under Brezhnev, but, given the regime's ideology, it could never be presented as an explicit doctrine of colonial conservatism. Instead, in China even more than in Russia, Marxism–Leninism's obsession with 'scientific method' and historical stages of development rigidified and turned into doctrine rather traditional assumptions about where peoples stood in the hierarchy of civilization and which road was the unique route to progress.

Notes

In the notes I confine myself to listing a very small number of sources for further reading, all of which are in West European languages. For a much more comprehensive coverage of this subject and a bibliographical essay on the subject see my forthcoming book, *Empire and Russia* (London, John Murray, 2000).

1 See, above all, R. Folz, *The concept of empire in Western Europe from the fifth to the fourteenth century* (Westport, CT, 1969).
2 C.H. Beck, *China Vielvolkerreich und Einheitsstaat* (Munich, 1997). For those without German, C. Blunden and M. Elvin, *Cultural atlas of China* (Oxford, 1983) is a very useful introduction, with excellent maps.
3 P.J. Marshall (ed.), *The Cambridge illustrated history of the British Empire*, (Cambridge, 1996) is the best single-volume introduction.
4 On the Habsburgs see J. Berenger, *A history of the Habsburg Monarchy 1278–1700*, (London, 1994) and C. Ingrao, *The Habsburg Monarchy 1618–1815* (Cambridge, 1994).
5 On empire in pre-1917 Russia, nothing in English remotely matches A. Kappeler, *Russland als Vielvolkerreich*, (Munich, 1993).
6 J.R. Seeley, *The expansion of England*, (London, 1885) best expresses this aspiration.
7 On Russian policy in the Western Borderlands see E.C. Thaden, *Russia's Western Borderlands 1710–1870*, (Princeton, NJ, 1984) and T.R. Weeks, *Nation and state in late Imperial Russia*, (De Kalb, IL, 1996).
8 On the millet see, above all, B. Braude and B. Lewis (eds), *Christians and Jews in the Ottoman Empire: the functioning of a plural society*, (New York, 1982).
9 On nationalities within the Habsburg Empire and the state's nationalities policy the best study is Band III/I, *Die Völker des Reiches*, in A. Wandruszka (ed.), *Die Habsburgermonarchie* (Vienna, 1980). On Austro-Marxism the best English-language introduction are the essays by Theodor Hanf and Alfred Pfabigan in U. Ra'anon *et al.* (eds), *State and nation in multi-ethnic societies*, (Manchester, 1991).
10 Parallels between the British and Austrian dilemmas exist but are not usually drawn. See I.R. Smith, *The origins of the South African War 1899–1902* (London, 1996) and S.P. Williamson, *Austria–Hungary and the origins of the First World War*, (London, 1991).
11 M. Duverger, *Le concept d'empire*, (Paris, 1980).
12 M. Doyle, *Empires* (Ithaca, NY, 1991).
13 On Rome, see A. Lintott, *Imperium Romanum: politics and administration* (London, 1993).
14 See N. Canny and A. Pagden (eds), *Colonial identity in the Atlantic world 1500–1800*, (Princeton, NJ, 1987), especially the introduction by J. Elliott.
15 See, for example, R.K.I. Quested, *'Matey' imperialists: the tsarist Russians in Manchuria 1895–1917* (Hong Kong, 1982).
16 It is now becoming a commonplace to describe the USSR as an empire. See e.g. K. Dawisha and B. Parrott (eds), *The end of empire? The transformation of the USSR in comparative perspective* (Armonk, 1997).
17 See, above all, volume VII of A.H. Toynbee, *A study of history* (London, 1954).
18 G. Fowden, *Empire to commonwealth: consequences of monotheism in late antiquity* (Princeton, NJ, 1993).
19 See Chapter 12 of T. Metcalf, *Ideologies of the Raj* (Cambridge, 1994).

2

How holy was Holy Russia? Rediscovering Russian religion

SIMON DIXON

Although Sergei Averintsev insists that Holy Russia was originally 'an almost cosmic category',[1] specific neither in geographical nor in ethnic terms, few would dispute that the idea later came to represent a messianic form of Russian national consciousness. It has attracted most interest as a potentially subversive political slogan, used to reproach rulers who abandoned the uniquely sacred legacy of medieval *Rus'*. Yet the notion that Holy Russia was the last remaining earthly sanctuary of authentic apostolic Christianity evidently carried practical implications in terms of popular religious belief. And among those who stressed these implications none was more explicit than Semen Denisov, who declared in his *Vinograd rossiiskii* (The Russian Vineyard), a martyrology of the early Old Believer leadership, that 'In Russia, there is not one single city which is not permeated with the radiance of faith, not one town which does not shine with piety, nor a village which does not abound with true belief'.[2]

Was such a claim ever anything more than a myth? Most foreigners thought not. Committed to stereotypical images of the Muscovite as a quasi-oriental barbarian, at best sunk in Greek superstition, Protestants in particular took a caustic view of the Russians and their ritual: 'As for whoredome and drunkennesse there be none such living', added Richard Chancellor in the 1550s, 'and for extortion, they be the most abhominable under the sunne. Nowe judge of their holinesse'.[3] Russians themselves remained divided on the question of their religious rectitude. It was still hotly debated in the nineteenth century, not least among radical populists anxious to discover a reliable means of communication with the *narod*. Whilst Osip Aptekman converted from Judaism to Orthodoxy specifically for the purpose, and did indeed gain peasants' trust by discussing religion with them in the 1870s, other *narodniki* dismissed the religiosity of the Russian peasant as a Slavophile fiction.[4] Churchmen found it no easier to reach a consensus, for whilst some drew a favourable contrast between peasant piety and the irreligion of the intelligentsia, others continued to bemoan the 'dark masses'' ignorance of even the most basic tenets of their faith.[5] It doubtless pleased the more arrogant Bolshevik atheists to suppose that the sceptics had right on their side. Yet Lenin was wary of attacking the church, lest persecution trigger either mass martyrdom or a clerical counter-revolution, and it was not until 1922 that a concerted plan to confiscate ecclesiastical valuables was launched under cover of a scheme for famine relief.[6] Neither of Lenin's fears was then realized. But the vigour with which individual congregations resisted persecution suggests that both the church and its religion retained their popular grip even in the most harrowing of circumstances.[7] Certainly, Stalin's regime was unnerved when the answers to question 5 in the 1937 census, which required all Soviet citizens aged 16 years and over to declare their religion, revealed an unexpectedly high proportion of Orthodox believers.[8]

It is only during the past decade that scholars have been prepared to take seriously the notion of widespread popular Christianity in modern Russia. Before the late 1980s, the dominant view – not only among the Soviet academic establishment but also in the West – was that Russia had long been indifferent to Orthodoxy. Richard Pipes went so far as to declare that 'The true religion of the Russian peasantry was fatalism'.[9] It would be misleading to claim that Christianity went wholly unrecognized. Beyond the confines of the two Russian capitals, sophisticated work could be done even within the limitations of a Marxist–Leninist framework. The anthropologist Marina Gromyko included in her study of peasant behaviour a section on pilgrimages (concealed under the innocuous heading 'noneconomic reasons for leaving the village'), and investigations of 'antifeudal protest', undertaken in Novosibirsk by N.N. Pokrovskii and his students, threw new light on the Old Belief in Siberia.[10] In the West, Brenda Meehan added a gendered dimension to the subject by revealing the significance of informal communities of female religious which first responded to (and in turn stimulated) popular spiritual demand in the wake of Catherine II's crackdown on convents at the secularization of the church lands in 1764, prompting the nineteenth-century church ultimately to recognize them as models of the ascetic way of life.[11]

But these historians were exceptions to the rule. Many failed to mention religion; most of those who did were dismissive. Anthony Netting, struck by 'the virtual absence of Christian symbols in peasant art', saw Christianity as 'part of but peripheral to peasant belief'.[12] Steven Hoch, in his outstanding study of the Gagarin estate at Petrovskoe, saw no reason to suppose that its serfs cared much about their church, attributing their neglect to 'the weakness of Russian Orthodoxy as a religion without content or theology'. There was, moreover, 'no evidence that the bailiff, the central estate office, or even Prince Gagarin himself was at all concerned with the peasants' spiritual well-being, participation in religious rites or church attendance'.[13] For historians guided by the preoccupations of some distinctly secular social scientists, life in the Russian countryside was bound to be dominated by socio-economic constraints.

How different the historiographical picture looks in 1998! Recovering the sectarian dimension of migrant peasant labour, Jeffrey Burds has turned the tables on conventional verdicts by claiming that

> it was through the prism of their religious beliefs that Russian peasants handled the tensions of their daily lives. In practice, the religious dimension was pervasive, defining every aspect of the everyday life of the community, overlaying and forming the language of rivalry between clans or socioeconomic groups.[14]

Such a bold conclusion is by no means untypical in the current revisionist climate. The anthropologist S.V. Kuznetsov argues that 'religious–moral conceptions, lying at the root of the Russian peasant's relationship with the land and with work, exerted a decisive influence on the formation of common law norms', whilst his compatriot, L.A. Tul'tseva, has suggested that

> The Christian map of the world, accepted by the Orthodox peasantry together with Christian teachings [and] their own ritual practices . . . played an invaluable role (the depth of which is hard to measure) in the formation and perfection of the peasant's inner spiritual world.[15]

Not that this world was as monolithic as scholars were once tempted to suppose. On the contrary, regional and local traditions generated sufficient variety for Gregory Freeze to claim, in his long-awaited study of religion and society, quoted in advance of its publication by Elise Kimerling Wirtschafter, that Russian Orthodoxy was in reality 'Russian Heterodoxy', consisting of an 'aggregate of local Orthodoxies, each with its own special cults, rituals and customs'.[16]

Orthodoxy, so recently portrayed as 'a religion without content or theology' in which almost no-one believed, is now apparently better understood as a religion with little shared content or theology in which almost everyone believed. How has this transformation been accomplished? Partly, it is attributable simply to a swing of the historiographical pendulum given added momentum by intensified interest in religion as an antidote to the discredited Soviet regime. More significantly, changed political circumstances have permitted unprecedented wide access to a range of central and local archives, so that the latest studies rest on a far broader basis of evidence than was previously available. However, since only the most determined of positivists could suppose that archival documents are sufficient in themselves to generate historical explanations,[17] the crucial element in the rediscovery of Russian religion has been the questions asked of the sources, and above all the assumptions about the nature of peasant religion that lie behind these questions. These assumptions are in many ways reducible to what I shall call 'the attack on *dvoeverie*'.

Since the late nineteenth century, most discussions of Russian spiritual-ity, be they sympathetic or hostile to Orthodoxy, have been informed by the notion of *dvoeverie*, or 'dual faith', which rests on the distinction between pagan and Christian elements. Fedotov, for example, made this distinction crucial to his dissection of *The Russian religious mind*, arguing that 'the deep and rich forms' taken by the Divine Womanhood cults prominent in the Russian Orthodox tradition were explicable only in the context of the 'Christian–Pagan syncretism' which he saw emerging from 'the gradual fusion of dying paganism with victorious Christianity'.[18] Most historians, doubting that such a fusion ever occurred, have spoken instead of an uneasy coexistence between the two, contending that Christianity was merely a veneer. It is this more critical conception of dual faith that underpins the account of 'not-so-holy Russia' in the dazzling history of the revolutionary period by Orlando Figes: for the peasant whose relation-ship with institutional Orthodoxy was no more than 'semi-detached', Figes suggests, Christianity remained but a 'thin coat . . . painted over his ancient pagan folk-culture'.[19]

And yet, according to Chris Chulos, the very notion of *dvoeverie* is 'one of the most trite misnomers about pre-revolutionary peasant religion'.[20] Part of the problem lies in the level of distortion implicit in any binary model. Eve Levin has shown that the assumption of a polarity between paganism and Christianity obscures the overlap between the two and exaggerates the coherence of each component.[21] To modern scholars, less sanguine than nineteenth-century intellectuals about the ease of draw-ing clear boundaries between the magical, the scientific and the religious, it seems doubtful that most Russian peasants made any such distinction. Conscious that outsiders have generally patronized the peasantry, histor-ians now prefer to characterize both the Old Belief and rural Orthodoxy not as uncomfortable amalgams between opposing forces of religion and 'superstition', but instead, as Moshe Lewin once suggested, as popular religions 'in their own right'.[22]

So vigorously has the attack on *dvoeverie* been prosecuted in the 1990s that it is easy to forget that it was first launched by Pierre Pascal at the beginning of his short study of *The religion of the Russian people*.[23] One reason why historians have found this book frustrating is its imprecision about time and place. But in his broader judgements about the nature of popular religion, Pascal nevertheless anticipated a number of current historiographical trends. Having emphasized the domestic focus of many Russian devotions (enforced in part by low population densities and the inadequate provision of worship in rural areas), he went on to claim that Russian popular religion was not only 'about as unclericalist as it could be, not in any way tied to the clergy', but also 'as little possible tied to the church', so that no Russian peasant believer would be deterred by 'priestly unworthiness'. In stark contrast to the dualist model of Russian culture subsequently advanced by Lotman and Uspenskii (a notable casualty of the attack on *dvoeverie*), Pascal explained these features of popular religion in terms of 'the general disdain in Russia for absolute division, prohibitions and precepts: why have watertight partitions between divine and profane?'[24]

Pascal stressed popular religion's independence from institutional constraints in order to explain Orthodoxy's resilience in the 1920s, when ecclesiastical provision was corrupted and forcibly disabled. But we should not allow this motive to blind us to three obvious difficulties with his account. First, his implicit assertion of Orthodox exceptionalism cannot withstand comparative investigation: a glance at other pre-industrial societies suggests that a reluctance to separate the divine from the profane was by no means confined to Russia. Second, Pascal underestimates the importance of institutions for even at the nadir of ecclesiastical fortunes in the 1920s it was an exaggeration for Solzhenitsyn to claim that 'the only church remaining was that church which, in accordance with the Scriptures, *lay within the heart*'.[25] Third, Pascal's vision of a 'cosmic Christianity', in which animism is integral to peasant reverence for God's creation, underestimates the magical content of Russian popular religion that needs to be explained rather than simply explained away.

Not only did the French peasantry fail to distinguish between superstition and dogma but, as Arlette Farge has stressed in a study based on the eighteenth-century police archives, 'neither Church nor monarchy found it in their interests to make the distinction over-clear'.[26] As this example suggests, questions to which historians of Russia have only recently turned their minds have long preoccupied students of Western Europe. Indeed, there is now a flourishing body of scholarship devoted to attempts to measure the relative strengths of magic and doctrine in the minds of the faithful and to understand the balance of their requirements for individual devotions and corporate worship. The most sophisticated writers have stressed the need to explore not only the tensions but also the interpenetration between 'official' and 'popular' religion. As the late Bob Scribner put it, in a study of Catholic Germany in the Reformation, 'Many people shared both official and popular religion, some more and others less, and there was a good deal of two-way flow between the two areas of experience'.[27] Scribner's expression of this conclusion in diagrammatic form (Figure 2.1) is of general application. First, it suggests that Russian holiness is probably best expressed not in the manner of the classic French studies of popular religion, in predominantly statistical terms, but rather by means of the sort of qualitative analysis preferred by a later generation of historians anxious to escape from linear models of 'secularization'.[28] Second, Scribner's model serves as a reminder that though magic and doctrine evidently overlapped the two are nevertheless separable. Third, to counteract the danger that modern secular historians may be no less condescending towards the clergy than were nineteenth-century intellectuals towards the peasantry, it emphasizes the need to take seriously both

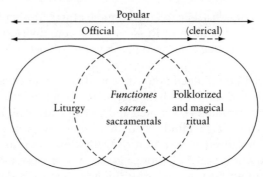

Figure 2.1 Popular religion and religious ritual. The broken lines at the top represent: for the laity, a degree of passive participation; for the clergy, a degree of participation in 'non-official' ritual.

lay participation in liturgical affairs and clerical participation in non-liturgical religion – what Robert Evans calls 'Christian magic' in his analysis of counter-Reformation spirituality in the Habsburg Empire.[29]

Gregory Freeze has already discussed some of these issues in relation to Russia between 1750 and 1850.[30] What follows is a preliminary attempt to consider the late nineteenth and early twentieth centuries. Since the topic is too vast to permit comprehensive coverage, the intention is merely to reflect on a few key points, infusing fragments from my own work, emphasizing the significance of religious rivalry as the motive force for eccesiastical change in a multidenominational empire, into a commentary on recent contributions to the field.

Let us begin by adopting Scribner's focus on the liturgy, taking as our starting point the records of prosecutions of clerical misdemeanours which survive in synodal and diocesan archives. At the most obvious level, these may be expected to tell us something about the severity and efficiency of diocesan justice (a key target for critics both within and outside the Church at the end of the nineteenth century), and even of the incidence of priestly indiscipline. But by reading 'against the grain' among the testimony of lay witnesses, we may also hope to learn something not only of popular attitudes to the clergy but also of the nature of people's religious beliefs. In this context, it is significant that Chulos found that of the 290 disciplinary cases against clergy that survive from the diocese of Voronezh between 1880 and 1917 no fewer than 129 (almost 45 per cent) involved liturgical errors.[31] How far does such a high proportion imply doctrinal sophistication on the part of the complainants? Might it, by contrast, offer grounds for supposing that peasants regarded the liturgy as a spell that relied on regularity of expression for its effect? How far does it simply suggest that parishioners were vexed when the services for which they had paid (sometimes over the odds) were unexpectedly interrupted or curtailed?

Answers to such questions must recognize that the surviving evidence is as indicative of ecclesiastical priorities as it is of lay concerns. By no means every charge was investigated. Even such an uncompromising devotee of clerical discipline as K.P. Pobedonostsev, Over Procurator of the Holy Synod between 1880 and 1905, acknowledged that the majority of the denunciations (*donosy*) he received were worthless. In line with this critical approach, Metropolitan Antonii (Vadkovskii) reported to the Synod in 1907 that most of the 850 accusations sent to the St Petersburg diocesan consistory in 1906 had been ignored in a year when only nine guilty verdicts were recorded from the 117 disciplinary cases currently under investigation.[32] Why, then, did the authorities pay such particular attention to liturgical error?

In some cases, liturgical infringements were merely the flashpoint at which long-standing clerical tensions were publicly exposed. Diocesan authorities felt bound to investigate any incidence of unseemly behaviour that further besmirched the clergy's already sullied reputation. Whilst rivals, and especially evangelical Protestants, appeared to be capable of practising what they preached, it mattered that some Orthodox priests lived visibly unsaintly lives. Take, for example, an incident in the impoverished hinterland of St Petersburg when the service was broken off and finally abandoned following an argument between the priest, Father Pavel Vishnevskii, and his junior clergy. Irritated by the deacon, who had left the church to relieve himself during the liturgy, Vishnevskii refused to bless him on his return and sought to dismiss him from the remainder of the service, provoking a quarrel not only with the offending deacon but also with the psalmist.[33] Here was a case where the peasantry required no great theological acumen to see that something had gone wrong. Mistakes committed as a consequence of the clergy's besetting sin – inebriation – were often equally unsubtle, a fact sufficient to ensure that charges of insobriety were gratuitously added by most lay complainants against the clergy, though only the most persistent offenders seem to have alienated parishioners who (consonant with Pascal's views on the insignificance of priestly unworthiness) tolerated individual weakness provided that the incumbent was not permanently incapacitated.[34]

It was not only the need to avoid public humiliation that persuaded diocesan consistories to punish liturgical error. Still more important was the need to preserve the authenticity of Orthodoxy in the face of rival claims to offer the true path to salvation. As archbishop of Finland (1905–17), where religion and nationalism were inextricably intertwined, the future patriarch Sergii (Stragorodskii), followed his predecessor in challenging Lutheranism by insisting on full and splendid Church Slavonic liturgies, delivered at a measured pace.[35] But it was not only on the periphery of the empire that liturgical politics mattered. Since no less an upheaval than the seventeenth-century schism had resulted from liturgical change, any reform was bound to be controversial. A powerful current in the Church therefore insisted on strict conformity in liturgical practice. The Oxford don, William Palmer, visiting Russia in 1840–41, heard the influential layman A.N. Murav'ev contrast the early church, when much was still 'indeterminate', with his own day, in which 'all things have been decided and classed and catalogued': 'We must not "move the landmarks"', he repeated, 'We do not live now in the age of the [seven great Ecumenical] Councils when . . . things could be changed'.[36] The same argument was encapsulated by Palmer's host in St Petersburg, Father Vasilii Fortunatov, in a sermon in the 1850s: the sacraments 'happen now and will happen until the world comes to an end precisely as they happened in Apostolic times and in the first centuries of Christianity'.[37]

Whilst leading churchmen might be expected to insist on accurate liturgical practice, an apparently unthinking commitment to ritual on the part of the laity is easily mocked. Aided by the circumstance that Anton Chekhov's father, Pavel, was also a sadist, the writer's modern biographer paints a portrait of a monstrous humbug whose mindless determination to maintain the splendour of the services at Taganrog Cathedral, where he became regent of the choir in 1864, led to his dismissal only three years later. It was his father's disciplinarian view of religion, Chekhov later claimed, that had led him to doubt his own faith.[38] By the same token, it is tempting to think that men such as Chekhov might have been saved for the church if only those 'renovationist' clergy (*obnovlentsy*) who sought to shorten the liturgy and to make it more accessible by conducting services in Russian rather than Church Slavonic had not struggled in vain. Renovationism was no shallow movement within Orthodoxy. Its roots ran sufficiently deep for archimandrite Feodor (Bukharev) – prominent in post-emancipation debates about the Church's social role – to be claimed as its 'spiritual father',[39] and for many intelligent priests in St Petersburg to have been touched by its concerns. Yet when the renovationists finally had the opportunity to implement their reforms in May 1922 they encountered intense popular hostility, not only to calendrical revision (as it transpired, the most offensive point in their programme) but also to liturgical change. 'Not unlike the Old Believers', Freeze remarks, 'regular members of the Orthodox Church still placed great importance on the performance of traditional rites in traditional ways and at traditional times'.[40]

The release within the Orthodox church, after 1917, of new men 'carrying out new measures and casting away the useless rubbish of past centuries' ultimately proved still more divisive in Russia than had the arrival in Barchester of the Reverend Obadiah Slope.[41] But allowance must be made for the exceptional upheaval of those post-revolutionary years. As everything they knew collapsed around them, it is not surprising that believers should have resisted change in the one institution that might have been expected to offer continuity to a civilization severed from its roots even more violently than it had been under Peter the Great. Who can say what might have been the fate of the renovationists' liturgical reforms had they been introduced in calmer times? They might have been greeted more positively. And yet any attempt to make the liturgy more comprehensible and accessible risked removing the mystery crucial to a religion dependent upon aesthetics. 'The Russian people are too sensitive to beauty not to appreciate the Liturgy', claimed Pascal, calling it 'the only perfect beauty on earth'.[42] National stereotypes rarely inspire trust, and yet this one is not wholly implausible. Tchaikovsky, whose reason made him suspicious of ecclesiastical doctrine, was attracted by liturgical poetry, whilst Chekhov's *On Easter night*, as Rayfield writes, 'transcends the author's own unbelief', imbued as it is 'with intense love of the archaic language of the liturgy which only he and Leskov could fuse into literary Russian'.[43] Men and women of lesser artistic sensibility may well have been equally drawn to the beauty of the divine service, though how often they experienced it is a question to which we will shortly return.

Widespread resistance to renovationism is evidence in itself that lay commitment to the church was less torpid than scholars have generally been tempted to suppose. Recent historians have sought various ways to illustrate its nature and intensity. Among those who have concentrated on the parish trusteeships sanctioned by the reformist government of the 1860s, Adele Lindenmeyr has studied their charitable activities, stressing that Father Aleksandr Gumilevskii, a key figure, saw in lay confraternities a tangible survival of authentic apostolic almsgiving.[44] Glennys Young's painstaking analysis of the published statistics on parish trusteeships has breathed new life into these much abused bodies.[45] It remains to be seen whether they were sufficiently vital to give parish life much meaning. As things stand, this seems unlikely: even within the Church it was acknowledged that, beyond the two capitals, many of these bodies existed only on paper, and parishes themselves remained poorly defined. But we may nevertheless find more direct evidence of lay piety in the construction of hundreds of small chapels in partial compensation for the inadequate provision of worship in the countryside. Here, in frequently very simple wooden buildings, often constructed in memory of the imperial family or of the community's salvation from natural disaster, peasants might hold prayer meetings led by laymen, though they could not normally celebrate the liturgy since priests were rarely present and chapels had no *antimins*, the cloth required by Orthodox liturgical practice.[46]

The proliferation of unsupervised chapels is but one among several obstacles to an accurate assessment of attendance. Since no Orthodox church had pews, and few pilgrims remained for the whole service, we have nothing to compare with the English census of 1851. Nevertheless, statistics of communion and confession indicate that only a tiny minority of pre-revolutionary Russians failed to fulfil this annual legal obligation, and parochial records allow us to make more detailed observations in some cases. Let us take, for example, the remarkably full series of early-twentieth-century records from the eastern Karelian parish of

Suojärvi, one of the most russified in the Orthodox diocese of Finland. Confessional records here show almost complete conformity.[47] But there is evidence that, at least for a core of fervent believers, religion was more than a matter of routine. Clerical reports, supplemented by the accounts of candle sales, record the maximum attendances during the Lenten fast followed by a secondary peak in August, when some parishioners confessed for a second time. By contrast, winter, autumn and early summer attendances were much lower; on occasion, there can hardly have been anyone in church at all.[48] Though he could not significantly affect its seasonal distribution, a zealous young priest, Father Alexander Loginevskii, was able to increase the attendance at his church, despite the handicap of a huge parish, by supplementing corporate worship with lay involvement, on the part of his most fervent followers, in the choir, the church school and, more generally, in the quasi-political work of the Orthodox Karelian Brotherhood.[49]

Although further research is required to establish whether a national pattern can be discerned, it is already clear that churchmen in areas affected by religious rivalry were prompted to investigate the reasons for low winter attendance by the suspicion that Orthodox absentees might be seduced by denominational competitors performing clandestine services in the depths of the forest.[50] Poor rural communications were a major deterrent, though since the spring thaw generated the highest attendance indifference cannot be ascribed wholly to inadequate roads and flooded rivers. As peasants complained, insufficient firewood and unreliable heating systems often made churches intolerably cold: Loginevskii reported from Suojärvi that in the winter of 1906–7 both the water and the lamp oil froze.[51] In consequence, many churches chose to sacrifice asceticism by serving in so-called 'warm' chapels during the winter.[52] Believers, however, found many of these interior chambers dark and confined, especially in comparison with the clean, bright churches used by Protestants. Nor were inner chapels the only offenders: the gloom at St Isaac's in St Petersburg was notorious.[53] In response, several of the capital's churches advertised the brightness of their newly restored decoration,[54] and the Society for the Propagation of Religious and Moral Enlightenment pioneered the more open design exemplified by its church on the Obvodnyi canal near the Warsaw Station, where the forbidding red brick belies a well-lit interior left free from columns so that the preacher could not only be heard but also be seen.[55] Electricity was a further option, adopted by all the capital's parish churches by 1911. But this innovation raised new contradictions of its own, for why, critics enquired, build churches in authentic Russian style only to flood them with 'uncanonical' artificial light?[56] 'Improvements' were in any case often accompanied by threats. Peasants gathered for the consecration of a new church in Gdov uezd, west of St Petersburg, were warned in 1898 that God had punished the Jews when their faith lapsed, and told that the provision of a spacious new building had removed any excuse for absenteeism.[57] It was probably this authoritarian approach to ecclesiastical affairs – in marked contrast to the communitarian ethos maintained by the Old Believers – that did most to alienate the faithful from their church.[58]

If the majority of Russians attended only annual confession and communion, then what was the nature of their experience? The secrecy of the confessional makes it hard to penetrate, but since we know that the sacrament was concentrated in the final weeks of Lent, when time was short, it seems certain that practice often diverged from the prescribed ideal.[59] Of course, exceptional circumstances generated exceptional cases. At Easter 1917 Father Afanasii Beliaev spent a full hour and 20 minutes hearing the tortured confessions of the recently deposed tsar Nicholas II, his wife and Grand Duchess Tatiana Nikolaevna: 'Oh, how unspeakably happy I am that I was favoured by God's grace to become the mediator between the Heavenly Ruler and the earthly one'. Yet less august consciences were dispatched more rapidly. That very lunchtime, Beliaev had heard 42 members of the household at Tsarskoe Selo confess in less than two hours; two days ealier, he had heard 54 servants in three hours.[60] The norm was probably swifter. Father Fortunatov claimed to have heard up to 2000 confessions in the Vyborg district of St Petersburg in the final weeks of Lent in 1840–41. He read out the preparatory text, as far as the questions, to the congregation gathered in the body of the church, and then sat behind a moveable screen on the *solea* as individual parishioners filed past in what can have been only limited privacy.[61] Most priests, by contrast, stood to hear confession, partly to cope with the numbers, partly to distinguish Orthodox practice from Catholic.[62] To give a sense of the burdens such a system imposed on the clergy, let us quote a letter sent in the 1880s to archpriest N.I. Rozanov, senior priest at St Petersburg's Smol'nyi Cathedral, by his brother, a rural clergyman then aged 68 years:

> In the 1st week [of the Lenten fast] I gave communion to 610 people, in the 2nd to 554, in the 3rd to 288, in the 4th to 648, in the 5th to 687, and in the 6th to 144. In Passion week, there will probably be more than 600. At my age, it's enough to exhaust me completely. And then there are daily baptisms, funerals and visits. I have also had an average of 515 confessions over the last five weeks.[63]

Rozanov knew what his brother meant. As he recorded in his own diary in 1901, he himself stood for seven and a half hours a day administering confession in the cathedral.[64] In the circumstances, it is hardly surprising that some priests should have put perfunctory confessions at the head of their list of apologies when leaving a parish.[65]

Beyond these somewhat arid annual observances, most Russians owed their contact with the church not to liturgical celebrations but instead to events associated with the life of the many confraternities (*bratstva*) established in the nineteenth century; to icon processions, which varied from the parochial celebration of a local community's recovery from cholera, to the imperial pomp and ceremony commemorating the millennium of the death of St Methodius in 1885;[66] and finally to pilgrimages, sometimes to Jerusalem, but more often to holy places in Russia, and especially to monasteries such as Valaam, a favoured destination for thousands of members of Orthodox temperance societies from St Petersburg, whose extensive traffic on packed steamships on Lake Ladoga generated sufficient business to attract the unwelcome, but characteristically vigilant, attention of Finnish tax and safety officials.[67] Since what united these various expressions of popular piety was a belief in the power of the supernatural, it is with a discussion of miracles that we conclude.

Though some historians of Western denominations have been tempted to treat miracles as an expression of conflict between 'popular' and 'official' religions, it is more revealing to investigate the accommodation between the two.[68] Russian ecclesiastical authorities were certainly nervous of unauthorized miracles, an anxiety which revealed itself in periodic attempts to restrict the movement of renowned miracle-working icons.[69] Yet there were also multiple attractions to the Church of widespread belief in miracles. The first such attraction was intellectual. As a clerical contributor to the spiritual journal *Strannik* stressed in its first year of publication (1860), there could be no better demonstration of the superiority of the supernatural over natural science than the recovery of a patient who was relieved of either physical or mental affliction by a miracle-working icon, having earlier been declared incurable by doctors.[70] Miracles might serve a punitive as well as a humanitarian function. A pamphlet published by the Synodal press alleged that, in 1891, the matron of the Trinity Charitable Society attached to the Izmailovskii regiment suffered a seizure of the shoulder and was confined to bed for several weeks having contemplated the unworthy thought that a highly-reputed icon from Mount Athos might be merely a means of luring the credulous to the St Petersburg monastery where it was displayed.[71] Although this was an extreme case, there was always a veiled threat: 'Do not think', warned a Moscow priest in a public lecture in December 1900, 'that it is possible to remain a believer having denied miracles' – a far from casual warning directed primarily at those followers of Leo Tolstoy who shared his conviction that faith in miracles was a sign of insanity.[72]

The second attraction of miracles in the eyes of the Church was what might be labelled their lack of social discrimination. British visitors to Russia often contrasted Orthodox services with the class-ridden corporate worship prevalent at home. As Maurice Baring remarked of Moscow at Easter 1906: 'There are no seats, no pews, no precedence nor privilege. There is a smell of incense and a still stronger smell of poor people, without which, someone said, a church is not a church'.[73] It can hardly be coincidental that almost every pamphlet published in celebration of a miracle-working icon in St Petersburg was careful to stress that its blessings could be conferred on each sector of society, from the highest to the lowest.[74] On the one hand, this strategy was intended to deflect suspicions that the urban clergy were preoccupied by afflictions of the wealthy. On the other hand, it formed part of a wider (and only partially successful) campaign to encourage the educated to remain actively committed to their church.[75]

The third, related, advantage was pecuniary. The presence of a miracle-working icon guaranteed the income of any monastery or church fortunate enough to hold one. Even a tangential association with the miraculous was beneficial. Such an association was crucial to Father Mikhail Galkin's attempts to defray the debts of his impoverished parish in the Petrograd district of the capital. After the Revolution, Galkin became infamous, under the pseudonym Gorev, as Trotsky's henchman and a lynchpin of the League of the Militant Godless.[76] Yet during the First World War, this 'scoundrel and renegade', as the historian Iu.V. Got'e described him in 1922, had not yet come to regard clerical assassinations as 'a good warning to the counterrevolution in cassocks'.[77] Galkin took his deacon to the Sarov *pustyn'*, from which they returned not only with a donation of 3000 rubles (roughly a tenth of what they needed to pay for repairs) but also, more significantly, with an icon of the recently canonized St Serafim, part of his mantle, and a fragment of the clothing in which he had been buried.[78] Serafim had been canonized in 1903 at the instigation of Nicholas II himself, an embattled ruler hoping to exploit the occasion as a symbol of national integration and divine legitimacy. But this was not to be, since the event itself was poorly organized and served largely to contrast the destitution of the sick pilgrims who attended in the hope of miraculous recovery to the opulence of the tsar and his suite. More important still, the popular demand for uncorrupted remains could not be satisfied in Serafim's case.[79] Not for the last time, Russian religion defied the expectations of those who sought to control it.

Russian popular religion – a subject whose validity was barely acknowledged but a decade ago – has swiftly become a modish area of research. Much remains to be done before we can establish social, geographical and chronological patterns of holiness, or alternatively deny their existence. Though pre-revolutionary Orthodoxy can no longer be ignored it may be premature to ascribe to it a dominant role in social life. Furthermore, for all the 'attack on *dvoeverie*', the distinction between doctrinal Christianity and peasant custom is still reflected in an historiographical spectrum ranging in emphasis from Chulos's acute sensitivity to the significance of folk traditions to Shevzov's demonstration that popular religion owed more to the clergy than Pascal, for one, supposed. Only a tiny part of the debate has been touched upon here. Much more could be said about the relative significance of the local and the national, the sacred and the profane, in popular religious culture. But enough has been said to show that it is crucial to restore the religious dimension to Russian history and that it is impossible to do so without understanding the dilemma of a national church in a multinational empire, torn between the need to assimilate its rivals' most successful pastoral techniques whilst seeking to differentiate its own spiritual and doctrinal identity.

Acknowledgements

This chapter is a by-product of research on Russian religious rivalry, sponsored by the British Academy, the Royal Society of Edinburgh and the Caledonian Research Foundation. I am grateful to all these bodies for their support.

Notes

Restrictions of space confine me throughout to illustrative rather than comprehensive references.

1 S. Averintsev, 'The idea of Holy Russia', in P. Dukes, ed. *Russia and Europe* (London, 1991), p. 16.
2 Quoted by G. Hosking, *Russia: people and Empire, 1552–1917* (London, 1997), p. 72.
3 Quoted by F.-D. Liechtenhan, 'Le Russe, ennemi héréditaire de la chrétienté? La diffusion de l'image de la Moscovie en Europe occidentale aux XVIe et XVIIe siècles', *Revue Historique*, 285, 1 (1991), p. 85, fn 4.
4 C.A. Frierson, *Peasant icons: representations of rural people in late nineteenth-century Russia* (New York and Oxford, 1993), pp. 45–6.
5 See C.J. Chulos, 'Myths of the pious or pagan peasant in post-emancipation Central Russia (Voronezh Province)', *Russian History*, 22, 2 (1995), pp. 181–216.
6 S. Dixon, 'Reflections on modern Russian martyrdom', in Diana Wood, ed. *Martyrs and martyrologies: studies in church history*, 30 (Oxford, 1993), pp. 404–5; J.W. Daly, '"Storming the last citadel": the Bolshevik assault on the church', in V.N. Brovkin, ed. *The Bolsheviks in Russian society: the Revolution and the civil wars* (New Haven, CT, 1997), pp. 235–68.
7 For documents on persecution, see N.N. Pokrovskii and S.G. Petrov (eds), *Arkhivy kremlia. 1: politbiuro i tserkov' 1922–1925gg* (Novosibirsk and Moscow, 1997); for discussion, see A. Luukkanen, *The party of unbelief: the religious policy of the Bolshevik Party, 1917–1929* (Helsinki, 1994), and A. Luukkanen, *The religious policy of the Stalinist state: a case study. The Central Standing Commission on Religious Questions, 1929–1938* (Helsinki, 1997); on popular reactions, see W.B. Husband, 'Soviet atheism and Russian Orthodox strategies of resistance, 1917–1932', *Journal of Modern History*, 70 (1998), pp. 74–107.
8 Conducted on Christmas Eve, 6 January, the census registered 42.29 per cent of the adult population as Orthodox, of whom 66.23 per cent were women. See F. Corley, 'Believers' responses to the 1937 and 1939 Soviet censuses', *Religion, State and Society*, 22, 4 (1994), pp. 403–17, especially table 1, p. 407; S. Davies, *Popular opinion in Stalin's Russia: terror, propaganda and dissent, 1934–1941* (Cambridge, 1997), pp. 73–82.

9 R. Pipes, *Russia under the Old Regime* (Harmondsworth, Middx, 1977), p. 161.

10 M.M. Gromyko, *Traditsionnye normy povedeniia i formy obshcheniia russkikh krest'ian XIXv* (Moscow, 1986), pp. 99–105; N.N. Pokrovskii, *Antifeodal'nyi protest uralo-sibirskikh krest'ian staroobriadtsev v XVIII v.* (Novosibirsk, 1974).

11 See, *inter alia*, B. Meehan, 'Popular piety, local initiative, and the founding of women's religious communities in Russia, 1764–1907', in S.K. Batalden, ed. *Seeking God: the recovery of religious identity in Orthodox Russia, Ukraine, and Georgia* (De Kalb, IL, 1993), pp. 83–105, an essay first published in 1986; B. Meehan-Waters, 'Metropolitan Filaret (Drozdov) and the reform of Russian women's monastic communities', *Russian Review*, 50 (1991), pp. 310–23.

12 A. Netting, 'Images and ideas in peasant art', in B. Eklof and S.P. Frank, eds *The world of the Russian peasant: post-emancipation culture and society* (London, 1990), pp. 186–7.

13 S.L. Hoch, *Serfdom and social control in Russia: Petrovskoe, a village in Tambov* (Chicago, 1986), pp. 146–7.

14 J. Burds, 'A culture of denunciation: peasant labour migration and religious anathematization in rural Russia, 1860–1905', in S. Fitzpatrick and R. Gellately, eds *Accusatory practices: denunciation in modern European history, 1789–1989* (Chicago, 1997), p. 42.

15 S.V. Kuznetsov, 'Vera i obriadnost' v khoziaistvennoi deiatel'nosti russkogo krest'ianstva', in V.P. Danilov and L.V. Milov, eds *Mentalitet i agrarnoe razvitie Rossii (XIX–XX vv.): materialy mezhdunarodnoi konferentsii. Moskva. 14–15 iiuniia 1994g* (Moscow, 1996), p. 286; L.A. Tul'tseva, 'Bozhii mir pravoslavnogo krest'ianina', in Danilov and Milov, eds *Mentalilet*, p. 304.

16 E.K. Wirtschafter, *Social identity in imperial Russia* (De Kalb, 1997), p. 50.

17 See Q. Skinner, 'Sir Geoffrey Elton and the practice of history', *Transactions of the Royal Historical Society*, 6th series, 7 (1997), pp. 307 ff.

18 G.P. Fedotov, *The Russian religious mind*, 2 vols (Belmont, MA, 1975), vol. 1, pp. 357, 360, 362. Fedotov's equally influential use of the term 'kenoticism' is exposed as anachronistic by J. Børtnes, 'Russkii kenotizm: k pereotsenke odnogo poniatiia', in V.N. Zakharov, ed. *Evangel'skii tekst v russkoi literature XVIII–XX vekov: tsitata, reminintsentsiia, motiv, siuzhet, zhanr* (Petrozavodsk, 1994), pp. 61–5.

19 O. Figes, *A people's tragedy: the Russian Revolution 1891–1924* (London, 1996), p. 66.

20 Chulos, 'Myths of the pious or pagan peasant in post-emancipation Central Russia (Voronezh Province)', p. 199.

21 E. Levin, '*Dvoeverie* and popular religion', in S.K. Batalden, ed. *Seeking God: the recovery of religious identity in Orthodox Russia, Ukraine, and Georgia* (De Kalb, IL, 1993), pp. 31–52. See also C.D. Worobec, 'Death ritual among Russian and Ukrainian peasants: linkages between the living and the dead', in S.P. Frank and M.D. Steinberg, eds *Cultures in flux: lower-class values, practices and resistance in late imperial Russia* (Princeton, NJ, 1994), pp. 14–15.

22 M. Lewin, *The making of the Soviet system* (London, 1985), p. 70; R.O. Crummey, 'Old belief as popular religion: new approaches', *Slavic Review*, 52, 4 (1993), pp. 700–12.

23 P. Pascal *The religion of the Russian people*, trans. R. Williams (London, 1976), pp. 8–15.

24 Pascal, *The religion of the Russian people*, p. 21; cf. Ju.M. Lotman and B.A. Uspenskij, 'The role of dual models in the dynamics of Russian culture (up to the end of the Eighteenth century)', in their *The semiotics of Russian culture*, ed. A. Shukman (Ann Arbor, MI, 1984), pp. 3–35.

25 A. Solzhenitsyn, *The gulag archipelago, 1918–1956: an experiment in literary investigation I-II*, trans. T.P. Whitney (London, 1974), p. 342.

26 A. Farge, *Subversive words: public opinion in eighteenth-century France*, trans. R. Morris (Cambridge, 1994), pp. 81–9; quote at p. 85.

27 R.W. Scribner, 'Ritual and popular religion in Catholic Germany at the time of the Reformation', *Journal of Ecclesiastical History,* 35, 1 (1984), p. 74 (figure at p. 75).

28 See, for example, J. Walsh, C. Haydon and S. Taylor, 'Introduction', in J. Walsh, C. Haydon and S. Taylor, eds *The Church of England c. 1689–c. 1833: from toleration to tractarianism* (Cambridge, 1993), p. 13; H. McLeod, 'Secular cities? Berlin, London and New York in the late nineteenth and early twentieth centuries', in S. Bruce, ed. *Religion and modernization: historians and sociologists debate the secularization thesis* (Oxford, 1992), pp. 85–6.

29 R.J.W. Evans, *The making of the Habsburg Monarchy, 1550–1700* (Oxford, 1979), p. 383, and ch. 11, *passim*. On the interrelationship between Christianity and magic in early modern Russia, see J.M. Hartley, *A social history of the Russian Empire, 1650–1825* (London, 1999), pp. 224–56, which draws on the forthcoming book by W.F. Ryan, *The bathhouse at midnight: an historical survey of magic and divination in Russia.*

30 G.L. Freeze, 'The rechristianization of Russia: the Church and popular religion, 1750–1850', *Studia Slavica Finlandensia*, 7 (1990), pp. 101–35.

31 C.J. Chulos, 'Myths of the pious or pagan peasant in post-emancipation Central Russia (Voronezh Province)', p. 212.

32 See my *Church, state and society in late imperial Russia: the diocese of St Petersburg, 1880–1914*, unpublished PhD. thesis (London: University of London, 1993), pp. 221–32; for the report cited in text, see Rossiiskii gosudarstvennyi istoricheskii arkhiv (RGIA), fond (f.) 796, opis' (op.) 442, delo (d.) 2229, list (l.) 8.

33 RGIA, f. 796, op. 173, d. 2558.

34 C.J. Chulos, 'Peasant perspectives of clerical debauchery in post-emancipation Russia', *Studia Slavica Finlandensia*, 12 (1995), especially pp. 41–5. Although Chulos's evidence is drawn solely from the diocese of Voronezh, his conclusions are universally plausible.

35 See, for example, his annual reports to the Synod: RGIA, f. 796, op. 442, d. 2125 (1905g.), l. 27. On Archibishop Nikolai's *ukaz* on the same point, 30 April 1902, see Mikkelin Maakunta-Arkisto, Suojäarven Ortodoksisen Seurakunnan Arkisto, [henceforth, MMA, Suojärvi], IIEa8 (unfoliated). The Finnish case will play a significant part in my study of religious rivalry.

36 *Notes of a visit to the Russian Church in years 1840, 1841 by the late William Palmer M.A. Selected and arranged by Cardinal Newman* (London, 1882), pp. 163, 225. See also, B.I. Sove, 'Problema ispravleniia bogosluzhebnykh knig v Rossii v XIX–XX vekakh', *Bogoslovskie trudy,* 5 (1970), 25–68.

37 *Besedy v pravoslavnoi vere khristianskoi govorennyia v tserkvi Sv. i Prav. Simeona Bogopriimtsa i Anny Prorochitsy sviashchennikom Vasiliem Fortunatovym v 1859 godu* (St Petersburg, 1860), pp. 33–4.

38 D. Rayfield, *Anton Chekhov: a life* (London, 1997), p. 13, and *passim*.

39 V.M. Lur'e, 'Dogmatika "religii liubvi". Dogmaticheskie predstavlieniia pozdnego Dostoevskogo', in V.A. Kotel'nikov ed. *Khristianstvo i russkaia literatura: Sbornik vtoroi* (St Petersburg, 1996), p. 294, n. 12. On Bukharev, see A.P. Dmitriev, 'A.M. Bukharev (arkhimandrit Feodor) kak literaturnyi kritik', in *Khristianstvo*, pp. 160–201, and G.L. Freeze, 'Die Laisierung des Archimandriten Feodor (Bukharev) und ihre kirchenpolitischen Hintergründe', *Kirche im Osten*, 28 (1985), 26–52.

40 G.L. Freeze, 'Counter-Reformation in Russian Orthodoxy: popular response to religious innovation, 1922–1925', *Slavic Review*, 54, 2 (1995), p. 318. See also, E.E. Roslof, 'The heresy of "Bolshevik" Christianity: Orthodox rejection of religious reform during NEP', *Slavic Review*, 55, 3 (1996), pp. 614–35.

41 Anthony Trollope, *Barchester towers*, The World's Classics (Oxford, 1980), vol. 1, p. 112. Cf. pp. 116–19.

42 Pascal, *The religion of the Russian people*, p. 22.

43 D. Rayfield, *Anton Chekhov: a life*, p. 132.

44 A. Lindenmeyr, *Poverty is not a vice: charity, society, and the state in Imperial Russia* (Princeton, NJ, 1996), pp. 133–4 and *passim*.

45 G. Young, '"Into Church matters": lay identity, rural parish life and popular politics in late Imperial and early Soviet Russia, 1864–1928', *Russian History*, 23, 1–4 (1996), 367–84.

46 V. Shevzov, 'Chapels and the ecclesial world of prerevolutionary Russian peasants', *Slavic Review*, 55, 3 (1996), especially pp. 593–607.

47 MMA, Suojärvi, IAa11–15: confessional records; IHa, filed in IFa1: altar books. I owe much to the Mikkeli archivist, Anja Jääskeläinen.

48 MMA, Suojärvi, IIIGa6, 9, 11, 12: candle accounts for 1892–1912; IIAb3–4: reports on the moral condition of the parish, 1907–13. Though candle sales tell us little about absolute attendance they seem, at least at this grass-roots level, a plausible indicator of seasonal distribution.

49 Compare J. Cox, *The English churches in a secular society: Lambeth, 1879–1930* (Oxford, 1982), who emphasizes (pp. 42–3) the significance of clerical effort and the need for a range of parochial activities involving lay volunteers in order to establish a vital parish life.

50 Apart from the sources quoted below, see priests' views on this question, in *Istoriko-statisticheskie svedeniia o S.-Peterburgskoi eparkhii*, 10 vols (St Petersburg, 1869–85), *passim*.

51 MMA, Suojärvi, IIAb3, f. 12v.

52 *Pis'ma preosviashchennago Leonida, arkhiepiskopa Iaroslavskago i Rostovskago k arkhimandritu Pimenu, nastoiateliu Nikolaevskago monastyria, chto na Ugreshe* (Moscow, 1877). A letter of 10 January 1869 condemns warm chapels as a breach of asceticism (p. 41).

53 *Proshchanie protoiereia P.A. Smirnova s prichtom i prikhozhanami kafedral'nago Isaakievskago sobora v S.-Peterburge 1 noiabria 1897 goda* (St Petersburg, 1897), p. 6.

54 For example, *Tikhvinskaia tserkov's farforovymi ukrasheniiami v Spasobocharinskom prikhode* (St Petersburg, 1882), p. 6, a building that had earlier been as dark as the catacombs (p. 3).

55 *Osviashchenie Voskresenskago khrama Obshchestva rasprostraneniia religiozno-nravstvennago prosvescheniia v dukhe pravoslavnoi tserkvi* (St Petersburg, 1909), p. 6. On the society and its preaching, see my 'The Church's social role in St Petersburg, 1880–1914', in G.A Hosking, ed. *Church, nation and state in Russia and Ukraine* (London, 1991), pp. 167–92.

56 I.N. Manasein, *Elektricheskoe osveshchenie v tserkvakh* (St Petersburg, 1912), pp. 6–7.

57 *Vospominaniia o Nikol'shchine, pogoste Gdovskago uezda, S-Peterburgskoi gubernii, po povodu osviashcheniia khrama 9–go maia 1898 goda* (St Petersburg, 1898), pp. 10, 19.

58 See R.R. Robson, 'Liturgy and community among Old Believers, 1905–1917', *Slavic Review*, 52, 4 (1993), 713–24; R.R. Robson, *Old Believers in modern Russia* (De Kalb, 1995).

59 For a manual urging priests to remember the curative rather than the punitive powers of penance, see Arkhiepiskop Platon, *Napominanie sviashchenniku ob*

obiazannostiakh ego pri sovershenii tainstva pokaianiia, 3rd edn, 2 parts (Moscow, 1896), especially I: 166–87.

60 M.D. Steinberg and V.M. Khrustalev, *The fall of the Romanovs: political dreams and personal struggles in a time of revolution* (New Haven, CT, 1995), pp. 145, 144 (Beliaev's diary, 31 March), 140 (29 March).

61 *Notes of a visit to the Russian Church in years 1840, 1841 by the late William Palmer M.A. Selected and arranged by Cardinal Newman*, pp. 320–1.

62 A.I. Al'mazov, *Tainaia ispoved' v pravoslavnoi vostochnoi tserkvi: opyt vneshnei istorii*, 3 parts (Odessa, 1894–95), I: 590; and 'Dozvolitel' no li sovershat' ispoved' sidia?', *Tserkovnyi vestnik*, no. 36, (1891), p. 571.

63 Excerpted in *Nashe pastyrstvo: Pamiati Protoiereia N.I. Rozanova*, compiled by Prot. S. Arkhangelov (St Petersburg, 1913), p. 53.

64 Rozanov's diary for 16–17 February 1901, Also excerpted in Arkhangelov, *Nashe pastyrstvo*, p. 55.

65 See, for example, Prot. V. Mikhailovskii, *Proshchal'naia rech', skazannaia v Spasobocharinskoi Tserkvi v kontse pozdnei obedni 8–go Ianvaria 1884 goda* (St Petersburg, 1884), p. 6, and *Slovo pri proshchanii s prikhozhanami Troitskago na Peterburgskago storone Sobora i pripisnoi k nemu krestovozdvizhenskoi Tserkvi, ona-zhe Nikolotrunilovskaia, Sviashchennika Polievkta Soboleva 25–go Marta 1902g* (St Petersburg, 1902), pp. 8–9.

66 For an example of the former, see RGIA, f. 796, op. 178, d. 2560; for the latter, see *Tseremonial krestnago khoda iz Kazanskago Sobora, v S.-Peterburge, v Kafedral'nyi Isaakievskii Sobor, 6 aprelia 1885 goda* (St Petersburg, 1885).

67 Kansallis Arkisto, Helsinki, KKK 7–5/1912, II osasto (tax); KKK 7–14/1916, I osasto (dangerous steamers). See *Palomnichestvo Sampsonievskikh trezvennikov v Valaamskuiu obitel'* (St Petersburg, 1910); *Finliandskaia gazeta*, 5/18 July 1909; *Izvestiia S.-Peterburgskoi eparkhii*, no. 12, (1908), pp. 22–5 (unofficial section).

68 In this sense, T. Kselman, *Miracles and prophecies in nineteenth-century France* (New Brunswick, NJ, 1983), is more persuasive than M.P. Carroll, *Madonnas that maim: popular Catholicism in Italy since the fifteenth century* (Baltimore, MD, 1992), and M.P. Carroll, *Veiled threats: the logic of popular Catholicism in Italy* (Baltimore, MD, 1996).

69 For example, see RGIA, f. 796, op. 187, d. 6929. For a superb treatment of this subject, published as this book went to press, see V. Shevzov, Miracle-working icons, laity and authority in the Russian Orthodox church, 1861–1917, *Russian Review*, 58, 1 (1999) pp. 26–48.

70 Diakon A. Lebedev, 'Razgovor sviashchennika s doktorom o chudesiakh', *Strannik*, 4, otdel II, (1860), p. 291.

71 *XXV-let, 1888–1913: Dukhovnoe torzhestvo po sluchaiiu dvadtsatipiatiletiia sv. khrama vo imia sv. ikony tverskoi Bozhiei Materi pri novo-afonskom podvorii v S. Peterburge* (St Petersburg, 1913), pp. 34–7.

72 Sv. I. Orfanitskii, 'Chto takoe chudo?', *Vera i tserkov'*, no. 1, (1901), p. 97; *Tolstoy's letters*, translated and edited by R.F. Christian, 2 vols (London, 1978), vol. II; p. 474.

73 M. Baring, *What I saw in Russia* (London, undated), p. 263.

74 See, *inter alia, Blagodatnyia deistviia i istseleniia ot Konevskoi ikony Bozhiei Materi, nakhodiashcheisia v monastyrskoi chasovne v S.-Peterburge na Zagorodnom prospekte, no. 7* (Pochaev, 1913), pp. 7–12.

75 G.L. Freeze, '"Going to the intelligentsia": the Church and its urban mission in post-reform Russia', in E.W. Clowes, S.D. Kassow and J.L. West, eds *Between tsar and people: educated society and the quest for public identity in late imperial Russia* (Princeton, NJ, 1991), pp. 215–32.

76 See D. Peris, 'Commissars in red cassocks: former priests in the League of the Militant Godless', *Slavic Review*, 54, 2 (1995), pp. 345–8.

77 *Time of troubles: the diary of Iurii Vladimirovich Got'e*, translated and edited by T. Emmons (Princeton, NJ, 1988), p. 457. Got'e ascribed Galkin's apostasy to his disappointed ambitions for episcopal preferment (p. 353). Got'e himself witnessed a 'miracle' when the red draping placed over the icon at Moscow's Nikol'skie gates on May Day 1918 'unraveled along its fibers just as if some kind of acid had been poured on it. A crowd gathered, buzzing about the miracle; there was a public prayer, and then firing in the air to disperse the crowd' (pp. 139–40).

78 Sv. M. Galkin, *Petrogradskii Spaso-Preobrazhenskii Koltovskii prikhod v 1915 godu* (Petrograd, 1916), p. 102.

79 G.L. Freeze, 'Subversive piety: religion and the political crisis in late imperial Russia', *Journal of Modern History*, 68 (1996), especially pp. 312–29; Freeze may nevertheless underestimate the impact of the Sarov canonization.

3

Restoring religion to Russian art

LINDSEY HUGHES

This paper was inspired by rereading James Billington's *The icon and the axe*, the evocative title of which, as the author explains in his preface, juxtaposes 'two artifacts of enduring meaning to Russians', objects which were 'traditionally hung together on the wall of the peasant hut in the wooded Russian north' and 'serve to suggest both the visionary and the earthy aspects of Russian culture'.[1] Orthodox Christianity produced 'the first distinctly Russian culture and provided the basic forms of artistic expression and the framework of belief for modern Russia'. An essential feature of that culture is 'a direct sense of beauty, a passion for seeing spiritual truth in concrete forms'.[2] Billington argued, in this book and elsewhere, that the 'intellectual silence' of Early Russia could be explained by the fact that 'Muscovite thought tended to crystallize in images', hence the importance which he accorded to the figurative arts and the built environment.[3]

Billington added substance to the idea that Russian artists, no less than writers – the icon painters who fasted and prayed before working, the nineteenth-century painter Alexander Ivanov attempting to encapsulate the essence of the gospels in a single painting, avant-garde artists trying to change the world – had a sense of mission above and beyond the work of art for its own sake. On the other hand, just as the rules of icon painting limited the scope for experimentation (indeed, anyone 'inventing' an icon was threatened with damnation), even post-medieval Russian artists often seemed constrained rather than liberated by ideals or ideology; they were prophets and servants. The very fact that Russians seemed more concerned with ideas than technique and composition reduced their appeal for Western art historians, with the latter's emphasis on stylistic and compositional innovation. It is instructive that the Russian artists best known in the West – Malevich, Kandinsky and Chagall – were the most radical stylistically.

My aim in this chapter is to explore a framework for the examination of religion in the arts in Russia, proceeding chronologically from the tenth century to the present and focusing on the figurative arts, but with some reference to architecture. I consider both Orthodox cult art created for devotional purposes (*ikonopis'*) and secular art (*zhivopis'*) on religious themes, the latter with reference to both Orthodox spirituality and Christianity in general. The interaction between these two spheres, sometimes in the work of one and the same artist, will also be examined. I revisit some Soviet preconceptions, which continue to hold sway even in Western studies of Russian art, review some new approaches and make some tentative suggestions for further research.

The survey begins with an extended 'medieval' period of more or less exclusively Orthodox art (albeit with pagan and folk elements), initiated by the conversion of Rus' to Christianity in 988–9 and prolonged by the Mongol occupation and the rift with the Latin West, which by and large cut off Russia from Western cultural developments (Gothic and Renaissance).

This period, which extends into the seventeenth century, has been used to demonstrate, on the one hand, Russia's cultural distinctiveness from the West (*samobytnost'*), on the other, its 'backwardness' (*otstalost'*) in relation to Western civilisation. Georges Florovsky summed up the dilemma:

> It has commonly been assumed that culture had to be autonomous, that is, secular. The whole history of European civilisation was usually presented in this way – as the story of the progressive emancipation of culture from the stiffening control of established religion, or of the Church.[4]

Soviet art historians, who were saddled with this essentially rationalist approach long after it had been discarded by their Western counterparts, coped with the potentially embarrassing fact of the prolonged 'control of established religion' over early Russian art (doubly problematical because of wholesale borrowing from Byzantium) by emphasizing the material and 'humanistic' background, in other words, denying the religiosity of religious art. The following passage (on the twelfth century) is characteristic:

> Although all the surviving monuments of Vladimir-Suzdal' sculpture and painting were linked with the upper echelons of feudal society (they were commissioned either by princes or members of the church hierarchy), they had very strong popular features [*narodnye cherty*].

Artists in Rus', it is claimed, rejected dead and sterile Byzantine canons to create their own more 'life-enhancing' (*zhizneradostnyi*) interpretation of the world and man.[5] Old Russian religious painting was scrutinized for evidence of the 'growth of realistic tendencies'; everyday (*bytovye*) details in icons and frescoes were seized upon for comment, divorced from the religious context. The absence of free-standing examples of genre painting, still life, landscape and portraits in early modern Russia, which apparently cut it off from the European mainstream, was compensated for by the discovery of these genres within cult art.

The highest praise was reserved for those artists who allegedly emphasized 'human' qualities. For example, Andrei Rublev in his famous icon of the Old Testament Trinity (1410–20s) is said to have expressed 'a profoundly humane, philosophical idea', symbolizing 'mankind's dream of a perfect world in which harmony, love and friendship would reign'.[6] The fifteenth-century painter Dionysius 'stressed the dignity of man and the idea of the unification of the human race'.[7] The mysteries of religion, heaven and hell, reincarnation and salvation, hardly figure, except as examples of superstition or folk *fantaziia*. Soviet citizens lost the key to understanding iconic images and may even have believed that medieval Russian art was indeed secular.

New writing, ranging from beginners' guides to iconography to the complex cultural history of icons, is restoring the spiritual content of medieval Russian art.[8] Of particular interest are examinations of the synthesis of the arts in their historical context, which decode the religious and symbolic landscapes of Early Russia.[9] Works in the latter category may be recommended to those historians who still attach supreme significance to the evidence of the written word. 'Theories' of Muscovite power politics, it can be argued, are reflected more strongly in buildings, icons, frescoes, regalia and ritual, in their complex interrelationships, than in written sources, which are relatively sparse and often controversial (for example, the correspondence between Ivan IV and Prince Aleksei Kurbskii). The Cathedral of the Protecting Veil of the Mother of God on Red Square (better known as St. Basil's), for example, probably offers richer evidence of the concept of *translatio imperii* in Russia than do written references to Moscow the Third Rome. Early Russian art, far from being sterile and unchanging or 'primitive', had sophisticated conventions and a peculiar dynamic which have yet to be revealed in full.

In the seventeenth century a short transitional (*perekhodnyi*) period saw the hesitant emergence of secular art forms (portraits, 'perspective' drawings, popular tales, drama, instrumental music) and a modest Westernization of elite culture ('Moscow Baroque' architecture in the 1680s–90s with stylized application of the Classical orders) against a background of foreign influences and internal crises (notably Nikon's reform of the Orthodox church).

But were both Western and Russian historians overeager to declare the triumph of secular culture? Some of the changes may indeed be attributed to 'Westernization' [Tsar Aleksei's short-lived theatre (1672–6), organized by foreigners, is a case in point], but new, subtler interpretations are needed to supplement the old Soviet arguments which equated 'secularization' (*obmirshchenie*) with 'progressiveness'. The Moscow icon painter

Simon Ushakov (1629–86), for example, is generally characterized in the literature as a pioneer of secular features in icon painting – naturalistic use of light and shade, inclusion of realistic elements of architecture and landscape and so on.[10] In a recent article, however, the Russian art historian Engelina Smirnova challenges the idea that Ushakov's work was a 'move towards a new artistic epoch', arguing that it belongs to the 'old system' and that he resurrected ancient subjects and forms – Muscovite, Kievan and Byzantine – in an art which she categorizes as 'late medieval'.[11] The work of other leading 'transitional' icon painters needs to be re-examined in this light.

A topic in particular need of fundamental research is the interaction of Muscovite and other Eastern Slavonic cultures in the later seventeenth century. It is often claimed that Western styles and genres reached Russia via Ukraine and Belarus. The theory of the cultural mediation of the 'fraternal' nations fitted comfortably, after adjustments, into the Soviet framework, but what, precisely, were the nature and results of this interaction, which took place overwhelmingly in the religious sphere, in church architecture, icons, printing and engraving? Recent research on the reception in Russia of Latinate book culture needs to be extended into the area of religious art.[12]

In the reign of Peter the Great (1682–1725), especially after the founding of St Petersburg in 1703, both Soviet and Western textbooks agree, cult art more or less disappears from elite culture. Alan Bird writes that 'as a generalisation one might say that religious painting in the traditional sense had ceased with Peter the Great'.[13] Billington placed the parting of the ways for religious and secular art somewhat later in the century: 'More than any other single person prior to the Leninist Revolution, Catherine [II] cut official culture loose from its religious roots, and changed both its physical setting and its philosophical preoccupations'.[14] Classicism followed by Romanticism linked Russia to the mainstream of European culture and the pagan world of antiquity.

In fact, the religious element in culture proved more resilient than is sometimes admitted. Even Peter the Great regarded St Petersburg not as a secular city but as a 'paradise' blessed with a new brand of holiness by his favourite saints Peter and Paul, Andrew and Alexander Nevskii.[15] It is certainly true that Peter furthered the development of *zhivopis'*, hiring foreign artists and dispatching Russians abroad to study. Official Petrine art was dominated by secular themes – images of the emperor and his supporters, records of the growth of the new capital, of battles, ships and captured towns. On the other hand, icons remained part of Peter's environment, as of every Othodox Christian's. He particularly venerated an image of the Saviour Not Made by Hands, which he carried on his campaigns, including Poltava.[16] In a sense, Peter endorsed the importance of cult art by regulating it, cracking down hard on hoaxes associated with 'miraculous' icons and in 1707 appointing the Ukrainian architect and sculptor Ivan Zarudnii as superintendant of religious painting. Icon painters were to be examined and awarded certificates after a period of study with a qualified master. Ancient rules on icons based on the resolutions of the Church Council of 1551 were reiterated.[17] In January 1723 a personal imperial decree complained that portraits (*zhivopisnye persony*) of the emperor and empress, 'painted unskilfully by ignorant persons', were being sold in Moscow and displayed in people's homes. Inspector Zarudnii was ordered to gather the offending paintings into the Holy Synod and ensure that no more were painted or sold and 'to order such portraits to be painted skilfully by artists with certificates of good workmanship, with all care and fitting assiduity.'[18] In other words, the Church retained considerable authority in respect of all images, not just cult art. In 1725 the Holy Synod refused permission for the publication of Nicholas Pineau's detailed description of the decorations for Peter's lying-in state on the grounds that they were 'pagan'.[19] In 1743–4, when the late Alexander Menshikov's private chapel was being refurbished, the Synod ordered workmen to add wings to some wooden cupids to turn them into angels and to destroy the rest.[20]

The Orthodox Church's continued disapproval of images in the round meant that sculpture, especially the lifelike imitation of the human form, was regarded as doubly 'progressive' by old-style Soviet art historians. But the carving of free-standing figures in stone and casting in metal made little impact in the hands of native Russian craftspeople until the second half of the eighteenth century. The only works of Petrine sculpture illustrated in general histories are those surviving from the workshop of the Italian artist C.B. Rastrelli. In fact, there was plenty of sculpture in Russia in the first half of the eighteenth century, but, like Menshikov's cupids, it was mainly intended for religious settings and carved from wood (the iconostasis of the Peter–Paul cathedral is an important example) and therefore did not support the accepted wisdom that Peter 'secularized' culture.[21] New studies of the wooden sculpture of the Russian north bear witness to vigorous traditions of relief carving and sometimes three-dimensional religious images in the provinces throughout the eighteenth century, whereas virtually all sculpture on antique themes had to be imported.[22]

Peter's reign also saw the importation of Western religious paintings, the most famous of which was Rembrandt's *David and Jonathan* (1642).[23] Such paintings were not regarded as devotional works, but as a branch of history painting, which, with the establishment of the Russian Academy of Arts in 1764, gained formal recognition as the highest sphere of artistic activity. The artist's mature technical skills were applied to the original creation of complex compositions based on narratives from ancient history, classical mythology and the Bible.

Thus, far from witnessing the demise of religious painting, the eighteenth century saw the continuation of an indigenous tradition (Orthodox cult art) and the development of an alien one (religious history painting). Russian painters working on both cult and secular art assimilated the freer conventions of Western religious art, thereby hastening the drawing together of *ikonopis'* and *zhivopis'*, so that the former, while maintaining rules of iconographic composition, drew closer to the latter both in style and in the materials used – oil on canvas rather than tempera on wood. Painters continued to paint icons because there was a lively market for 'devotional artefacts', whereas secular works such as portraits were confined to the homes of the nobility and better-off merchants. In Russia's age of Classicism, which can be extended to the 1830s and beyond, virtually all major Russian artists working in the capitals painted icons as well as secular works. Many began their careers as icon painters, including Ivan Vishniakov (1699–1761), I.P. Argunov (1727–1802), Dmitrii Levitskii (1735–1822, the son of a priest) and Vladimir Borovikovskii (1757–1825), the latter two both Ukrainians who spent most of their working lives in Russia. In 1764 the painter A.P. Antropov sent a petition for payment to Catherine II, reminding her that for her coronation he had painted an icon of the Nativity of Christ, two shrouds with Christ's image (*plashchanitsy*) and two portraits of the empress, a not uncharacteristic mix.[24]

In the capitals the Byzantine idiom (increasingly regarded by sophisticated taste as archaic and ugly) was often rejected in favour of a more Italianate style (what a recent catalogue refers to as *ikony zhivopisnoi manery*).[25] But many icon painters remained faithful to the Byzantine manner, at the same time as many early Russian portraits, in the hands of provincial artists, have distinctly icon-like or 'naive' features – static two-dimensionality, decorative treatment of details and so on.[26] The problem for the modern researcher attempting to study this synthesis is that so few examples of eighteenth-century and early-nineteenth-century Russian icons and religious history painting are available for study, either in galleries or in books. Thus Russia's leading Classical painter, Anton Losenko, is usually characterized by his composition from early Russian history, *Vladimir and Rogneda* (1770), rather than his *Miracle of the Fishes* (1762) or *Abraham Sacrificing his Son Isaac* (1765).[27]

The only religious history painting to gain acceptance in the Soviet canon was Alexander Ivanov's gigantic canvas *The Appearance of the Messiah to the People* (1837–57), although even that was partially 'secularized'. For example, the small, distant Christ in the background was presented as less significant than the life-sized representatives of the *narod* in the foreground; critics focused on the realism of the *narodnyi* types and the original treatment of landscape rather than on the theological content. For the Soviet art historian Dmitrii Sarabianov, Ivanov's painting is great precisely because it 'progressed beyond the depiction of a miraculous event and portrayed an actual historical episode'.[28] Of course, the whole context of Ivanov's life and work challenges such interpretations and recent Russian publications are restoring his credentials as a religious painter.[29]

I will conclude this part of the discussion by pointing out that even in the age of Enlightenment it was still possible to create new religious landscapes. Ivanov devised a temple in Moscow to 'the golden age of all humanity', featuring frescoes of the Holy Land in Christ's time and of contemporary 'Holy' Russia, with the emperor Nicholas I in the centre. Charles Cameron's model town of Sophia near Tsarskoe Selo, commissioned by Catherine the Great, has references to Hagia Sophia in Constantinople[30] and Catherine's Greek project (the idea of the conquest of Constantinople and the establishment of a new Byzantine empire) was reflected in a number of church designs by Nikolai L'vov.[31] Religious architecture flourished in eighteenth-century provincial Russia, with remarkably original buildings created from a fusion of Classical and traditional devices.[32]

The second half of the nineteenth century officially saw the triumph of Realism in the work of the Itinerants (*peredvizhniki*), whose subject matter was presented as overwhelmingly secular and 'humanistic', although a few pictures on Biblical themes, religious history and some antireligious subjects enter the canon. In fact, a reassessment of religious (although rarely overtly Orthodox) themes in the work of nineteenth-century Realist painters is overdue. Nearly all the first generation of *peredvizhniki* trained in the Academy of Arts, where they duly produced history paintings for their diplomas. For example, Il'ia Repin's first major work was not his famous *Volga Barge Haulers* but *The Raising of Jairus's Daughter* (1871). Vasilii Polenov is known for his *Moscow Courtyard* (1874), but an exhibition held in Moscow in 1994 restored the true balance of his life's work, which centred on a huge series on the 'Life of Christ'. His major canvas was *Christ and the Woman Taken in Adultery (Which of You is without Sin)?* (1888).[33]

The *peredvizhniki* had their origins in a revolt against the Academy's emphasis upon Classical models and themes from distant eras. Their preference for genre painting – subjects from contemporary life – allowed a new type of religious subject matter to emerge. The most acceptable to the Soviet canon were works such as Vasilii Perov's *Village Easter Procession* (1861) and Repin's *Easter Procession in Kursk Province* (1880–3), both of which 'unmask' the Church's hypocritical indifference to suffering and its endorsement of social hierarchies but also reveal the vital role of religious ritual in everyday life. Soviet historians were less eager to draw attention to paintings on religious themes produced by these same two artists towards the end of their lives. Critics roundly denounced Perov's 'growing reaction' as a result of his 'departure from democratic foundations' (*otkhod ot demokraticheskikh ustanovok*)[34] as demonstrated in such subjects as The Crucifixion, the head of the Mother of God, Mary Magdalene and the Angel of Death. The later Perov is now rehabilitated, his huge canvas *Nikita Pustosviat: The Dispute About the Faith* (1881), depicting a clash between official churchmen and Old Believers in Moscow in 1682, again on display in the Tret'iakov gallery. Repin's final works, a Biblical series, including the dark *Golgotha* (1921), were omitted from the major Soviet albums of his work, probably because they seemed at odds with his approved 'democratic' subject matter.[35]

The Soviet canon was generally able to accommodate compositions which focused on Christ's human nature. Ivan Kramskoi's *Christ in the Wilderness* (1872) earned the endorsement of the radical critic Vladimir Stasov on the grounds that it was a sort of embodiment of Chernyshevskii's question 'What is to be done?', an image of contemporary man refusing to accept the easy way out and sacrificing himself for higher ideals. Nikolai Ge's *The Last Supper* (1863) portrayed 'the farewell meal of Christ with his disciples as a real event; it stripped it of its mystical significance and knocked the Gospel subject off its pedestal'.[36] Ge's powerful 'Passion Week' series (1880s) won approval because it was 'engendered by the epoch of reaction, executions and persecution of the progressively-minded intelligentsia and the inhumane exploitation of the people', which made Ge 'acutely, even morbidly, sensitive to the sufferings of the innocent'.[37] None of these paintings were devotional works. They treat the Biblical subjects freely and dramatically, without set references to Orthodox iconography.

Nineteenth-century artists could also win a place in the Soviet canon by depicting key moments from Russian religious history. A major example is Vasilii Surikov's *Boiarinia Morozova* (1887), in which a defiant Old Believer woman is taken away to be executed, while the 'mass of the people' look on. (The Old Belief, it will be recalled, was characterized as *narodnoe dvizhenie*.) Perhaps the richest source of religious motifs in nineteenth-century Russian art were landscapes, in which images of Orthodox churches featured prominently. One of the most evocative is Isaak Levitan's *Above Eternal Rest* (1894), in which expanses of horizon and water and a tiny church and graveyard viewed from above hint at timeless spiritual values.

There was no place in the canon for cult art, however, even when it was painted by otherwise approved artists. Few Russians know of Surikov's frescoes of the Ecumenical church councils (1870s), commissioned for the Cathedral of Christ the Redeemer,[38] or his striking history painting *The Apostle Paul Explains the Dogma of the Faith in the Presence of King Agrippa* (1875).

At the end of the century religion reasserts itself, not only in narrative and genre paintings which explore specifically Orthodox spirituality but also in the creation of new devotional art and church architecture and in the rediscovery of ancient icons. These developments are generally presented in the framework of national identity and consciousness (*russkii stil'*). In Evgeniia Kirichenko's view, the new prominence of religious art at the turn of the century 'reflects a change in attitude towards religion on the part of the intelligentsia' which led to 'a closing of the gulf that had divided religious and secular art . . . throughout the post-Petrine period. The task for all the arts was now seen as the affirmation of the beautiful and the good, and the promotion of beauty as a transfiguring spiritual force' under the influence of the new religious philosophy.[39] This trend, which encompassed literature as well as art, is associated with the rejection of materialism and the abandoning of contemporary social interests, of the here and now, in favour of other worlds: the past, the imagination, the spirit, the future.

An early landmark was the Orthodox church designed and built in 1882–3 by the artists of the colony at Abramtsevo, the 'cradle of modern Russian art'.[40] Several of the Abramtsevo artists painted icons and frescoes for the church – notably Viktor Vasnetsov, the son of a priest from Viatka – but the key figure there in the revival of Orthodox themes was Mikhail Nesterov (1862–1942), Perov's pupil.[41] One of Nesterov's earliest memories was of lying sick under an icon, with another small icon of Saint Tikhon Zadonskii laid on his breast. Nesterov's family venerated the popular Russian saint Sergii of Radonezh, who later featured in the artist's work (for example, in *The Vision of St Bartholomew*). Nesterov worked on church frescoes and mosaics, for example in the Moscow convent of Martha and Mary, but is best known for a series of paintings of the holy men and women of modern Russia, culminating in the monumental canvas *Na Rusi. Dusha Naroda* (1914–6): a peasant boy walks by the river in front of a crowd of God-seeking Russians gathered from various epochs (including Tolstoy, Dostoevskii and the philosopher Vladimir Solov'ev). This work is now displayed in the Tret'iakov Gallery (1997), along with Nesterov's portrait of the religious philosophers P.A. Florenskii and S.N. Bulgakov (1917).[42]

In the eyes of Russian avant-garde artists of the 1910s-20s, painters such as Nesterov had outlived their day. Yet for all their loud rejection of the past and embracing of the future, radical artists gave yet another new lease of life to religious images. The 'iconic impulse' in the Russian avant-garde has long been a popular topic among Western specialists on Russian art, from Camilla Gray onwards, but it could be explored in print in Russia only fairly recently, when artists such as Malevich and Filonov were rehabilitated and their works restored to the national galleries.[43]

In the nineteenth century the radical intelligentsia regarded icons, if they thought about them at all, as distasteful cult objects. (Belinskii's denial of Russian Orthodox spirituality – peasants, according to him, said of icons 'If you can't use them for praying, use them for covering pots' – probably had a profound influence.[44]) But attitudes began to change as icons were 'seen' for the first time, first by dedicated enthusiasts who went on collecting expeditions (for example, Abramtsevo artists, led by Polenov), then by a wider public as they were cleaned of centuries of grime and overpainting and displayed in exhibitions.[45] These revelations struck chords at a time when artists were exploring antihistorical, antirealistic approaches to art, planning their escape from objective reality. Icons (along with 'primitive', Oriental, children's and folk art) provided a 'new' pictorial language.[46] Natalia Goncharova (1881–1962) was perhaps the most prolific exponent of this trend.

The incorporation of iconic images into the vocabulary of the artistic avant-garde was facilitated by the fact that so many artists had direct experience of working in an Orthodox idiom or in a religious environment. The roll call includes Filip Maliavin (1869–1940), who studied icon painting on Mount Athos as a lay brother; Pavel Filonov (1883–1941), who copied icons; Vladimir Tatlin (1885–1953), who did religious 'jobbing' and studied church frescoes; Boris Kustodiev (1878–1927), who had a theological training; Aristarkh Lentulov (1882–1943), the son of a priest, educated in Penza seminary; Mikhail Vrubel' (1856–1910), who worked on the restoration of St Cyril's Church and St Vladimir's Cathedral in Kiev; Kuz'ma Petrov-Vodkin (1878–1939), who decorated churches and visited Constantinople. Kazimir Malevich (1878–1935) explained his early relationship with icons and his discovery of the 'spiritual side' of peasant art in his autobiography. His *Black Square* (1914–5) may be regarded as 'a new age icon', while many of his slightly later Suprematist works contain religious symbols.[47]

Some early Soviet artists, especially the Constructivists, appreciated the 'democratic' credentials of icons. Icons were necessary and public, an essential part of life, not elitist or hidden away in the homes of the rich. In traditional society they were everywhere – in houses, shrines, on people. Such endorsement was short-lived, for Bolshevik policies toward religion required the destruction of churches and icons. By the time Socialist Realism was declared in the 1930s, religious themes had virtually disappeared from Soviet art, except in antireligious posters and displays in museums of religion and atheism. The production of cult art virtually ceased, although (see above) selected monuments of the religious art of the past were exhibited and studied in the context of national heritage.

For Western historians, demolished churches and desecrated icons become symbols of the aggressively atheistic state, which, despite its best efforts, proved incapable of suppressing Orthodox traditions, evidence of which would be perceived everywhere, from the *krasnyi ugolok* in public institutions to the panapoly of Soviet 'saints' on posters and banners, not to mention the incorruptible Lenin in his shrine.[48] It has been argued that Socialist Realism – an art which looks beyond the here and now to the bright future – transformed Soviet men and women rather as icons transfigured the saints. Transcendental images based on stereotypes deleted the transient and the accidental in order to express a higher reality: short Stalin could appear taller than his (in reality taller) companion; Lenin, ravaged by illness in his last years, looked eternally healthy and serene; collective farm workers were happy and well-fed even in time of famine. A striking example of Soviet 'iconography' is the photograph of Mikhail Gorbachëv with birthmark erased in a pack of Politburo portraits dating from 1980.

Positive references to Orthodox spirituality in paintings by Soviet artists tended to indicate dissident credentials, although towards the end of the Soviet period such phenomena become semi-official, notably in the work of Il'ia Glazunov, whose work in many ways echoed that of Nesterov.

Since the late 1980s explicitly religious art has made a comeback.[49] The most visible examples are architectural, as, for example, the Cathedral of Christ the Redeemer (a polemic with the Stalinist era?) and the Poklonnaia Gora memorial complex in Moscow, where Soviet-style 'totalitarian Classicism' rubs shoulders with Novgorod revival.[50] The building of new churches and the reconsecration of old ones (the refurbishment of the Danilov monastery as the patriarch's new residence was an early major project) have in turn created work for icon painters, as has the revival of personal devotion. The quality of the new *ikonopis'* and the attitudes of the new *ikonopistsy* have yet to be assessed.

The new relationship between Church and State have brought to the surface conflicts between museums and churches, as the latter seek to resanctify icons and cult objects. Orthodox scholars, too, attempt to wrest religious art from the clutches of art historians, for example, M.M. Dudaev, whose recent survey published by the Moscow Academy (which begins with the question 'What is Truth?') offers a thinly veiled Slavophile critique of modern Russian society through references to the growth of materialism, professional individuality and rationalism which undermined Russian religious art from the seventeenth century onwards.[51] In the Tret'iakov gallery believers ostentatiously cross themselves in front of the Vladimir *Mother of God*, one of the great miracle-working icons of Muscovite Rus'. To the best of my knowlege, no one has suggested that Ivanov's *Appearance of the Messiah* should be removed to a church (it was not created for such a setting), but priests have been observed giving a commentary on it.[52] Meanwhile, on the streets mass-produced cardboard icons and pictures of onion domes by pseudo-Levitans, Kustodievs and Nesterovs tempt tourists in search of affordable mementos of 'Holy Russia'. A new chapter in the history of Russian religious art has begun.

Notes

1 J. Billington, *The icon and the axe: an interpretive history of Russian culture* (New York), 1966, p. vii.

2 J. Billington, *The icon and the axe*, p. x, 6; also p. 9 ('the desire to see spiritual truth in tangible form').

3 See J. Billington, 'Images of Muscovy', *Slavic Review*, 21 (1962), p. 31. See also G. Florovsky, 'The problem of Old Russian culture', *Slavic Review*, 21 (1962), pp. 1–15; N. Andreyev, 'Pagan and Christian elements in Old Russia', *Slavic Review*, 21 (1962), pp. 16–23; G. Florovsky, 'Reply', *Slavic Review* 21 (1962), pp. 35–42.

4 G. Florovsky, 'The problem of Old Russian culture', p. 3.

5 I.E. Grabar', ed. *Istoriia russkogo iskusstva*, vol. 1 (Moscow, 1953), p. 504.

6 See A. Dmitrenko, ed. *Fifty Russian artists* (Moscow and London), 1985, p. 13, a useful popular guide to the late Soviet art historical canon.

7 *Fifty Russian artists*, p. 20.

8 See, for example, Iu. G. Bobrov, *Osnovy ikonografii drevnerusskoi zhivopisi* (St Petersburg, 1995); V.V. Bychkov, *Dukhovno-esteticheskie osnovy russkoi ikony* (Moscow, 1995); O. Iu. Tarasov, *Ikona i blagochestie: ocherki ikonnogo dela v imperatorskoi Rossii* (Moscow, 1995) (the latter is an encyclopedic, richly illustrated guide to icon studies).

9 See R.O. Crummey, 'Court spectacles in seventeenth-century Russia: illusion and reality', in D.C. Waugh, ed. *Essays in Honor of A.A. Zimin* (Columbus, OH, 1985), pp. 130–46; N.S. Kollmann, 'Pilgrimage, procession, and symbolic space in sixteenth-century Russian politics', in M.S. Flier and D. Rowland, eds *Medieval Russian culture: II* (Berkeley, CA, Los Angeles, CA, and London, 1994), pp. 163–81; D. Rowland, 'Biblical imagery in the political culture of early modern Russia: the Blessed Host of the Heavenly Tsar', in Flier and Rowland, eds *Medieval Russian culture II*, pp. 182–212; M.S. Flier, 'Breaking the code: the image of the tsar in the Muscovite Palm Sunday ritual', in Flier and Rowland, eds *Medieval Russian culture II*, pp. 213–42; D. Miller, 'Creating legitimacy: ritual, ideology and power in sixteenth-century Russia', *Russian History*, 21 (1994), pp. 289–35; M. Pliukhanova, *Siuzhety i simvoly moskovskogo gosudarstva* (St Petersburg, 1995); R. Milner-Gulland, *The Russians* (Oxford, 1997).

10 See my own article on this topic, 'The age of transition: 17th-century Russian icon-painting', in S. Smyth and S. Kingston, eds *Icons 88* (Dublin, 1988), pp. 63–74.

11 E.S. Smirnova, 'Simon Ushakov – "Historicism" and "Byzantinism". On the interpretation of Russian painting from the second half of the seventeenth century', in S.H. Baron and N. Shields Kollmann, eds *Religions and culture in early modern Russia and Ukraine* (De Kalb, IL, 1997), pp. 170–83.

12 See M. Okenfuss, *The rise and fall of Latin humanism in early-modern Russia: pagan authors, Ukrainians, and the resiliency of Muscovy* (Leiden and New York, 1995). On the theoretical framework of 'secularization', see V.M. Zhivov, 'Religious reform and the emergence of the individual in Russian seventeenth-century literature', in Baron and Shields Kollmann, eds *Religions and culture*, pp. 184–98

13 A. Bird, *A history of Russian painting* (Oxford, 1987), p. 146; but on the same page he claims that Nikolai Ge's painting of the Last Supper (1863) 'horrified St Petersburg by its departure . . . from iconographical traditions'.

14 J. Billington, *The icon and the axe*, p. 227.

15 See, for example, S. Baehr, 'From history to national myth: *Translatio imperii*

in 18th-century Russia', *Russian Review*, 37 (1978), pp. 1–13; *idem, The paradise myth in eighteenth-century Russia* (Stanford, 1991), pp. 1–13.

16 Alexander III's survival from a train accident in 1888 was attributed to this icon. See D.G. Bulgakovskii, *Domik Petra Velikogo i ego sviatynia v S. Peterburge* (St Petersburg, 1891), pp. 19–20, who attributes the icon to the workshop of Simon Ushakov.

17 See decrees in *Polnoe Sobranie Zakonov (PSZ)*, VI, no. 4079 (31 August, 1722); VII, no. 4154 (31 January, 1723). See chapter 43 of the 1551 Stoglav (Council of a Hundred Chapters). See also J. Cracraft, *The Petrine revolution in Russian imagery* (Chicago, IL, 1997), L. Hughes, *Russia in the age of Peter the Great* (New Haven, CT, 1998), pp. 228–40.

18 *PSZ*, VII, no. 4148, pp. 16–17.

19 N.V. Kaliazina and G.N. Komelova, *Russkoe iskusstvo Petrovskoi epokhi* (Leningrad, 1990), ill. 172.

20 Kaliazina and Komelova, *Russkoe iskusstvo*, ill. 79.

21 I am grateful to Dr Elena Mozgovaia of St Petersburg for discussions of the iconostasis and of her difficulties earlier in her career in publishing her conclusions on religious sculpture. Kaliazina and Komelova do not include any examples. I.E. Grabar. ed. *Istoriia russkogo iskusstva*, vol. 5 (Moscow, 1960), illustrates some examples of wooden folk sculpture to demonstrate 'the materialistic basis of the popular understanding of the world, so contrary to the very essence of religious thought' (p. 432). The crucified Christ and the severed head of John the Baptist are said to have reflected the people's own sufferings.

22 See *Reznye ikonostasy i dereviannaia skul'ptura Russkogo Severa. Katalog vystavki* (Archangel–Moscow, 1995).

23 R. Kistemaker *et al.*, *Peter de Grote en Holland* (Amsterdam, 1996), pp. 275–62. Works by Juvenet bought in Paris in 1717 included *St Peter Fishing, The Raising of Lazarus, The Healing of the Man with Palsey* and *The Driving of the Moneylenders from the Temple*: J. Stahlin, *Podlinnye anekdoty o Petre Velikom* (Leningrad, 1990), p. 43.

24 I.E. Grabar ed., *Istoriia russkogo iskusstva*, vol. 5, p. 368, note 3.

25 I. Iarygina, A. Mal'tseva and G. Belovolov, *Pozdniaia russkaia ikona: Konets XVIII–XIX vek* (St Petersburg, 1996), is the catalogue of a 1994 exhibition 'rehabilitating' late icons, which Soviet museums rejected as being of little artistic or scholarly interest.

26 See Cracraft: 'the cult art of Russia was never *transformed* by the standards of the new imagery such as it had been in Europe itself' (p. 300).

27 Some examples are illustrated in I.E. Grabar, ed. *Istoriia russkogo iskusstva*, vol. 5, and described in vol. 7 (Moscow, 1961), for example, pp. 95–6 ('Together with this generally archaic tradition, in icons one can undoubtedly discover the influence of contemporary secular art').

28 D. Sarabianov, *Russian art from neo-classicism to the avant-garde* (London, 1990), p. 84.

29 N.K. Gavriushin, ed. *Filosofiia russkogo religioznogo iskusstva* (Moscow, 1993), reprints articles by Vasilii Rozanov and Vladimir Kozhevnikov on Ivanov as a religious painter. See the forthcoming PhD dissertation by Andrew Curtin, *Alexander Ivanov's Appearance of the Messiah and the medieval revival in XIX century European art and architecture*, School of Slavonic and East European Studies, University of London.

30 D. Shvidkovskii, *The empress and the architect: British architecture and gardens at the court of Catherine the Great* (New Haven, CT, 1996), pp. 106 ff.

31 See the doctoral thesis by A. Makhrov, 'The Architecture of Nikolai L'vov. A study of the architectural relationships between Britain and Russia at the end of the eighteenth century', St. Andrews, 1998.

32 See W.C. Brumfield, *Lost Russia: photographing the ruins of Russian archi-tecture* (Durham and London, 1994).

33 E. Paston *et al.*, eds *Vasilii Dmitrievich Polenov. K 150–letiiu so dnia rozhde-niia. Katalog vystavki* (Moscow, 1994); A. Remezov's 1915 article on Polenov's 'Life of Christ', in N.K. Gavriushin, ed. *Filosofiia russkogo religioznogo iskusstva* (London, 1990), pp. 189–94.

34 A.A. Fedorov-Davydov, *V.G. Perov* (Moscow, 1934), pp. 64–5, 71, 76.

35 See E. Valkenier, *Ilya Repin and the world of Russian art* (New York, 1989), p. 192.

36 A.G. Vereshchagina, *Nikolai Nikolaevich Ge* (Leningrad, 1988), p. 31.

37 Vereshchagina, *Nikolai Nikolaevich Ge*, p. 90.

38 N.G. Mashovtsev, *V.I. Surikov* (Moscow, 1994). He tried to 'enliven these iconic pictures by including national Greek features to correspond with actual historical reality, but was forbidden from doing so by the church authorities' (p. 12).

39 E. Kirichenko, *The Russian style* (London, 1991), p. 199. See also the catalogue *The twilight of the tsars: Russian art at the turn of the century* (South Bank Centre, 1991).

40 See W.C. Brumfield, 'The "new style" and the revival of Orthodox church architecture, 1900–1914', in W.C. Brumfield and M. Velimirovic, eds *Christ-ianity and the arts in Russia* (Cambridge, 1991), pp. 105–23.

41 M.V. Nesterov, *Davnie Dni. Vstrechi i vospominaniia* (Moscow, 1959), p. 48.

42 See A.A. Rusakova, *Mikhail Nesterov* (Leningrad, 1990), pp. 17–18.

43 See, for example, J. E. Bowlt, 'Orthodoxy and the avant-garde: sacred images in the work of Goncharova, Malevich and their contemporaries', in Brumfield and Velimirovic, eds *Christianity and the arts in Russia*, pp. 145–50. Also, see O. Tarasov, 'Russian icons and the avant-garde: tradition and change', in R. Cormack and D. Caze, eds *The art of Holy Russia: icons from Moscow, 1400–1660* (London, 1998), pp. 93–9. This topic awaits a thorough examination.

44 V. Belinskii, *Letter to Gogol* (1847), reprinted in W.J. Leatherbarrow and D.C. Offord, eds *A documentary history of Russian thought* (Ann Arbor, 1987), p. 133.

45 Landmarks include the 1901 'Art Works from Antiquity' exhibition in Moscow; the cleaning of Rublev's Trinity (1903–4); public exhibitions of cleaned icons in St Petersburg in 1911 (the Ostroukhov collection, seen by Henri Matisse) and in Moscow in 1913 (for the Romanov Jubilee).

46 See Robin Milner-Gulland's list of 14 qualities in icons which appealed to avant-garde artists: spirituality, transcendancy, symbolism, abstractions, imper-sonality, musicality, stylization, naiveté, picture-space, colour, materiality, utility, humanism, 'national' quality, in *The Russians* (1997), pp. 200–1.

47 *Kazimir Malevich, 1878–1935* [Exhibition catalogue, Stedelijk Museum] (Amsterdam, 1988), p. 108.

48 J. Billington, *The icon and the axe* (New York, 1966), p. 37.

49 See M. Cullerne Bown, *Contemporary Russian art* (Oxford, 1989), on early examples.

50 With thanks to John Klier for his talk in the earlier seminar series on 'Re-intrepreting Russia', both for illustrations and for ideas.

51 M.M. Dudaev, *Svoeobrazie russkoi religioznoi zhivopisi. XII-XX vek* (Moscow, 1997).

52 Overheard in 1997: 'Ivanov was not a believer in the formal sense, but he was a religious man'.

4

The problem of social stability in Russia, 1598–1998

DAVID MOON

In 1964–5 Leopold Haimson published his famous article, 'The problem of social stability in urban Russia, 1905–1917'.[1] He wrote about instability in Russia's towns and cities among the rapidly growing numbers of industrial workers in the last years of the tsarist regime. For the title of this chapter, I have adapted Haimson's title by dropping the 'urban' and greatly expanding the time period. The main focus is on relations between different social groups and the state[2] in the three centuries between two major crises that shook the Russian state and society: the 'Time of Troubles' of 1598–1613 and the revolutions of 1905–7 and 1917–21. Some remarks are also made about the Soviet state, from its inception in October 1917 to its collapse in 1991, during the most recent of Russia's recurring crises.

Much historical writing on the problem of social stability throughout the history of tsarist Russia, not just the twelve years before 1917, has concentrated on instability. Most obviously, Soviet historians followed Marx's assertion about the centrality of 'class struggles' in the history of human societies.[3] They wrote about a rising tide of 'class struggle' against the 'ruling classes' of tsarist Russia, for example: the four 'peasant wars', led by Bolotnikov in 1606–7, Razin in 1670–1, Bulavin in 1707–8 and Pugachev in 1773–4; the urban riots of the seventeenth century; the peasant and working-class 'movements' in the nineteenth and early twentieth centuries, all of which allegedly culminated in the revolutions that broke out in 1905 and 1917 and led to the downfall of the tsar in February–March 1917, and the victory of the Bolshevik revolution in October. Many Western historians, especially since Haimson's article, have examined the social origins of the early twentieth century revolutions, as well as previous popular movements.

As a result of these large bodies of scholarship, we know a great deal about the long-term background to the revolutions of 1905–7 and 1917–21 and about earlier social tensions and conflicts, but rather less about the reasons why the social order in Russia under the Romanov tsars lasted for so long. Tsarist Russian society was hierarchical and based on the exploitation of the mass of the population (mainly peasants) by higher elites (mostly nobles), the tsars and the state. The most striking example is the institution of serfdom. Between the 1590s and 1861 very roughly half the peasantry were the serfs of noble landowners. Nevertheless, for long periods of Russian history before the twentieth century, social stability, or at least the acquiescence of much of the population, was the norm.

The main purpose of this chapter is to suggest three possible explanations for the durability of the social order in tsarist Russia.[4] Comparisons with the social order in the Soviet Union (which was also hierarchical and exploitative) may shed some light on its relatively short duration in contrast to the system which preceded it.

Co-optation of elites: divide and rule

One of the ways in which the tsars, the state and 'higher elites' [mainly the noble and clerical social estates (*sosloviia*)[5]] maintained their positions at the top of the social order of tsarist Russia was by co-opting elites of segments within Russian society. These elites were granted privileges and support for their status in their segments of society at local levels in return for allegiance to the state and higher elites, and paying tribute, which they collected from other members of their segments. A result was that segments of society became divided and fought amongst themselves for access to the privileged status to be gained from 'collaborating' with their 'superiors'. Thus, the state and higher elites were able to maintain their control, and extract tribute, through intermediaries, with minimal expenditure on officials and administration.

This idea of co-opting elites is perhaps most familiar from literature on the expanding frontiers of the Russian state. One of the ways the state expanded its borders, brought new peoples under control and extracted tribute from them was, by extending the privileged status of Russian nobles to the social elites of other peoples, for example, the nobles of the Tatar khanates annexed in the sixteenth centuries, the German nobles of the Baltic provinces conquered in eighteenth century, and the Cossack *starshina* of Ukraine, the Don and other frontier regions over the seventeenth and eighteenth centuries.[6]

Russia's rulers and 'higher elites' also co-opted the 'lower elites'[7] of segments of society in the Russian heartland, in particular the communities of peasants that made up the overwhelming majority of the population. Almost all Russian peasants lived on estates that were the property of the state or higher elite landowners, in particular the Orthodox church (until the secularization of church lands in 1762–4) and noble landowners (until 1861). The main forms of tribute extracted from peasants were obligations in labour (*barshchina*), cash or kind (*obrok*) for landowners (including the dues state peasants paid to the treasury). All peasants paid taxes for the state (the poll tax from 1724), and supplied recruits for the army in levies held in most years from 1705.

Some nobles and monasteries with small estates administered their lands and peasants directly, but many noble and clerical landowners relied on intermediaries, such as bailiffs or estate managers. The state administered its vast lands partly through lower officials. In additions, however, many elite landowners and the state devolved some of their authority over the peasant communities on their lands onto lower elites from the peasants themselves. In return for support to maintain their status in their village communities, peasant elites maintained social order, and extracted tribute from their communities, most of which they passed on to their landowners and the state. The system of mutual responsibility (*krugovaia poruka*) for the obligations owed by peasant communities collectively to their landowners and the state also served to maintain the social order, and fostered mutual suspicion. To some extent, the elites of peasant communities collaborated with bailiffs, estate managers and local officials, who supported each others' interests.[8]

The local elites in many village communities were the older generation of (usually male) peasants. They were the heads of large, multigenerational households, and also to the elders who dominated their village communes. They made sure that most of their communities' obligations, especially labour services, were fulfilled by the younger generation of adult peasants, who lived under their authority in their households and communities. The peasant elites enjoyed, at their expense, some degree of leisure, status and authority. Many members of the younger generation of peasant men and women conformed to the authority of the heads of their households and communal elders because most could reasonably expect to live long enough to become heads of households, or the wives of heads, themselves, when they would be able to exploit their sons and daughters and share in the privileges that accrued from supporting seigniorial authority. The maintenance of large, multigenerational households, by preventing younger adults from breaking away from their parents' households and setting up on their own, was very important if the older generations of peasants were to retain their status.[9]

In other villages, the local elites were factions of peasants who had gained control over village communes through networks based on kinship and patronage. These village elites controlled the distribution between peasant households of the communal land and the obligations the community as a whole owed to their landowners and the state. Village factions used the power this gave them to further their own interests and those of their kin and clients. Other peasants formed rival factions and manoeuvred to oust the existing village elites so that they could run the villages in their interests. In villages run by factions of peasants, the maintenance of large households was not central to the power of peasant elites.[10]

In villages dominated by the older generation or factions of peasants, of central importance in maintaining their authority was control over the selection of recruits. Under the system of recruitment in operation between 1705 and 1874, men were sent to the army in levies held in most years to serve for life (until 1793) or 25 years (until the 1860s). Most never returned home. The loss of a young man to the army was a major blow to a peasant household, and effectively a life sentence to penal servitude for the recruit. Most peasants were prepared to go to great lengths to avoid losing a son or being conscripted themselves.[11]

Thus, the local elites of peasant communities, either the older generation or factions of peasants, used the authority that had been devolved onto them by their landowners and the state in order that they participate in enforcing the hierarchical and exploitative social order to further their own interests at the expense of other peasants in their communities. Case studies of peasant communities[12] suggest that peasants spent a great deal of time and effort fighting amongst themselves, rather than joining forces against the landowning and ruling elites that exploited them. In 1881, Alexander Engelgardt, a perceptive observer of peasant life, famously wrote:

> Every peasant, if the circumstances are favourable, will exploit everyone else in the most splendid fashion, it is all the same whether it be a peasant or a lord, he will squeeze the juice out of him, will exploit his need.[13]

The fractiousness of peasant communities should not be overstated, however. Village life was also marked by elements of cooperation. Under certain circumstances, village communes offered assistance (*pomoch'*) to households that had fallen on hard times, but had the chance to recover and once again make a full contribution to the village economy. Village festivals also served to promote lines of solidarity.[14] Moreover, at times when the interests of all peasants were threatened by outside power, communities acted in unison.[15]

At times when social stability was threatened, one response by the Russian state was to extend the status and privileges of the higher elites to other groups in society, with the aim of widening the basis of support for the existing order and/or dividing possible adversaries. In 1648, during riots in Moscow, tsar Alexis and his boyars granted the demand of the lesser gentry for the abolition of the time limit during which landowners could sue for the return of peasants who had fled their estates or been kidnapped by other (usually wealthier) landowners. This marked the final legal consolidation of serfdom, and was an important stage in the creation of a single social estate of nobles.[16] In 1775, in her proclamation after the defeats of the Pugachev revolt and the Turkish Empire, Catherine the Great created a new elite social estate of merchants (*kuptsy*) from the wealthiest members of the urban population.[17] During the Pugachev revolt, some townspeople had joined the rebels, although not to the extent that urban inhabitants had taken part in riots and revolts in the seventeenth century. Fear of social revolts was one of the factors that united most members of the privileged social estates and Russia's rulers. A decade after Pugachev's defeat, the rights and privileges of the nobility and urban populations were confirmed by Catherine in her Charters of 1785.[18]

The development of a hierarchy of elites with the tsars at the top, the nobility and other privileged elites (the clergy and merchantry) at a higher level, and local elites at a lower level, all of whom acquired some status, authority and wealth by supporting the existing social order, went some way to maintaining social stability in tsarist Russia prior to the social and economic changes, in particular urbanization and industrialization, that began to gather pace in the late nineteenth century.

The co-optation of elites, and the resulting social disunity, has some relevance to understanding the problem of social stability among the working classes in urban Russia at the turn of the twentieth century. It should be noted straight away, however, that most urban workers were outside the hierarchy of authority in the old social order. The large literature on the working classes in late-tsarist Russia has paid a lot of attention to the different focuses and levels of working-class loyalties, identities and 'consciousness'.[19] Some were 'peasant-workers' whose primary identification was with their home villages and regions. They formed self-help associations (*zemliachestva*) of peasants from the same areas, and many intended to return to their home villages after earning some money in the cities.[20] For much of the time, other urban workers identified with their workshops, trades, factories and towns or cities, but not with a cohesive Russian (or worldwide) 'proletariat'. Workers were as likely to take part in pogroms against local Jewish communities as strikes against their bosses or demonstrations against the regime.[21]

Studies of better-off, skilled workers, for example some metal workers and print workers, suggest that many saw themselves as a cut above 'peasant-workers' and semiskilled workers. Higher status and respectability for themselves, as a 'worker aristocracy' or even members of the bourgeoisie, were far more important than notions of uniting with all workers in a proletarian, socialist revolution.[22] Lenin was probably right when he feared that, left to their own devices, Russian workers would press only for economic concessions rather than political change.[23] What needs explaining is not disunity among Russian workers, but the solidarity that emerged in 1905 and 1917.

Studies of workers in Soviet Russia provide some evidence for the idea that the social order was preserved (or, rather, a new social order was constructed and maintained) after 1917 by the co-optation of elites and by the fostering of disunity among the mass of the urban population. The ideal of workers' control did not long survive the October Revolution: it was soon replaced by one-man management, the rehiring of 'bourgeois specialists', labour discipline enforced by trade unions, and piecework rates. In the short run, these policies led to worker protests during the years of War Communism (1918–21).[24]

In the longer term, the industrialization drive of the late 1920s and the 1930s created opportunities for a small minority of workers for advancement through accommodation with the Soviet state and communist party. The creation of brigades of elite shock-workers during the first Five-Year Plan (1928–32) and the Stakhanovite movement of the mid-1930s seem almost to have been designed to foster working class *disunity* by favouring the few, who were rewarded, against the interests of the vast majority, who saw their production norms increased with little or no reward, and who endured great sacrifices. The communist party leaders were well aware of the potential power of solidarity among industrial workers, and did their best in the 1930s to atomize the Soviet working class while claiming to be building socialism and a 'workers' state'.[25]

The policy of training 'red specialists', to replace the 'bourgeois specialists', during the first Five-Year Plan, gave opportunities for personal advancement to thousands of young, upwardly mobile proletarians, some of whom did relatively well in the 1930s. Contrary to the views of some 'revisionist' scholars, this group was too small and became too closely involved in the apparatuses of the party and state to have constituted broad 'social support' for the Soviet regime. Rather, many of its members became a 'new elite', which staffed the relatively privileged *nomenklatura* and provided the next generation of party leaders after the death of Stalin in 1953.[26]

The party also tried to 'divide and rule' the peasantry. In June 1918, the party introduced the short-lived 'Committees of Poor Peasants' (*Kombedy*) to extract grain from richer peasants (the so-called 'kulaks'). The attempt failed because it was based on the false premise that the peasantry had become polarized into a small, rich, rural 'bourgeoisie' and a large, poor, rural 'proletariat'.[27] The forced requisitioning that followed alienated many peasants, leading to serious revolts in 1920–1, which compelled the party to introduce the more moderate New Economic Policy in March 1921.[28] When the party resumed the 'socialist offensive' in rural Russia in 1929–30, with the forced collectivization of agriculture, little or no attempt was made to manufacture a 'new elite' inside the peasantry. Instead, in a mirror image of this strategy, a large minority, labelled 'kulaks', were singled out for 'liquidation' to coerce the rest to join the collective farms.[29]

The degree to which the state and party elite in the Soviet Union succeeded in 'dividing and ruling' the population can be gauged from the increasingly widespread practice of denunciation, especially in the 1930s. Thousands of people were prepared to denounce their neighbours, workmates, even members of their families, to the authorities, motivated by jealousies, grievances, malice or hope of personal gain. Some complaints, however, were less self-serving attempts to draw attention to abuses and corruption among the managerial and party elites.[30] The argument should not be taken too far, however. The atomization of Soviet society was never total, even at the height of the purges and terror in the 1930s. Throughout the Soviet period, some degrees of mutual support were maintained by such strategies as subversive gossip and malicious jokes about the regime. People tried to get around the hierarchy of privilege by drawing on informal personal contacts, based on reciprocity, to obtain scarce goods and services: the pervasive networks of '*blat*'.[31]

'The ties that bound': exploitation, protection and dependence

The phrase 'the ties that bound' is Marx's, from *The Communist manifesto*, first published in 1847:

> The bourgeoisie, wherever it has got the upper hand, has put an end to all feudal, patriarchal, idyllic relations. It has pitilessly torn asunder the motley feudal ties that bound man to his 'natural superiors', and has left remaining no other nexus between man and man than naked self-interest, than callous 'cash payment'.[32]

In the same year, but from a different political perspective, Nikolai Gogol wrote in his letter 'to a Russian landowner':

> Let your thoughts not be confused, as though the former bonds uniting landowners with peasants have disappeared forever. That they have disappeared is true; that it is the landowner's fault is also true; but that they have disappeared for good and all – spit on such words: only he can speak them who sees no further than the end of his nose.

After advising him how to manage his peasants, Gogol concluded:

> Work diligently just one year, and then everything will be operating so well that you will not have to apply your hand. You will grow rich as Croesus, contrary to those weak-sighted people who think that the advantage of the landowner is different from the advantage of the peasants. You will prove the point . . . that if the landowner simply regards his obligation with the eye of the Christian he can not only strengthen the old bonds . . . , but bind them with new, stronger bonds – the bonds in Christ, than which nothing can be stronger.[33]

A few years earlier, the conservative Baron von Haxthausen had travelled around Russia and 'discovered' a patriarchal society such as he believed had once existed in his native Germany.[34] All three men – Marx, Gogol and Haxthausen – were influenced by the Romantic movement, which looked back into the past and saw a paternalistic, organic society.

These ideas about social relations were not just intellectual constructs. A second way in which the tsars, the state and 'higher elites' maintained their positions at the top of the social order of tsarist Russia was by a combination of exploiting the mass of the population, offering in exchange some degree of 'protection' of their welfare, which in turn created ties of mutual dependence between them.

Most tsars' accession and coronation proclamations, which were read out in churches all over Russia, were conscious attempts to create and support an image of the benevolent, paternal *'batiushka'* ('little father') tsar, who cared for his subjects like his children. The eighteenth-century empresses used maternal imagery.[35] Some nobles, especially absentee magnates, presented themselves in similar ways.[36]

Behind the rhetoric was the self-interest, albeit clothed in fine garments, of the ruling and landowning elites. The main purposes of 'protection' were to enable the lower orders to meet their obligations and to keep them quiescent. These concerns were articulated by rulers and state officials in the eighteenth century, before the advent of Romanticism. For example, in the 1750s, Count Peter Shuvalov noted that the 'basic resource' in Russia was the poll-tax paying population, because it provided recruits for the army, the material means to support the armed services, the government, nobility and clergy, and the labour force for industry, agriculture and transport. Thus, he argued, the 'well-being of this basic resource . . . ought to be the center of attention for government policy, and anything that would lead to its diminution . . . ought to be avoided'.[37] At the same time, some 'enlightened' landowners redefined their relationship with their peasants 'in moral as well as economic terms'. Their main motive, however, was to secure their incomes from their estates.[38]

The idea of protection did exist in practice. The Russian state and landowners offered many peasants access to land, protection against cruelty and excessive exploitation and some measure of famine relief.

Russian peasants were bound to the land as part of the process of enserfment that stretched from the 1580s to 1649. As well as restricting their freedom, however, being bound to the land also meant that the land was bound to the peasants, that is, they had an entitlement to land.[39] Over the course of the seventeenth century, many previously landless labourers were allocated land by landowners and village communes.[40] Communal and repartitional land tenure, which ensured that many peasant households had enough land to support themselves and meet their obligations, became widespread in central Russia in the eighteenth century, and later in some outlying regions. It was supported by the state and landowners as well as village elders.[41] In the first half of the nineteenth century, tsars Alexander I and Nicholas I took some tentative steps to prevent nobles from selling parts of their estates if it would leave their peasants with insufficient land. At the same time, more decisive steps were taken to ensure that state and appanage peasants had adequate land allotments.[42]

The state and nobles also offered peasants some degree of protection against exploitative and cruel landowners. Peter the Great instructed landowners not to reduce their peasants to ruin by demanding unreasonable obligations or treating them harshly. The ultimate sanction was that estates would be taken away from offending nobles and managed by trustees. This threat was given greater force in law and in practice by rulers in the late-eighteenth and first half of the nineteenth centuries. In 1797, tsar Paul issued a proclamation banning labour services on Sundays, and recommending that landowners divide peasants' labour during the rest of the week equally between their demesne and the peasants' allotments. Efforts to protect peasants from excessive exploitation were not very successful, however, since they depended largely on noble-dominated local authorities to enforce them.[43]

The state and nobles also offered peasants some measure of famine relief. This was particularly important in Russia. Large parts of the population lived close to the margins of subsistence and the periodic crop failures could spell disaster. The ruling elites regularly made some effort to provide for their starving subjects. Tsar Boris Godunov, who took power after the demise of the old ruling dynasty in 1598 and is often considered the founder of serfdom, took steps to mitigate the impact of the widespread famine of 1601–3. The obligation of nobles to provide for their peasants in times of dearth was laid down in law in the early eighteenth century, and tightened up over the subsequent period. In the early nineteenth century, the provision of reserve granaries or cash reserves was required by law on noble, state and appanage land. Throughout the tsarist period, rulers, officials and landowners sometimes made loans or grants of grain or cash to peasants in times of dearth. More frequently, they reduced, postponed or waived the obligations, taxes and levies of recruits they demanded from peasants if they were too destitute to fulfil them. Their efforts, together with those of the peasants themselves, certainly did not eliminate the threat of starvation, but went some way to reducing it. In the worst famines, such as that of 1832–3, however, the central authorities admitted that they lacked the resources to feed entire regions struck by crop failure.[44]

These ways in which members of the ruling and landowning elites of tsarist Russia offered 'protection' to peasants met with some support. Peasants certainly preferred 'good masters', who took account of their subsistence needs, to 'bad masters', who did not. There were even a few cases of peasants choosing to remain the serfs of 'good' landowners to the uncertainties of 'freedom'.[45] To some extent, therefore, the rulers, the state and members of all sections of Russian society, high and low, shared in what has been called a 'moral economy' that predated industrialization, capitalism and *laissez-faire* attitudes to state intervention in national economies.[46] It is very important, however, not to romanticize pre-industrial societies such as tsarist Russia. The degrees to which members of the elites 'protected' the lower orders should not be overstated, nor should it be forgotten that, to the extent that they did, it was in their own best interests, since their privileged position in the social order was based on the domination and exploitation of the vast majority of the population.

The extent of 'protection' offered by the ruling and landowning elites was a result not just of the whims of the privileged few. It was also influenced by demands by members of the lower orders for elites to live up to the paternal image they projected. The tsars, central and local officials and landowners received constant streams of petitions requesting redress of grievances and protection against ruinous exploitation, harsh treatment or the threat of hunger. Many peasants had a surprisingly good understanding of laws that protected them or gave them some opportunities to further their interests. Peasants were not averse to some creative misunderstandings. On occasions, moreover, they claimed to be 'rebels in the name of the tsar', who were opposing the 'evil boyars' or unjust officials who were allegedly concealing his true wishes from his loyal subjects. Daniel Field has called this 'the myth of the tsar'.[47]

The 'great reforms' of the 1860s-80s and the social and economic changes of late-nineteenth and early-twentieth-century Russia went some way towards undoing 'the ties that bound' the old social order together, and replacing the 'moral economy' with a new socio-economic order. The system of extracting 'tribute' from the lower orders alone, leaving the higher elites exempt, was gradually phased out. Serfdom was abolished in 1861 and similar reforms of the state and appanage peasants were enacted in the same decade. The military service reform of 1874 made all young men, not just peasants and townsmen, liable to conscription. The maximum term of active service was cut to only seven years, and later reduced further. The poll tax was abolished in the 1880s, and replaced by taxes on business and commerce, as well as increased indirect taxes on consumer goods, which were paid by people regardless of their social estate.

There were also elements of continuity from the old social order. The system of social estates, and the privileges that went with noble status, were very resilient. After 1861, nobles retained large amounts of land, including parts that had been 'cut off' from peasants' former allotments, and were compensated for the loss of the parts of their land they ceded to the freed serfs. Men with higher education, mostly nobles, served for far shorter terms (six months) in the army if they were conscripted. Elections to the local councils (*zemstva*) set up after 1864 and the State Duma after 1905 were organized by social estate. Peasants and urban workers were greatly underrepresented compared with nobles.[48]

The idea of 'protection' also survived. The terms of the abolition of serfdom and reforms of the other categories of peasants in the 1860s guaranteed the peasants land. Indeed, they were compelled to take land, and to pay for it.[49] When the pressure of population increase led to 'land hunger' among the peasantry, the government took some steps to alleviate it. The government of Alexander III set up the Peasant Land Bank in 1883, which helped peasants buy millions of acres of land.[50] Some provision was made to assist peasant migration to Siberia, where large amounts of land were made available for settlement.[51] But, these steps, together with Stolypin's land reforms of 1906–11, did not solve the land shortages faced by peasants in late-tsarist Russia.[52] In another area of 'protection', the government deserves more credit than it got at the time for its efforts to alleviate the consequences of the massive famine in 1891–2. Lack of resources, rather than concern, were the main reasons why state relief measures did not achieve more.[53] People also continued to demand 'protection' from the tsars and the legitimate authorities. Some peasants who were disappointed by the terms of the abolition of serfdom in 1861 believed that the 'real' freedom was being concealed from them by the nobles and corrupt local officials, and sought somehow to find it. Attempts by radical members of the intelligentsia, who were opposed to the tsarist regime, to win the support of peasants often met with indifference and suspicion.[54]

There is less evidence for 'protection' of the mass of the population by the state and elites in the rapidly growing and industrializing cities of late-tsarist Russia. The modest welfare measures enacted in the late nineteenth and early twentieth centuries did little to alleviate the appalling conditions many workers lived in. Again, perhaps, lack of resources rather than disregard were to blame. It would stretch the argument too far, however, to claim that the trade unions set up by the tsarist police under Zubatov before 1905 aimed to improve the economic conditions of workers. Their real aim was to keep workers away from revolutionaries who wanted to turn their demands for improvements in economic conditions into calls for political change. However, the peaceful appeal by workers to the 'paternal tsar' for justice and redress of grievances in St Petersburg in January 1905 met only with gunfire. The massacres of demonstrators on 'Bloody Sunday', and seven years later in the Lena goldfields, cast long shadows over any attempt to redeem the government of late-tsarist Russia in the area of concern for the well-being of its industrial workers.[55]

The 'ties that bound' the tsarist state and elites with the lower orders were unravelling in the late nineteenth and early twentieth centuries. However, steps in the direction of a new social order were slow and uneven. The result, among the lower orders, was uncertainty, increasing discontent, and even less prospect than before of articulating their grievances through accepted channels. Among the elites and inside the state bureaucracy there was also uncertainty, and divided opinions about how to reform the system of governance to deal with the increasing pace of social, economic and cultural change.[56]

Did the Soviet state and ruling party succeed in establishing any 'ties that bound' state and society together? The genuinely 'popular' movements among workers and peasants in 1917–18, which aimed at workers' control of factories, peasants' control over the land, and grass roots democratization, strongly suggest that the mass of the population did not want to be 'protected' by their 'natural superiors', but wanted to control their own lives. In contrast, the Bolsheviks claimed to represent the interests of the mass of the people in 1917, but did so on the basis of their interpretation of these interests, which differed sharply from what most people seem actually to have wanted. The gains of the popular movements were soon lost as the Bolsheviks reestablished a centralized state and resorted to dictatorship.[57]

Peasants did take over the land in 1917–18, in a massive agrarian revolution, and were authorized to do so by Lenin's 'Decree on land' in October 1917. However, the ensuing conflict between peasants and the party over the latter's policies of requisitioning grain in 1918–21 and collectivizing agriculture in 1929–30 (when peasants were deprived of their land) led to two of the most devastating famines in Russian history, in 1921–2 and 1932–3, during which millions died. Tsarist agrarian policies and famine relief measures certainly had serious shortcomings. Nothing that happened in tsarist Russia, however, stands comparison with the horrors of violence and starvation in rural Russia the decade and a half after 1917. Rather than offering 'protection', the Soviet state and ruling party under Lenin and Stalin waged intermittent war against the rural population.[58]

The Soviet state did make basic provision for many of its citizens, for example food, housing, education, welfare, etc., and living standards rose after Stalin's death in 1953. Khrushchev and Brezhnev both recognized the political need to divert some resources in the Soviet economy into the production of consumer goods after decades of emphasis on heavy industry. In return for improving material standards of living, the Soviet leadership expected quiescence and acceptance of party rule. Nevertheless, in spite of the promises and propaganda, many Soviet citizens were all too well aware of how far their living standards lagged behind those of much of Eastern Europe, let alone the capitalist West. In contrast to the West, the Soviet constitution guaranteed the 'right to work'. But, those who did not work were liable to arrest for 'parasitism'. Moreover, there was no guarantee that the work on offer was worthwhile or adequately remunerated. The Soviet centrally planned economy failed to meet the growing and changing demands of consumers, and most had to resort to '*blat*' (see above) or turn to the 'black' economy. The attitude of many Soviet citizens was summed up by the aphorism: 'You pretend to pay us, and we pretend to work'. This hardly constituted meaningful 'ties that bound' the Soviet social order together.[59]

Social control and coercion

A third mechanism used to maintain social order in tsarist Russia was social control and coercion. The points I have emphasized about the social order in tsarist Russia show some similarities to a protection racket. People who refused to pay their protection money, that is, their obligations to the state and elites, and people who refused to accommodate to the elites and the social order, were punished. In many cases, social control and coercion were carried out not by representatives of the state but by intermediaries. In peasant communities, heads of households, village elders, bailiffs and estate managers usually dealt with recalcitrant peasants. The ultimate punishment for people who refused to accommodate to the social order and submit to authority was to be excluded from the community, that is, denied 'protection'. The right of exclusion and exile was granted in law in 1760 to landowners and to village and urban communities. To the extent that peasants depended on their communities and higher authorities, in particular for access to land, exclusion was a very serious punishment. There were two main forms of exclusion: exile to Siberia; and, before 1874, recruitment into the army. The threat of exclusion was a powerful weapon in the hands of village elders and their superiors in the hierarchy of authority. This is why control over selecting recruits was so important (see above, p. 57).[60]

Some people chose to exclude themselves from their communities and the social order by fleeing to frontier areas, further from the power of the state and social elites, where they would have to rely more on their own initiatives. Flight thus acted as a 'safety valve', removing people less willing to submit to authority, thereby helping maintain social stability in central Russia.[61]

When social control by local elites in the community failed, or when communities turned against village elites, then landowners' representatives and local officials could call on detachments of soldiers to restore order. In spite of the limited numbers of local officials in rural Russia ('under-government'), the balance of power lay with the state, backed up by the threat or use of force. Most peasants were well aware of this, and behaved accordingly. The brutal suppression of the few outbreaks of open protest that did take place in tsarist Russia served as warnings to other would-be rebels.[62] Moreover, the pre-reform (pre-1874) Russian army was relatively successful in socializing its peasant recruits into loyal soldiers by harsh discipline and indoctrination.[63]

There were limits nevertheless to the scale of force that the state authorities were able or prepared to use. Even the vast tsarist army was not able to fight external enemies and large-scale revolts inside its frontiers at the same time. The Pugachev revolt of 1773–4 was not suppressed until after Catherine the Great had ended the war with Turkey (1768–74).

Catherine's proclamation of 17 March 1775 put an end to the repression and executions that followed the revolt, and forgave other participants on the grounds that they had been led astray by their ignorance, stupidity and superstitious nature, rather than being guilty of treason.[64] Daniel Field noted the willingness of the authorities to forgive peasants who took part in smaller-scale protests in the nineteenth century, on the grounds that they had allegedly been misled by outside 'instigators' as a result of their gullibility; he called it 'the myth of the peasant'.[65]

As the old mechanisms for maintaining the social order began to fall apart in the late nineteenth century, and as new social groups outside the old order emerged, in particular urban workers and the educated middle classes, some of whom became openly disaffected with the regime, the tsarist authorities had to rely more on force to suppress discontent and protest. In the decades after the assassination of Alexander II in 1881 there was an escalating cycle of revolutionary terror and repression.[66]

At the same time as the tsarist regime became more reliant on the use of force to uphold the old social order, the Russian army became less dependable. This was a direct result of the military service reform of 1874. Because the term of active service was radically reduced to a maximum of seven years, and the number of men who served in the army for the shorter terms greatly increased, the reformed army was far less successful than the pre-reform army in socializing recruits into loyal soldiers. After 1874 many soldiers retained their loyalty to their original social groups, which most returned to after a few years. In John Bushnell's telling phrase, many soldiers were 'peasants in uniform'. Furthermore, after the reform, the young men who served were selected by ballot. This took away from communal elders the threat of sending to the army for 25 years recalcitrant men who defied their authority. The failure of the late-tsarist Russian state to create a national conscript army whose primary loyalty was to the state was to cost it dear in 1905–6, when many troops mutinied, and, above all, in February 1917, when soldiers of the Petrograd garrison refused to fire on demonstrators precipitating the collapse of the tsarist regime.[67]

The Soviet state and ruling party relied more heavily than its predecessor on the use and threat of coercion, force and terror both to take power in 1917 and to maintain power afterwards. The Soviet regime, especially under Stalin, resorted to mass violence and terror even when there was no direct threat to it. This has been so well documented that there is no need to discuss it here. Heavy dependence on coercion, or the threat of force, is evidence for lack of legitimacy and instability. The failure, or inability, of Stalin's successors as party leaders ever fully to deal with this legacy pre-doomed any attempts to place the Soviet social order on a more secure basis. In August 1991, during the abortive coup by party hardliners, it was the reluctance, or inability, of its leaders to use force on the streets of Moscow that precipitated not just their failure, but also that of the increasingly tenuous communist hold on power in the disintegrating Soviet Union.[68]

Conclusions

This chapter has suggested some possible reasons for the endurance of hierarchical and exploitative social orders in Russian history in *la longue durée*. In a chapter of this length it is not possible to present an alternative framework for understanding social conflict in Russia in place of Marx's concept of 'class struggles'. Nor is there room to address other related questions, such as the failure of liberal democratic political systems to become established in Russia. These are subjects for other essays and other authors.

The three crises mentioned in the introduction to this chapter, the 'Time of Troubles' of 1598–1613, the revolutions of 1905–7 and 1917–21, and the collapse of the Soviet Union in 1989–91 were all periods when the three mechanisms described here by which the social order was maintained failed to work. In between these crises, the most stable and enduring social order was that of tsarist Russia. For much of the period between 1613 and 1905 the hierarchical and exploitative social order was able to sustain itself by co-opting elites at different levels of society and sharing with them some of the benefits of supporting the existing order. The state and social elites took some account of the basic welfare of the mass of the population and recognized as legitimate the 'subsistence ethic' of the peasantry. In the last resort, they used force to suppress discontent. It is a measure of the relative success of the tsarist social order until the turn of the twentieth century that most major revolts, in particular those led by Razin, Bulavin and Pugachev, were confined to the frontiers of the state and involved mostly people who were outside or just getting drawn into the 'ties that bound' the social order together.[69]

The most striking common feature of the three major crises was not social conflict but divisions inside the ruling elites and confrontations between potential elites. Social interpretations of the 'Time of Troubles' have been replaced by notions of civil wars between factions of nobles or Cossacks competing for power, sometimes under the banners of 'preten-ders' to the throne.[70] A major (and arguably the decisive) factor in the fall of Nicholas II and the tsarist regime in February–March 1917 was disunity among the elite. It was the commanders of his armies who persuaded Nicholas to abdicate in the face of imminent military defeat by the German army and the mutiny by the garrison on the streets of Petrograd. The demise of the old order took the lid off Russian society and allowed decades of suppressed discontent to overflow in a 'social revolution'. The most important feature of the ensuing four years, however, was the strug-gle for power between moderate liberals and socialists, conservative and reactionary Whites, and the Bolsheviks. It was the last group that won, and which then promptly suppressed the 'social revolution'.[71] The immediate cause of the demise of party power and the collapse of the Soviet social order in 1991 was the depth of the divisions within the party hierarchy over the continuation of the increasingly radical, and increasingly unsuccessful, reforms by Gorbachëv, the last leader of the Communist Party of the Soviet Union.

At the time of writing (late summer 1998) the Russian economy is in a state of collapse, the government in total disarray, and striking miners, whose pay is months in arrears, are camped outside government offices in central Moscow. Whether the next generation of leaders of post-Soviet Russia will succeed in establishing a durable social order will be a topic for future historians.

Acknowledgements

The author would like to thank participants in the conference 'Reinterpreting Russia', especially Roger Bartlett, for comments on earlier drafts of this chapter.

Notes

1 *Slavic Review*, 23 (1964), pp. 619–42; 24 (1965), pp. 1–22.
2 Limitations of space preclude discussion of gender and ethnicity. On the former, see D. Moon, 'Women in rural Russia from the tenth to the twentieth centuries', *Continuity and Change*, 12 (1997), pp. 129–38. On the latter, see the chapter by John Klier in this volume (chapter 12).
3 K. Marx, and F. Engels, *The Communist manifesto* (Harmondsworth, Middx, 1967), p. 79.
4 For other interpretations along similar lines to this chapter, see J.P. LeDonne, *Absolutism and ruling class: the formation of the Russian political order, 1700–1825* (Oxford and New York, 1991); E.K. Wirtschafter, *Social identity in Imperial Russia* (De Kalb, IL, 1997).
5 See G.L. Freeze, 'The *soslovie* (estate) paradigm and Russian social history', *American Historical Review*, 91 (1986), pp. 11–36. See also E.K. Wirtschafter, *Structures of society: Imperial Russia's 'people of various ranks'* (De Kalb, IL, 1994).
6 See M. Raeff, 'Patterns of Russian imperial policy towards the nationalities', in *Political ideas and institutions in Imperial Russia* (Boulder, CO, 1994), pp. 129, 133–6; Z.E. Kohut, *Russian centralism and Ukrainian autonomy: imperial absorbtion of the Hetmanate, 1760s–1830s* (Cambridge, MA, 1988), pp. 237–98; P. Longworth, *The cossacks* (London, 1969). For a more detailed, and nuanced, analysis, see LeDonne, *Absolutism and ruling class*.
7 I have made a (rather clumsy) distinction between 'higher elites', for example nobles, whose privileged status was recognized at national level, and 'lower elites', who enjoyed some privileges and status only at the local, sometimes village, level.
8 See D. Moon, 'Reassessing Russian serfdom', *European History Quarterly*, 26 (1996), pp. 483–526, and the works cited therein, especially those by S.L. Hoch. See also the chapter by Roger Bartlett in this volume.

9 See P. Czap, '"A large family: the peasant's greatest wealth": serf households in Mishino, Russia, 1814–1858', in R. Wall, ed. *Family forms in historic Europe* (Cambridge, 1983), pp. 105–51; S.L. Hoch, *Serfdom and social control in Russia: Petrovskoe, a village in Tambov* (Chicago IL, and London, 1986). See also R.D. Bohac, 'Widows and the Russian serf community', in B.E. Clements, *et al.*, eds *Russia's women: accommodation, resistance, transformation* (Berkeley, CA, and Oxford, 1991), pp. 95–112.

10 See E. Melton, 'Household economies and communal conflicts on a Russian serf estate, 1800–1817', *Journal of Social History,* 26 (1993), pp. 559–85.

11 See S.L. Hoch, *Serfdom and social control in Russia*, pp. 151–8; Melton, 'Household economies'; R.D. Bohac, 'The mir and the military draft', *Slavic Review,* 47 (1988), pp. 652–66. See also E.K. Wirtschafter, *From serf to Russian soldier* (Princeton, NJ, 1990).

12 For example, those by Bohac, Hoch and Melton cited above.

13 C.A. Frierson, (ed. and trans.), *Aleksandr Nikolaevich Engelgardt's letters from the country, 1872–1887* (New York and Oxford, 1993), p. 223.

14 See the slightly idealized account in M.M. Gromyko, *Traditsionnye normy povedeniia i formy obshcheniia russkikh krest'ian XIX v.* (Moscow, 1986).

15 This is the central argument of T. Shanin, *The awkward class: political sociology of peasantry in a developing society, Russia, 1910–1925* (Oxford, 1972).

16 R. Hellie, *Enserfment and military change in Muscovy* (Chicago and London, 1971), pp. 135–40.

17 *Polnoe sobranie zakonov Rossiiskoi imperii* [hereafter *PSZ*], series 1 (St Petersburg, 1830), XX, pp. 82–6, no.14275 (17 March 1775), especially point 47.

18 See Hellie, *Enserfment*, pp. 246–9; R.E. Jones, *The emancipation of the Russian nobility, 1762–1785* (Princeton, NJ, 1973); I. de Madariaga, *Russia in the age of Catherine the Great* (London, 1981), pp. 295–304. See also the chapter by Roger Bartlett in this volume.

19 See, in particular, S.A. Smith, *Red Petrograd: revolution in the factories, 1917–18* (Cambridge, 1983).

20 See J.H. Bater, 'Transience, residential persistence, and mobility in Moscow and St. Petersburg, 1900–1914', *Slavic Review,* 39 (1980), pp. 239–54; J. Bradley, *Muzhik and Muscovite: urbanization in late imperial Russia* (Berkeley, CA, and Oxford, 1985); J. Burds, *Peasant dreams and market politics: labor migration and the Russian village, 1861–1905* (Pittsburgh, PA, 1998); B.A. Engel, *Between the fields and the city: women, work and family in Russia, 1861–1914* (Cambridge, 1994); R.E. Johnson, *Peasant and proletarian: the working class of Moscow in the late nineteenth century* (Leicester and New Brunswick, NJ, 1979).

21 See C. Wynn, *Workers, strikes, and pogroms: the Donbass–Dnepr Bend in late imperial Russia, 1870–1905* (Princeton, NJ, 1992).

22 See, for example, T.H. Friedgut, *Iuzovka and revolution: life and work in Russia's Donbass, 1869–1924* (Princeton, NJ, 1989), p. 330; M. Steinberg, *Moral communities: the culture of class relations in the Russian printing industry, 1867–1907* (Berkeley, CA, and Oxford, 1992), pp. 89–122.

23 V.I. Lenin, *What is to be done?*, with an introduction by R. Service (Harmondsworth, Middx, 1988).

24 C. Read, *From tsar to soviets: the Russian people and their revolution, 1917–21* (London, 1996), pp. 238–57.

25 For differing perspectives on Soviet workers, see H. Kuromiya, *Stalin's industrial revolution: politics and workers, 1928–1932* (Cambridge, 1988); L.H. Siegelbaum, *Stakhanovism and the politics of productivity in the USSR, 1935–1941* (Cambridge, 1988); D. Filtzer, *Workers and Stalinist*

industrialization: the formation of modern Soviet production relations, 1928–1941 (London, 1986).

26 See S. Fitzpatrick, 'Stalin and the making of a new elite, 1928–1939', *Slavic Review*, 38 (1979) pp. 377–402; J.F. Hough, *Soviet leadership in transition* (Washington, DC, 1980), pp. 13–14, 40–8; J. Keep, *Last of empires: a history of the Soviet Union, 1945–1991* (Oxford, 1996), pp. 210–16.

27 See Shanin, *The awkward class*. See also R.E. Johnson, 'Family life-cycles and economic stratification: a case-study in rural Russia', *Journal of Social History*, 30 (1997), pp. 705–31.

28 See O. Figes, *Peasant Russia, civil war: the Volga countryside in revolution (1917–1921)* (Oxford, 1989); T. Osipova, 'Peasant rebellions', in V.N. Brovkin, ed. *The Bolsheviks in Russian society: the revolution and the civil wars* (New Haven, CT, and London, 1997), pp. 154–76; D. DuGarm, 'Peasant Wars in Tambov Province', also in Brovkin *The Bolsheviks*, pp. 177–98.

29 See S. Fitzpatrick, *Stalin's peasants: resistance and survival in the Russian village after collectivization* (New York and Oxford, 1994); L. Viola, *Peasant rebels under Stalin: collectivization and the culture of peasant resistance* (New York and Oxford, 1996). James Hughes has recently argued that the Soviet authorities did try, with some success at least in the short term, to create some social support for collectivization among 'poor' and 'middle' peasants in Siberia: *Stalinism in a Russian province: a study of collectivization and dekulakization in Siberia* (Basingstoke, Hants, and London, 1996). For a review of Hughes' book by Viola, see *Russian Review*, 57 (1998), pp. 142–3.

30 See S. Fitzpatrick, 'Signals from below: Soviet letters of denunciation of the 1930s', *Journal of Modern History*, 68 (1996), pp. 831–66; N. Lampert, *Whistleblowing in the Soviet Union: complaints and abuses under state socialism* (Basingstoke, Hants, and London, 1985).

31 S. Davies, *Popular opinion in Stalin's Russia: terror, propaganda and dissent* (Cambridge, 1997); A.V. Ledeneva, *Russia's economy of favours: 'blat', networking and informal exchange* (Cambridge, 1998); S. Lovell, ed. *Bribery and blat in Russia* (Basingstoke, Hants, and London, forthcoming).

32 Marx and Engels *The Communist manifesto*, p. 82.

33 N. Gogol, *Selected passages from correspondence with friends*, translated by J. Zeldin (Nashville, TN, 1969), pp. 137, 144–5.

34 See A. von Haxthausen, *Studies on the interior of Russia*, translated by L.M. Schmidt and edited by S.F. Starr (Chicago, IL, and London, 1972).

35 See M. Cherniavsky, *Tsar and people* (New Haven, CT, 1961), pp. 44–99; R. Wortman, *Scenarios of power: myth and ceremony in Russian monarchy*, vol. 1 (Princeton, NJ, 1995), pp. 62–4, 114–16, 217, 229–31, 305, 318; I.L. Abramova, 'Politika samoderzhaviia v otnoshenii chastnovladel'cheskikh krest'ian v 1796–1801 gg.', *Vestnik Moskovskogo Universiteta. Seriia istoriia*, no. 4 (1989), pp. 53–6. On 'monarchist populism', see the chapter by Maureen Perrie in this volume.

36 P. Roosevelt, *Life on the Russian country estate* (New Haven, CT, and London, 1995), pp. 173–91, 233–42.

37 A. Kahan, *The plow, the hammer and the knout: an economic history of eighteenth-century Russia* (Chicago, IL, and London, 1985), pp. 327, 377 note 6. See also R.P. Bartlett, 'Defences of serfdom in eighteenth-century Russia', in M. Di Salvo, and L. Hughes, eds *A window on Russia: papers from the Vth International Conference of the Study Group on Eighteenth-Century Russia, Gargano, 1994* (Rome, 1996), p. 67; R.E.F. Smith, and D. Christian, *Bread and salt: a social and economic history of food and drink in Russia* (Cambridge, 1984), pp. 194–5, 227; Moon, 'Reassessing Russian serfdom', p. 501.

38 See E. Melton, 'Enlightened seigniorialism and its dilemmas in serf Russia, 1750–1830', *Journal of Modern History,* 62 (1990), pp. 675–708.

39 S.L. Hoch, 'The serf economy and the social order in Russia', in M.L. Bush, ed. *Serfdom and slavery: studies in legal bondage* (London and New York, 1996), p. 312. See also Moon, 'Reassessing Russian serfdom', pp. 487–8, 501–2.

40 See J. Blum, *Lord and peasant in Russia from the ninth to the nineteenth century* (Princeton, NJ, 1961), pp. 240–2.

41 See V.A. Aleksandrov, 'Land reallotment in the peasant communes', in R.P. Bartlett, ed. *Land commune and peasant community in Russia* (Basingstoke, Hants, and London, 1990), pp. 36–44; S.G. Pushkarev, *Krest'ianskaia pozemel'no-peredel'naia obshchina v Rossii* (Newtonville, MA, 1976).

42 See Blum, *Lord and peasant in Russia from the ninth to the nineteenth century,* pp. 424–8, 532, 539; W.M. Pintner, *Russian economic policy under Nicholas I* (Ithaca, NY, 1967), pp. 73–5, 117–19, 153–81; B.F. Adams, 'The Reforms of P.D. Kiselev and the history of N.M. Druzhinin', *Canadian–American Slavic Studies,* 19 (1985), pp. 35–8.

43 See Moon, 'Reassessing Russian serfdom', pp. 505–6.

44 See Smith and Christian, *Bread and salt,* pp. 109–12; A. Kahan, 'Natural calamities and their effect on the food supply in Russia', *Jahrbücher für Geschichte Osteuropas,* 16 (1968), pp. 353–77; Moon, 'Reassessing Russian serfdom', pp. 504–5.

45 See Moon, 'Reassessing Russian serfdom', pp. 502–3, 523, note 82.

46 See E.P. Thompson, 'The moral economy of the English crowd in the eighteenth century', *Past and Present,* no. 50 (1971), pp. 76–136; J.C. Scott, *The moral economy of the peasant: rebellion and subsistence in South East Asia* (New Haven, CT, and London, 1976); D. Hardiman, 'Usury, dearth and famine in Western India', *Past and Present,* no. 152 (1996), pp. 113–56. For a contrasting view, see S.L. Popkin, *The rational peasant: the political economy of rural society in Vietnam* (Berkeley, CA, and London, 1979).

47 See D. Field, *Rebels in the name of the tsar* (Boston, MA, and London, 1976); G. Freeze, *From supplication to revolution: a documentary social history of Imperial Russia* (New York and Oxford, 1988); D. Moon, *Russian peasants and tsarist legislation on the eve of reform, 1825–1855* (Basingstoke, Hants, and London, 1992); Moon, 'Reassessing Russian serfdom', pp. 494–5; V. Kivelson, 'The devil stole his mind: the tsar and the 1648 Moscow uprising', *American Historical Review,* 98 (1993), pp. 733–56. See also the chapter by Maureen Perrie in this volume (chapter 10).

48 For surveys of the 'great reforms' and wider changes after 1861, see A.J., Rieber, 'Alexander II: a revisionist view', *Journal of Modern History,* 43 (1971), pp. 42–58; D. Saunders, *Russia in the age of reaction and reform, 1801–1881* (London and New York, 1992), pp. 204–77; B. Eklof, *et al.* (eds), *Russia's great reform, 1855–1881* (Bloomington, IN, 1994); H. Rogger, *Russia in the age of modernization and revolution, 1881–1917* (London and New York, 1983); P. Waldron, *The end of Imperial Russia, 1855–1917* (Basingstoke, Hants, and London, 1997). See also D. Moon, 'Estimating the peasant population of late imperial Russia from the 1897 Census', *Europe–Asia Studies,* 48 (1996), pp. 141–2.

49 See L.G. Zakharova, 'Autocracy and the Abolition of serfdom in Russia, 1856–1861', *Soviet Studies in History,* 24 (1987), pp. 12–115; S.L. Hoch, 'The banking crisis, peasant reform, and economic development in Russia, 1857–1861', *American Historical Review,* 96 (1991), pp. 795–820.

50 See H.S. Vasudevan, 'Peasant land and peasant society in late imperial Russia', *Historical Journal,* 31 (1988), pp. 212–16.

51 See S.G. Marks, *Road to power: the Trans-Siberian Railroad and the coloniza-tion of Asian Russia, 1850–1917* (Ithaca, NY, 1991), pp. 141–5, 153–69, 220–2.

52 See J. Pallot, and D. Shaw, *Landscape and settlement in Romanov Russia, 1613–1917* (Oxford, 1990), pp. 164–92; Vasudevan, 'Peasant land and peasant society in late imperial Russia', pp. 218–20.

53 See R.G. Robbins, *Famine in Russia, 1891–1892* (New York and London, 1975).

54 See T. Emmons, 'The peasant and emancipation', in W.S. Vucinich, ed. *The peasant in nineteenth-century Russia* (Stanford, CA, 1968), pp. 41–71; D. Field, *Rebels in the name of the tsar,* idem, 'Peasants and propagandists in the Russian movement to the people of 1874', *Journal of Modern History,* 59 (1987), pp. 415–38.

55 See Rogger, *Russia in the age of modernization and revolution, 1881–1917,* pp. 109–11, 115–17, 240–1.

56 On differing attitudes to change among bureaucrats and senior officials, see F. Wcislo, *Reforming rural Russia: state, local society, and national politics, 1855–1914* (Princeton, NJ, 1990).

57 See Read, *From tsar to soviets;* G. Swain, *The origins of the Russian civil war* (London and New York, 1996). See also the 'libertarian' interpretation in E. Acton, *Rethinking the Russian Revolution* (London, 1990).

58 See A. Graziosi, *The great Soviet peasant war: Bolsheviks and peasants, 1917–1933* (Cambridge, MA, 1996); M. Wehner, 'Golod 1921–1922 gg. v Samarskoi gubernii i reaktsii sovetskogo pravitel'stva', *Cahiers du Monde Russe,* 38 (1997), pp. 223–42; R. Conquest, *The harvest of sorrow: Soviet collectivisation and the terror famine* (London, 1986).

59 See Keep, *Last of empires,* pp. 84–7, 93–102, 137–40, 216–43; J. Millar, 'The "little deal": Brezhnev's contribution to acquisitive socialism', *Slavic Review,* 44 (1985), pp. 694–706.

60 See Hoch, *Serfdom and social control in Russia,* especially pp. 152–5, 160–86; C.D. Worobec, *Peasant Russia: family and community in the post-emancipa-tion period* (Princeton, NJ, 1991), pp. 175–216. See also Melton, 'Household economies and communal conflicts on a Russian serf estate, 1800–1817'.

61 See D. Moon, 'Peasant migration and the settlement of Russia's frontiers 1550–1897', *Historical Journal,* 30 (1997), pp. 889–92; Pallot and Shaw, *Landscape and Settlement in Romanov Russia, 1613–1917,* p. 27.

62 See, for example, P. Avrich, *Russian rebels 1600–1800* (New York, 1972), pp. 43–4, 103–15, 167–72, 239–45.

63 See J.S. Curtiss, *The Russian army under Nicholas I* (Durham NC, 1965); Wirtschafter, *From serf to Russian soldier.*

64 See J.T. Alexander, *Autocratic politics in a national crisis: the Imperial Russian Government and Pugachev's revolt, 1773–1775* (Bloomington, IN, 1969); *PSZ,* XX, series 1, pp. 82–6, no. 14275 (17 March 1775), especially point 38.

65 Field, *Rebels in the name of the tsar, 1881–1917,* pp. 208–14.

66 Rogger, *Russia in the age of modernization and revolution,* pp. 132–62; P. Waldron, 'States of emergency: autocracy and emergency legislation, 1881–1917', *Revolutionary Russia,* 8 (1995), pp. 1–25.

67 See J. Bushnell, 'Peasants in uniform: The tsarist army as a peasant society', *Journal of Social History,* 13 (1980), pp. 565–76; *idem, Mutiny amid repression: Russian soldiers in the revolution of 1905–1906* (Bloomington, IN, 1985); Read, *From tsar to soviets,* pp. 43, 121–5. See also D. Moon, 'Peasants into Russian citizens? A comparative perspective', *Revolutionary Russia,* 9 (1996), especially pp. 46–9, 64–7.

68 On the coup and its aftermath, see Keep, *Last of empires,* pp. 400–11.

69 See M. Khodarkovsky, 'The Stepan Razin uprising: was it a "peasant war"?', *Jahrbücher für Geschichte Osteuropas,* 42 (1994), pp. 1–19; G.-G. Nol'te,

'Russkie "krest'ianskie voiny" kak vosstaniia okrain', *Voprosy istorii*, no. 11 (1994), pp. 31–8; V.M. Solov'ev, 'Aktual'nye voprosy izucheniia narodnykh dvizhenii (polemicheskie zametki o krest'ianskikh voinakh v Rossii)', *Istorii SSSR*, no. 3 (1991), pp. 130–45.

70 See C. Dunning, 'R. G. Skrynnikov, the Time of Troubles, and the "first peasant war" in Russia', *Russian Review*, 50 (1991), pp. 71–81; *idem*, 'Does Jack Goldstone's model of early modern state crises apply to Russia?', *Comparative Studies in Society and History*, 39 (1997), pp. 572–92; M. Perrie, *Pretenders and popular monarchism in early modern Russia: the false tsars of the Time of Troubles* (Cambridge, 1995); A.L. Stanislavskii, *Grazhdanskaia voina v Rossii XVII v.: Kazachestvo na perelome istorii* (Moscow, 1990).

71 See Read, *From tsar to soviets*, especially pp. 42–5; Swain, *The origins of the Russian civil war*; E. Mawdsley, *The Russian civil war* (London, 1987).

|5|

Liberty and Property, Land and Freedom: landownership and agriculture in Imperial, Soviet and post-Soviet Russia

ROGER BARTLETT

Land has never been a scarce resource in Russia. The country's ever-increasing size and its geography were such that this item was never in short supply. Land might be inconveniently located; it might be inconveniently distributed; but in absolute terms it has always been plentiful. The problem, historically, has been, first, how it was to be obtained; second, on what terms it should be held; and, third, how it was to be made productive. These three questions, of course, face all agrarian societies. But in Russia such questions and the answers to them have been particularly influential in shaping societal relations for the last half-millenium. *Agrarnyi vopros*, the agrarian question – the status of landowner and of peasant farmer, of agricultural organization and productivity – fundamentally conditioned the history of Imperial and Soviet Russia and its outcomes, and continues to be a determining factor in the post-Soviet period.

The Imperial period saw radical and contrasting developments in noble and peasant landholding. In 1700 there were four principal landowning or landholding groups: the Church; the Crown and state; the nobility; and the peasantry. The Church was stripped of its lands in the ensuing century. The Crown remained the pre-eminent landowner. Theoretically, at least from the time of Ivan IV onwards, all privately held land (including *votchina*, allodial holdings) carried service obligations and was subject to confiscation by the Crown: absolute property rights did not exist. Nevertheless, already by the seventeenth century, state-granted and state-protected property rights for servitors in land had evolved which provided a strong incentive for military and state officials to support the autocracy.[1] Still, the *Ulozhenie* (Law Code) of 1649, which finally consolidated serfdom and satisfied the land and labour demands of the middle service class, did not stabilize the state's service regime. The 1682 abolition of *mestnichestvo* prefigured Peter I's fundamental redefinition of state service and the function of servitors. Peter's reforms both created a new corporate nobility, the *dvorianstvo*, and redefined its relationship to land. Under the Muscovite dispensation, landholding and landownership at once carried an obligation to serve and (although servitors could also receive cash payments) were the essential reward and payment for service. Peter's law of 1714, which equalized *pomest'e* (conditional service tenure) with *votchina*, and his introduction of salaries for state service broke the link of land to service; and this process was completed in 1762 when the nobility was freed altogether from compulsory service without any change in noble landowning rights. The Nobles' Charter of 1785 confirmed and extended these prerogatives; and it is, of course, a great irony that the term for a state serviceman holding crown land in conditional service tenure, *pomeshchik*, came to designate the autonomous noble landowner. Nobility and ownership of serf estates became synonymous, but they no longer carried serious obligations to the state. The nobility thus came to enjoy real private property rights; one can say that they acquired both liberty and property in this process during the eighteenth and nineteenth centuries. No subsequent government sought seriously to infringe these prerogatives until 1856–61, with the one exception of Paul I (1796–1801), and his fate – assassination – was emblematic. In other words, there was in Imperial Russia before 1861 a firm and developing tradition of civil rights, those of the nobility.[2]

These rights, however, were built on others' lack of rights. This encouraged a broad disregard for civic legality, which is normally based upon mutual recognition of rights, however unbalanced these may be. Noble ownership of serfs became a fundamental obstacle to the abolition of serfdom; it also defined social attitudes and economic relations through to the end of the autocratic regime. When the post-Crimean crisis finally prompted the abolition of serfdom, Alexander II was very anxious to represent the 1861 emancipation as a result of noble initiative: the nobility magnanimously limiting their own privileges. But the majority of the nobility were hostile to the reform and, unable to prevent it, did what they could to limit its impact. The next major attempt at changing peasants' status, Stolypin's reform programme of 1906, was likewise forced upon the government by a realization of impending crisis.[3] It met with equally strong opposition from the noble landowners' lobby.[4]

While Muscovite servitors' conditional control of land (and serfs) thus metamorphosed into the absolute Western-style private property of the Imperial nobility, peasant land-tenure evolved in the opposite direction. Most peasants on landlords' and monastic estates had never been owners or independent holders of their land, but other categories of peasantry regarded their land as their own, under God and the tsar. This was particularly true of the black-ploughing (*chernososhnye*) peasants in the north where serfdom never penetrated and, during the eighteenth century, of the *odnodvortsy* in the south, former chartered petty servicemen whom Peter I reduced to the status of state peasants. These groups initially had complete control of their land; they bought, sold, bequeathed or mortgaged it as they saw fit: they considered themselves in practice to be its owners.[5] During the eighteenth century this claim was denied by the state,[6] which, while allowing the development of Roman-law concepts for nobles, chose to reinforce norms of Muscovite state-controlled and service-determined tenure among the peasantry. It made peasant land-tenure dependent upon higher authority, intervened with decrees regulating holding and disposal of land and prescribing allotment size (partly, certainly, in order to protect peasants from outside encroachment), and resettled members of these groups onto other land according to its own priorities. The middle decades of the eighteenth century thus form a watershed in the development of land and property relations in Russia, fundamentally separating nobles and peasants: it is not surprising that this was also the point at which the peasant question – the problem of serfdom and the social and economic status of the peasantry – first emerged as a preoccupation of government and educated society.[7]

One major reason for this new state concern with peasant landholding was that Imperial policies had led to a shift in the burden of state service, from the nobility to the peasantry. While noble state servitors now received salaries for such service as they chose to perform, and held land (and its population) as unconditional private property, Peter I's legislation compelled peasants to man the armed forces and state industrial enterprises through conscription, and to maintain them through quartering of troops and through taxation: the poll tax of 1722, which remained the principal Russian tax up until the 1880s, was designed expressly to fund the armed forces, and it rapidly became the symbolic divider of social classes – broadly speaking, *podlye* (the base people, commoners, plebeians) paid it whereas *blagorodnye* (well-born, nobles) and *tserkovniki* (churchmen) did not. Thus the compulsion to serve and to service the state's institutions passed from those who owned land to those who worked it: although many nobles continued to serve, by choice or from need, and the tiny urban population also carried certain service burdens, the peasantry had become the essential compulsory load-bearer within the polity.[8] The emergence in the nineteenth century of the notorious noble estate-owning 'superfluous man' (*lishnii chelovek*), cultured, materially secure, and without aim in life, was a natural outcome of this process.

At the same time the authorities were correspondingly concerned to ensure that these new peasant categories of state servant had sufficient resources to carry out their obligations. The spread of repartitional communal tenure among state peasants at this time reflects the official wish to ensure a positive correlation of landholding with state burdens. Communal tenure was reinforced, repartition officially encouraged, and additional land allocated to peasant communities whose land fund fell below government-determined levels: the 1766 Survey Instruction set a norm of 60 *desiatinas* per family (15 per head).[9] These government-prescribed land norms and relative equalization of holdings in the state villages paralleled the situation encouraged in serf villages by serf owners who were either simply concerned for their rents or genuinely sought to avoid the impoverishment of their peasants.[10] This situation locked the peasantry, state and serf into a cycle of subservience and obligation, bound them to the land and the authority of their masters or administrators and so perpetuated existing social and economic relations. It also tended to limit differentiation, whether of wealth, of experience and world-view or of agricultural practice.

The effects of these developments on the agrarian economy and on social mores up to 1917 were multifarious: let us pick out those relevant to this chapter. First, under the nobles' monopoly or pre-eminent position in landownership, Imperial Russian agriculture as a whole failed to develop into a really prosperous and technically efficient economic sector. The servile system allowed nobles to live off unpaid serf labour in a technically primitive, cost-ineffective and relatively undynamic agrarian regime dominated by the three-field system and peasant methods and inventory. From the eighteenth century onwards noble economic requirements were inflated by the growth of a noble culture of conspicuous consumption, which was not adequately met by growth in estate productivity. While small landowners sank into poverty, or worked their peasants into the ground, others found additional ways to support their lifestyle. They took advantage of the land grants newly available in border areas, developing agriculture extensively rather than intensively; they exploited the noble monopoly of vodka distilling which used up quantities of grain and produced great profits; they created other low-technology estate industries using estate-produced raw materials and serf labour. They benefited from the Russian price revolution of the eighteenth century, when Russian prices rose to European levels, which brought great gains to those involved in marketing agricultural products as well as increasing the value of land and buttressing the financial strength of the national economy.[11] Noble landowners also simply went into debt – in the short term, the mortgaging of serfs was a rational response to financial pressure; in the long term, failure to increase estate productivity sufficiently to service such debts led increasingly to insolvency. In the early nineteenth century the servile landowner economy adapted to changing market conditions by extending *barshchina* (forced labour) in fertile areas, and the Southern Ukraine, conquered and brought into the market sphere by Catherine II, became the breadbasket of Europe. But innovation and technical advance at this time were the exception rather than the rule in agriculture, and much of what there was took place within the parameters of existing traditions, making more rational use of existing methods.[12] This was partly because serfdom, ignorance and lack of investment capital made innovation difficult and risky,[13] partly because there was little incentive or awareness of the need to innovate so long as existing economic circumstances provided an acceptable living.

In the decades after the emancipation servile labour became less and less available to landowners, and at the same time, during the so-called Long Depression in the 1870s and 1880s, the terms of world trade became much less favourable to Russia. Generalizations are risky here: one emphasis of recent writing has been on regional differences, both among landowners and among peasants. Nevertheless Seymour Becker's overall thesis seems broadly to hold: this period sees not so much the traditionally trumpeted decline of the gentry as a redisposition and redefinition of noble activity. A minority of noble landowners succeeded in adapting to the new economic situation on the land, either by changing their farming methods or by tailoring their lifestyles to the new reality, or both; as the market in farmland developed, nobles were buyers as well as sellers. The majority retreated from active involvement in agriculture, but found other rational solutions in renting out or selling their land or in entering other occupations. Success for those who succeeded in agriculture did not come only from modernization, however. The most recent work in this area, by Andreas Grenzer, focusing rather unsatisfactorily exclusively on very large estates, emphasizes the presence simultaneously of modern farming methods using hired labour and machinery, and the retention of strip farming, primitive rotations and labour-rent (*otrabotka*): 'any more decisive willingness to innovate among pomeshchiki was hindered by the persistence of elements of the old servile system which continued to exist'. Grenzer refuses to comment on the Seymour Becker – Roberta Manning argument, on the alleged grounds of insufficiency of sources; there are, in fact, indications that more commercial, 'capitalist' farming was to be found among the middle or smaller gentry.[14] The point to stress, however, is that such modernization and commercialization as occurred among gentry farmers was incomplete, evincing the notorious *feodal'nye perezhitki*, remnants of the old agrarian regime, while the political and ideological views of the surviving noble landowners remained largely hostile to the possible emergence of a fully independent and prosperous peasantry which could endanger their economic security and social preeminence. In sum, right up to the end of the Old Regime the social and agricultural predominance of noble landowners and their entrenched legal rights tended to inhibit the modernization of agriculture and society in Imperial Russia.

Let us turn back now to the peasantry. The emancipated peasantry did not supply the modern efficient agricultural sector which their former masters had failed to produce, either. Nevertheless, recent research has emphasized the economic successes of post-reform agriculture, in which the peasant economy played a growing role. The famous Leninist formulation, '1861 gave rise to 1905', defective emancipation allegedly leading to agrarian revolution, has been largely called into question: the peasants did not simply decline, any more than the nobles. Not only did post-emancipation agricultural productivity keep pace with the huge growth in population 1860–1914, peasants became responsible for a growing proportion of agricultural production, increasingly adapted to the market, and appear to have had more disposable income than proponents of the immiseration thesis generally allowed. Recent writing has emphasized the leading peasant role in the pre-revolutionary Russian agrarian economy, and the fact that average Russian crop yields in the period compare relatively favourably with those elsewhere in Europe. It has also been suggested that the commune as a socio-economic structure did not necessarily hinder flexibility or technical advance in agriculture; peasant agriculture suffered rather from the unfavourable general environment in which it had to operate.[16]

Nevertheless, peasants' adaptation towards more modern forms of agrarian and economic relations did not eradicate old attitudes or habits of mind, which were reinforced by government policies. The 1861 settlement imposed and reinforced communal tenure, burdensome redemption payments and collective responsibility; it entrenched peasant customary law and second-class civic status. And in the subsequent decades the authorities failed to do anything incisive or effective to develop agriculture and rural society which might have compared to contemporary official programmes of industrialization – nothing like the 1840s attempts to lead and guide of Kiselev's Ministry of State Domains, and only palliative measures to support peasant finances. The authorities failed equally to make or allow serious provision for the huge growth of rural population.[17]

Economic growth and diversification were thus paralleled by social conservatism and peasant alienation from the larger world around. Here again the picture is diverse. In some respects and some places the Russian peasant's world underwent radical change over the half century 1860–1914. Yet it seems to be true that at the start of the twentieth century the great Russian peasantry as a whole still broadly lived in a world determined by the horizons and relations of its villages, devoted to communal land-tenure and risk-averse farming, and more at ease with the traditional ways of peasant agriculture than with modern practice and innovation. Above all, a majority of peasants held to their own communal ethic: they rejected the legitimacy of Western-style private property norms. The lure of risk-based individual farming attracted only a minority, and peasants naturally distrusted the world of landowner, official and urbanite which at all times and in all ways, it seemed, sought only to exploit the peasant. Peasant society was strengthened in this by its own long-term experiences: it should be emphasized that peasant behaviour was rational within its own terms. The relatively small success of Stolypin's reform programme is testimony to the inertia, structural[18] difficulties and clearly-framed alternative values which any modernization of Russian peasant society from without would have to overcome, just as peasant actions during the revolution and civil war – expropriation of *pomeshchiki*, equalization of holdings, reinforcement of communal authority and subsequent peasant attitudes during the New Economic Policy to former landowners, who were sometimes given land shares provided they farmed for themselves on an equal footing with the peasants[19] – testify to the vitality of the 'moral economy' of the nineteenth-century village, well into the twentieth century.

Land and Freedom (from outside constraint) remained the peasant ideal. In sum, the dynamic of landownership and landholding, intimately linked with the requirements of the state and with serfdom, was one of the basic factors in Imperial Russia contributing to social rigidity and inequality, economic inefficiency and to the exclusion of the mass of the population from social rights and the civil society which began to develop at the end of the nineteenth century.

What has been said so far in this chapter, however, risks one-sidedness: it may give an impression of the peasantry as a more or less passive object of events unfolding around it, that the peasants simply suffered what impositions government, landlord and environment thrust upon them. This underemphasizes a vital and powerful dimension of the interaction between the peasantry and the larger world. A strong counterargument has been made that peasant society influenced and moulded the upper echelons and government just as much as the reverse, and not only in such times as 1773–74, 1905–06 or 1917–21, when peasant aspirations were expressed in mass action during societal breakdown, but constantly, in the very structures which ensured the normal running of Imperial society. This is a theme which George Yaney has made very much his own;[20] it has been developed more recently for the eighteenth and nineteenth centuries by Steven Hoch, Edgar Melton and David Moon,[21] who have analysed the persistence of serfdom and the problems of agrarian reform in terms of the interacting interests of peasants with other peasants in the village, and of peasants with landlord or estate representative. It is explicit in Christine Worobec's study of the pre-revolutionary peasantry,[22] and for the Soviet period it has been recently explored by Sheila Fitzpatrick and Lynne Viola.[23]

Of particular relevance here is the work of the German rural sociologist Gerd Spittler, introduced into the literature by Edgar Melton, which takes these ideas further than hitherto and may illuminate both the Imperial and the Soviet periods. Spittler developed his ideas on peasants and society during field work in Africa, principally the former French colony of Niger, in the 1970s. The problems facing the French colonial and ex-colonial administration in Niger have striking parallels with those facing Imperial and Soviet Russian governments. Spittler also applied his analysis to eighteenth-century Prussia.[24]

Spittler's model is that of the 'peasant state' (*Bauernstaat*): a preindustrial, agrarian polity and economy in which peasants supply the main sources of wealth. The model applies most clearly to countries with authoritarian governments and poor market development. This is a state, governed by non-peasants, in which (to repeat) the fundamental sources of wealth are provided by peasants, and in which local peasant administrative organs, representatives or leaders constitute an essential link between government and people.[25] In Niger the French had perforce to deal with local chiefs and elders, who mediated between them and the mass of the population; in Russia the government faced the serf owner or the commune. This relationship carries with it certain inevitabilities. First, it allows effective pursuit of coercive resource mobilization – taxation, labour and military levies, imposition of particular crop production – but makes any attempt to co-opt, communicate with or influence the population dependent upon the cooperation and the culture and interests of both the middlemen and of the population at large. The Russian authorities could collect taxes and other tribute from their population more or less successfully, but efforts to modernize the peasants' agricultural practices foundered on the traditional culture of the village. Not only was the village hostile to the outside world, viewing all outside intervention as deception or threat but also it had its own values and social mores and its own agenda. In particular, village communities had their own network of social relations and clientele systems, which combined with an oral culture and customary law to make rational and bureaucratic approaches invalid. Success for a villager in the village depended not on the justice of his or her cause, not on the decrees of government or the orders of the lord, but on the decision of the community, which was defined by internal dynamics; it was often for sale to the highest bidder or most powerful faction, or else it depended on the strong man's (almost never woman's) ability to provide patronage to friends and clients and on the weak man's to find a patron. Village elders derived their power less from carrying out outside orders than from their ability to implement or distort or ignore such orders to their own advantage, and to the advantage of their friends or of the village as a whole. Government and landlord stood outside this interface, though sometimes it was a matter of landlord or steward conniving with peasants against the government. Thus state (and often landowners') interventionist policies depended in large measure on the cooperation of a countryside or a populace in no way necessarily ready to cooperate. Nineteenth-century attempts by the Russian government to penetrate and co-opt the countryside, with peace arbitrators or land captains, brought state power much closer to the workings of village life, but incompletely, and only in a personal, arbitrary form as unsystematic and oppressive as the power of the community's officials. How does this compare with the relationship between party secretary, collective farm chairman and *kolkhozniki* in the Soviet period? In the eighteenth century in Russia this situation was not of great direct importance at the national level: it did not yet radically constrain the state's ability to develop its power. As time passed, however, the distance between the two sides became increasingly critical, and especially so in the revolutionary period. And the Soviet solution to the problem, enforced collectivization, succeeded neither in the short nor the long term: it failed to control sufficiently the dynamics of peasant society, to win peasant allegiance or adequately to solve the problem of agricultural production.

A second aspect of this problem is that of information flows, between town and country, between administrator and administered. Here the problem for those whom George Yaney called 'capital-city minds' lies in understanding and reciprocally communicating with the rural society they were trying to govern. Spittler emphasizes the ignorance, misunderstanding, condescension with which French-educated French officials met African peasant society; they brought their own theories and preconceptions and applied inappropriate yardsticks. Seeking rational interpretations, they created their own version of the countryside and its relationships which amounted in the end simply to fiction or myth. And they interpreted their almost inevitable failures in terms of their own understandings and by blaming the peasantry. Part of the problem was that French officials had great difficulty in obtaining reliable information, without which rational administration was also impossible. Bureaucratic written culture confronted peasant oral culture; the autarchy of peasants in an incompletely marketized economy defied efforts to measure economic activity and wealth. *Mutatis mutandis*, much the same was true in Russia. In short, French colonial, tsarist and Soviet power wielders developed their own view of the countryside and the treatment appropriate to it, cast in the terms of their own ideology, informed by inadequate factual knowledge, and self-justifying because any insuccess was clearly a result of peasant recalcitrance or peasant vices. The peasants on the other hand pursued their own agendas, acted and reacted according to their own values, understanding and advantage. This syndrome tends to affect all bureaucratic ruling structures.[26] In Niger in the 1930s, crop failure attributable to the French administration's policies caused famine conditions; but taxes were collected as usual, and the crop failures were explained by alleged peasant laziness, indifference and fatalism, and inactivity on the part of local chiefs.[27] In Russia and Ukraine of the same period famine was also a result of the Stalin regime's refusal to understand or treat peasant society in any except Stalinist terms. At the same time, as Sheila Fitzpatrick and Lynne Viola have demonstrated, peasants evolved their own strategies in attempting to preserve their lives and their culture under these conditions.[28]

Now, as Russia currently pursues its 'third great land reform of the twentieth century',[29] the economic environment is as hostile to successful farming as at any of the periods discussed so far, and at the same time old attitudes persist and continue to affect the outcome – in particular, entrenched peasant attitudes which were sanctified by Soviet practice. The idea that private property in land is evil, that land-tenure is conditional and must be justified by appropriate land-use, bedevils attempts to revitalize the modern Russian rural economy. The Rural Development Institute (RDI) of Seattle recently reported a survey just conducted in Russia which emphasized that 'although purchase and sale of agricultural plots is authorised by Presidential Decree [. . .], purchase and sale of land remains a highly charged issue, with many officials opposed to the very concept that land can be a commodity'.[30] No other issue mentioned in the report was associated with emotionally charged convictions in this way. The investigators also recorded that the threat of land confiscation is a powerful potential source of tenure insecurity. *Raion* administrators continue to confiscate privately held agricultural land without compensation on the supposed basis of violations of legal obligations, including the obligation to use the land, or 'if the lessee was not using the land properly'.[31]

The Seattle RDI appeals to empirical 'world experience' to demonstrate its own truth that 'smaller farms operated by single families and small groups consistently out-produce collective farms' and that a market in privately owned land must underpin this.[32] This is the case accepted and championed on one side of the argument which is proceeding inside Russia: as a letter-writer to *Izvestiia* put it in December 1997,

> In short, the *kolkhoz* represents beggary, and the impoverishment of everyday life. . . . a market in land is essential. Without it the rebirth of the countryside is impossible. Without it both town and village will drag out a half-starved existence. Without it Russia will always be beggarly.[33]

On the other side of the argument, traditionalist kolkhoz workers find justification for their scepticism towards private property and individual farming in the tribulations of pioneer *fermery*:[34] once again there is a real, rational basis for such peasant scepticism in a situation where available investment capital is principally in the hands of 'new Russians' and other outsiders, and neither legal authority, business security nor commercial infrastructures are yet strong enough to encourage private agricultural enterprise. At the same time a majority of politicians in the Duma are hostile to purchase and sale of land, on principle or in practice.[35] Some 14 federal (provincial) Russian authorities currently deny even country dwellers any legal property right in their shares of their reformed collective farm;[36] and, as can be seen from the Seattle survey, many local officials share this perspective. The Land Code proposed in 1997 remains mired in controversy, while negotiations for a compromise and discussions over the nature of controls required to regulate land sales continue. Meanwhile, at the time of this writing (March 1998), local initiative has outflanked the national debate: first in Nizhnii Novgorod, Sverdlovsk and St Petersburg, and now more completely in the Saratov region, local laws have been promulgated allowing free sale and purchase of land. The first unrestricted land auction was reported from Saratov on 6 March.[37]

In Russia as elsewhere old values, myths and assumptions die hard; ever since the coming of systematic thought on Russian agriculture in Peter I's time, and systematic attempts to shape the countryside from outside or above, such attitudes both peasant and official have combined with difficult material conditions and social tensions to play a crucial role in the evolution of land-tenure and agricultural practice. While the situation gradually evolves, they evidently still continue to do so.

Notes

1 G.G. Weickhardt, 'The pre-Petrine law of property', *Slavic Review*, 52 (1993), pp. 663–79; R. Hellie, *Enserfment and military change in Muscovy* (Chicago and London, 1971), especially ch. 3.

2 O.A. Omel'chenko, '*Zakonnaia monarkhiia*' *Ekateriny II. Prosveshchennyi absoliutism v Rossii* (Moscow, 1993), pp. 357–9; N.V. Kipriianova, 'K voprosu o dvorianskom zemlevladenii v zakonodatel'stve XVIII v.', *Vestnik Moskovskogo Universiteta*, Seriia 8: Istoriia, 1 (1983), pp. 57–68.

3 The decision in principle predated 1905, however: first indications were given in a decree of 1904, following on the Witte and Kokovtsov commissions.

4 A.P. Borodin, 'Ob'edinennoe Dvorianstvo i agrarnaia reforma', *Voprosy istorii*, 9 (1993), pp. 33–44; *idem*, 'Gosudarstvennyi Sovet i ukaz 9 noiabria 1906 g.: iz istorii agrarnoi reformy Stolypina', *Otechestvennaia Istoriia*, 2 (1994), pp. 74–89; D.A.J. Macey, 'Zemel'naia reforma i politicheskie peremeny: fenomen Stolypina', *Voprosy istorii*, 4 (1993), pp. 3–18.

5 V.I. Semevskii, *Krest'iane v tsarstvovanie Ekateriny II*, 2 vols (St. Petersburg 1900–1), II, *passim*; E. N. Shveikovskaia, 'K kharakteristike mirovospriiatiia chernososhnykh krest'ian (XVII vek: sever)', *Istoriia SSSR*, 1 (1992), pp. 75–86; J. Pallot and D.J. Shaw, *Landscape and settlement in Romanov Russia 1613–1917* (Oxford, 1990), ch. 2.

6 V.I. Semevskii, *Krest'iane v tsarstvovanie Ekateriny II*, II, pp. 624, 733 *et al.*

7 R. Bartlett, 'The question of serfdom. Catherine II, the Russian debate, and the view from the Western periphery. . .', in Roger Bartlett and Janet Hartley, eds *Russia in the Age of Enlightenment: essays for Isabel de Madariaga* (Basingstoke, Hants, and London, 1990), pp. 142–66.

8 Now, as before, service was enforced by violence if necessary – whereas reluctant servitors (*netchiki*) had been subject to arrest, peasants could suffer confiscation of movable property for non-payment of taxes, and recalcitrant recruits were sent to the army in chains.

9 'Instruktsiia mezhevym gubernskim kantseliariiam i provintsial'nym kontoram', 25th May 1766, *Polnoe Sobranie Zakonov Rossiiskoi Imperii*, Sobranie Pervoe, 44 vols (St Petersburg, 1830), vol. XVII, pp. 716–94, no. 12659, chs XII (§ 6), XIV (§ 12), XIX (§§ 1, 2); XX (§§ 1, 5, 10); *et al.* The Survey Instruction explicitly excluded non-peasants from such landholding. Its prescriptions were valid 'do budushchego po general'nym planam rassmotreniia' (XIX, § 15 *et al.*). 1 desiatina = 2.7 acres. See, generally, S.G. Pushkarev, *Krest'ianskaia pozemel'no-peredel'naia obshchina v Rossii* (Newtonville, MA, 1976); Ya. Firestone, 'Land equalization and factor scarcities: holding size and the burden of impositions in imperial central Russia and the late Ottoman Levant', *Journal of Economic History*, 41 (1981), pp. 813–33.

10 H.E. Melton, 'Enlightened seignorialism and its dilemmas in serf Russia 1750–1830', *Journal of Modern History*, 62 (1990), pp. 675–708; H.E. Melton, '"Bauernstaat Russland"': Das Problem aufgeklärter Agrarreform in der Zeit Katharinas', paper presented at the conference on 'Katharina II, Russland und Europa', Zerbst, August 1996, preprint; A.A. Preobrazhenskii, ed. *Sel'skokhoziastvennye instruktsii (pervaia polovina/seredina XVIII v.)*, 3 vols (Moscow, 1984–87) (Inst. Istorii Akad. Nauk SSSR, Materialy po istorii sel'skogo khoziaistva i krest'ianstva Rossii). Cp. Survey Instruction (as endnote 9), ch. XIII, §§ 4, 7.

11 A. Kahan, 'The costs of "Westernization" in Russia: the gentry and the economy in the eighteenth century', *Slavic Review*, 25 (1966), pp. 40–66; B.N. Mironov, 'Vliianie revoliutsii tsen v Rossii XVIII veka na ee ėkonomicheskoe i sotsial'no-politicheskoe razvitie', *Istoriia SSSR*, 1 (1991), pp. 86–101 (an English version appeared in *Journal of Economic History*). The recent work of Boris Mironov and of Ian Blanchard raises questions and perspectives on the eighteenth-century Russian agrarian economy which cannot be addressed here. See further B.N. Mironov *Russkii gorod v 1740–1860e gody* (Leningrad, 1990); I. Blanchard, *Russia's 'Age of Silver': precious-metal production and economic growth in the eighteenth century* (London and New York, 1989), critically reviewed by Mironov in *Slavonic and East European Review*, 69 (1991), pp. 361–63; and Blanchard, 'Eighteenth-century Russian economic growth: state enterprise or peasant endeavour?', *Studies in Economic and Social History: Discussion Papers*, ed. I. Blanchard, no. 95–1, Department of Economic and Social History, University of Edinburgh (1995).

12 N.W. Cornwell, *The role of the nobility in agricultural change in Russia during the reign of Catherine II*, PhD dissertation, University of Illinois, Illinois, IL (1972).

13 M. Confino, *Domaines et seigneurs en Russie vers la fin du XVIIIe siècle: étude de structures agraires et de mentalités économiques* (Paris, 1963); Melton, 'Enlightened seignorialism and its dilemmas in serf Russia 1750–1830'.

14 S.J. Becker, *Nobility and privilege in late imperial Russia* (De Kalb, IL, 1985), a necessary corrective to R.T. Manning, *The crisis of the Old Order in Russia: gentry and government* (Princeton, NJ, 1982); A. Grenzer, *Adel und Landbesitz im ausgehenden Zarenreich. Der russische Landadel zwischen Selbstbehauptung und Anpassung nach Aufhebung der Leibeigenschaft* (Stuttgart, 1995), p. 211.

15 See endnote 4.

16 J. Y. Simms, 'The crisis in Russian agriculture at the end of the nineteenth century', *Slavic Review*, 36 (1977), pp. 377–98, and ensuing discussion; E.M. Wilbur, 'Was Russian peasant agriculture really that impoverished? New evidence from a case study from the "impoverished center" at the end of the nineteenth century', *Journal of Economic History*, 43 (1983), pp. 137–47; P. Gatrell, *The tsarist economy 1850–1917* (London, 1986), pp. 119–40; N.B. Selunskaia, 'Krest'ianskoe khoziaistvo evropeiskoi Rossii nakanune Oktiabria', *Istoriia SSSR*, 5 (1987), pp. 110–28; R. Bideleux, 'Agricultural advance under the Russian village commune system', in R. Bartlett, ed. *Land commune and peasant community in Russia: communal forms in Imperial and early Soviet society* (Basingstoke, Hants, and London, 1990), pp. 196–218; E. Kingston-Mann, 'Peasant communes and economic innovation: a preliminary enquiry', in E. Kingston-Mann and T. Mixter, eds *Peasant economy, culture, and politics of European Russia 1800–1921* (Princeton, NJ, 1991), pp. 23–51; see also E. Wilbur, 'Peasant poverty in theory and in practice: a view from the "impoverished center" at the end of the nineteenth century', in Kingston-Mann and Mixter, eds *Peasant economy, culture and politics*, ch. 2, and

S. Wheatcroft, 'Crises and the condition of the peasantry in late Imperial Russia', in Kingston-Mann and Mixter, eds *Peasant economy, culture and politics*, ch. 3; P. Gregory, 'Rents, land prices and economic theory: the Russian agrarian crisis', in L. Edmondson and P. Waldron, eds *Economy and Society in Russia and the Soviet Union 1860–1930* (London, 1992), pp. 6–23; S.L. Hoch, 'On good numbers and bad: Malthus, population trends and peasant standards of living in late imperial Russia', *Slavic Review*, 53 (1994), pp. 41–75; *et al.*

17 On the development of peasant agriculture and institutions 1861–1914 see I.A.G. Yaney, *The urge to mobilize: agrarian reform in Russia 1861–1930* (Urbana and Chicago, IL, and London, 1982); D.A.J. Macey, *Government and peasant in Russia, 1861–1906: The origin of the Stolypin reforms* (DeKalb, IL, 1987); Bartlett, ed. *Land commune and peasant community in Russia*; Kingston-Mann and Mixter, eds *Peasant economy, culture, and politics in European Russia 1800–1921*; C.D. Worobec, *Peasant Russia: family and community in the post-emancipation period* (Princeton, NJ, 1991); V.S. Diakin, 'Den'gi dlia sel'skogo khoziaistva (vybor puti ekonomicheskogo razvitiia Rossii, 1892–1914 gg.)', *Istoriia SSSR*, 3 (1991), pp. 64–82.

18 See J. Pallot, 'Open fields and individual farms: land reform in pre-revolutionary Russia', *Tijdschrift voor Economische en Sociale Geografie*, lxxv (1984), p. 60.

19 J. Channon, 'Tsarist landowners after the revolution: former pomeshchiki in rural Russia during NEP', *Soviet Studies*, 39 (1987), pp. 575–98.

20 G.L. Yaney, *The systematisation of Russian government: social evolution in the domestic administration of Imperial Russia 1711–1905* (Urbana and Chicago, IL, and London, 1973); *idem*, *The urge to mobilize*.

21 S.L. Hoch, *Serfdom and social control in Russia: Petrovskoe, a village in Tambov* (Chicago, IL, and London, 1986); Melton, 'Enlightened Seignorialism' and its dilemmas in serf Russia 1750–1830'; *idem*, '"Bauernstaat Rußland"'; *idem*, 'The Russian peasantries 1480–1861', in T. Scott, ed. *The European Peasantries 1400–1800* (London, 1998); D. Moon, 'Reforms in historical perspective: tsarist Russia, peasant society and the constraints on reform 1840s–1890s', unpublished paper presented to CREES Annual Conference, Windsor Great Park, 1991; *idem*, *Russian peasants and tsarist legislation on the eve of reform: interaction between peasants and officialdom, 1825–1855* (Basingstoke, Hants, and London, 1992); *idem*, 'Reassessing Russian serfdom', *European History Quarterly*, 26 (1996), pp. 483–526; *idem*, 'Peasants into Russians: a comparative perspective', *Revolutionary Russia*, 9 (1996), pp. 43–81; see also David Moon's chapter in this book (Chapter 4).

22 Worobec, *Peasant Russia*, pp. 8–9.

23 S. Fitzpatrick, *Stalin's peasants: resistance and survival in the Russian village after collectivization* (New York and Oxford, 1994); L. Viola, *Peasant rebels under Stalin: collectivization and the culture of peasant resistance* (New York, 1996); see also N. Vakar, *The taproot of Soviet society* (New York, 1961).

24 G. Spittler, 'Staat und Klientelstruktur in Entwicklungsländern. Zum Problem der politischen Organisation von Bauern', *Europäisches Archiv für Soziologie*, 17 (1977), pp. 57–83; *idem*, 'Peasants and the state in Niger (West Africa)', *Peasant Studies*, 8 (1979), pp. 30–47; *idem*, 'Abstraktes Wissen als Herrschaftsbasis. Zur Entstehungsgeschichte bürokratischer Herrschaft im Bauernstaat Preußen', *Kölner Zeitschrift für Soziologie und Sozialpsychologie*, 32 (1980), pp. 574–604; *idem*, 'Die Struktur der Bürokratie in Agrarstaaten und ihre Auswirkung auf die Agrarpolitik', in R. Hänisch and R. Tetzlaff, eds *Staat und Entwicklung. Studien zum Verhältnis von Herrschaft und Gesellschaft in Entwicklungsländern* (Frankfurt am Main, 1981), pp. 297–318; *idem*,

Verwaltung in einem afrikanischen Bauernstaat, das koloniale Westafrika 1919–1939 (Wiesbaden, 1981); *et al.*

25 G. Spittler, *Verwaltung in einem afrikanischen Bauernstaat*, p. 13.

26 Daniel Brower has described its workings in Imperial Russian government attempts in the late nineteenth century to oversee the mushroom growth of Russian towns, what Brower calls 'fugitive cities', which constantly escaped the straitjackets of planning and control which the state's officials wanted to impose on them. D.R. Brower, *The Russian city between tradition and modernity 1850–1900* (Berkeley and Los Angeles, CA, and Oxford, 1990).

27 G. Spittler, in Hänisch und Tetzlaff, *Staat und Entwicklung*, p. 316.

28 S. Fitzpatrick, *Stalin's peasants*; L. Viola, *Peasant rebels*. Recent reinterpretations of the pre-revolutionary and revolutionary periods along similar lines include O. Figes, *A people's tragedy: The Russian Revolution 1891–1924* (London, 1996), and A. Jones, *Late-imperial Russia: an interpretation. Three visions, two cultures, one peasantry* (Berne, 1997).

29 S.K. Wegren, 'Land reform and the land market in Russia: operation, constraints and prospects', *Europe–Asia Studies*, 49 (1997), pp. 959–87.

30 R.L. Prostermann, R.G. Mitchell and B.J. Rorem, 'Prospects for family farming in Russia', *Europe–Asia Studies*, 49 (1997), pp. 1383–1407 (1390).

31 R.L. Prostermann *et al.*, 'Prospects for family farming', p. 1392.

32 R.L. Prostermann *et al.*, 'Prospects for family farming', pp. 1383, 1402.

33 'Bez rynka zemli Rossii ne vyzhit', letter from pensioner V. Bogoiavlenskii, Aznakaevo, Tatarstan, *Izvestiia*, 6 December 1997. I am indebted to Andrew Pospielovsky who supplied press reports and informed comment on the current debate.

34 'Fermer Bezgod'ko na trope voiny', *Izvestiia*, 21 November 1997.

35 'Russkoi zemle – "kupliu-prodazhu"'!', *Izvestiia*, 31 October 1997. As indicated, the problem is greatly complicated by the indebtedness and unprofitability of existing kolkhoz agriculture and the absence of financial stability and cheap investment capital.

36 'Zemlia stala tovarom', *Izvestiia*, 6 March 1998.

37 'Zemlia stala tovarom', *Izvestiia*, 6 March 1998. A full account of the sale appeared in the following issue.

6

Poor Russia: environment and government in the long-run economic history of Russia

PETER GATRELL

The collapse of the Soviet Union lends more than a little piquancy to the study of Russian economic history. The hesitant and tortuous search for a viable economic system to replace the command economy offers an opportunity to set the relatively short-lived Soviet economic experiment in a longer-term perspective. There is less temptation to interpret Russia's economic past as a series of preliminaries to the revolution of 1917. The planned economy is, like the serf economy or the post-emancipation economy, a subject for historical investigation, not a blueprint. What occurred between 1917 and 1991 was an experiment, not a definitive and irrevocable turning point in world economic history.[1]

How, then, can we make sense of Russian economic history in the long run? The overarching problem, in my opinion, is to explain how it is that an economy, evidently capable of periods of uninterrupted growth in total output, has, over the long term, been unable to close more of the gap with the West. The issue may be posed another way: why, under different forms of political organization and a changing social system, has the performance of the Russian economy not been more dynamic, save for periodic, but unsustained, bursts of growth?

I emphasize that my main concern is with the failure of Russia to sustain increases in output per capita over the long term, and not with evidence of and explanations for intermittent bursts of industrialization during the early eighteenth century, the later nineteenth century and the 1930s. These great leaps forward should not be underestimated, but they did not fundamentally alter the international economic status of Russia or its endemic poverty in the long run – and I pass over the fact that they ended badly, in traumatic social conflict, in two major political revolutions and in environmental catastrophe.[2] I also recognize that there were pockets of intensive development, creating regional disparities. In a land mass as great as the Russian Empire/USSR this is hardly a startling observation. It was well understood even in the eighteenth century. Herder, for example, maintained that Russia consisted of three regions: the 'completely culti- vated, the half cultivated, and the wild regions . . . the wild peoples are on the borders, the half mannered is the country, then the mannered seacoast . . .'.[3] Economic indicators confirm regional differences. In 1913, tsarist Russia – excluding European Russia – boasted income per capita some 24 per cent higher than the corresponding figure for the heartland of European Russia. The Baltic region, in particular, stood out as a region of relative prosperity, closer in development terms to Austria than to the European Russian core. In Siberia, too, no one can fail to be struck by the dramatic and sustained economic development that took place in the generation before 1914.[4] But I do not have space to pursue this important issue here.

Russian poverty

How can I support my contention about the international economic status of Russia and the persistence of poverty? Paul Bairoch has shown that, in terms of total output per capita, the gap with Europe widened during the nineteenth century.[5] Between 1913 and 1940 Soviet economic performance barely kept pace with the United Kingdom and the USA and was heavily outclassed by Germany and Japan. Who can doubt that the gap between Russia and the West has widened still further during recent decades?[6] Inevitably it is more difficult to establish the growth and development of the Russian economy for earlier periods. We should not assume that the Russian economy stagnated. Kievan Russia (878–1237) enjoyed a signifi- cant degree of economic prosperity by medieval standards, at least to judge by society's capacity to sustain urban growth (urban population probably represented around 13 per cent of the total on the eve of the Mongol invasion).[7] Following the Mongol invasion, whose demographic distur- bance is in dispute, further economic expansion took place during the fifteenth and especially sixteenth centuries. Growth came to an abrupt halt during the early seventeenth century. Urban population estimates again shed some light on the course of economic change. According to Vernadsky, the Russian population in 1650 stood at 10 million, of whom just 5 per cent lived in towns and cities. Thus, between *c.* 1300 and 1650 – representing the era between the peak of Mongol influence and the stabi- lization following the Time of Troubles – such growth as there was did not reverse the trend of de-urbanization.[8]

Most of the premodern growth, it appears, was associated with terri- torial expansion (for example, between 1530 and 1630 the area under Russian control grew by 7 million square kilometres, taking the territory from 3 million to 10 million square kilometres). During the sixteenth century we see the extension of arable farming to the banks of the Volga; during the seventeenth, the consolidation of Russian control over vast tracts of Siberia. There is some evidence of urbanization in the later seventeenth century, but this was not sustained during the eighteenth and early nineteenth centuries. The urban population declined from 11 per cent of the total in the 1740s to around 7 per cent in the 1860s.[9]

Further evidence of slow growth is presented by the historical geographer Aleksandr Dulov. Dulov estimated total energy consumption from animate and inanimate sources (draught animals; timber, peat and coal; and water and wind power). His estimates (Table 6.1) suggest that total energy use during the late fifteenth century was equivalent to between 5.3 and 5.7 times the standard human biological capability. Two centuries later the corresponding figure had risen to between 6.5 and 6.9. By the middle of the nineteenth century, energy availability in Russia was equivalent to between 7.4 and 7.8 times the human capacity. The record suggests sluggish growth, rather than dynamism; an increase of around 40 per cent over three and a half centuries in energy consumption per person suggests not only that Russia had scarcely begun to exploit fossil fuels but also that animate sources of power remained disappointingly underdeveloped.

To sum up so far. There is evidence of growth in total output in the medieval and early modern period, but largely as a function of territorial acquisition, allowing the supply of resources to keep pace with population growth. Russia's dramatic growth during the post-1850 period was mostly extensive rather than intensive. Russia was relatively poor (although not intolerably poor) at the dawn of the modern industrial era and did not share in the rapid growth in income per head that is observed in the more dynamic nineteenth-century and twentieth-century economies.

This lack of dynamism is a serious problem. Do we locate its sources in domestic conditions or to the so-called 'underdevelopment' by Europe's 'core' of the Russian 'periphery'? The underdevelopment hypothesis does not seem to me to be very helpful in accounting for 'backwardness' in the

Table 6.1 Estimated consumption of energy (in kcal) in Russia (expressed as a percentage of human potential)

Century	Fuel use		Livestock	Wind and water power[a]	Total estimated range
	domestic	productive			
Late fifteenth	400	30	120	5	530–550
Late seventeenth	400	50	200	17	650–690
Mid nineteenth	400	130	200	30	740–780

[a] Water power used in flour milling
Source: A.V. Dulov, *Geograficheskaia sreda i istoriia Rossii konets XV–seredina XIXv* (Moscow, 1983), p. 142.

long term, because Russia's contacts with the international economy only became significant during the second half of the eighteenth century. Furthermore, when they were established, they played an important role in helping to improve growth rates. Foreign trade yielded substantial benefits to the later eighteenth century economy.[10] During the nineteenth century, the integration of Russia in the international economy brought undeniable gains: foreign investment (which did not create enclaves, with the possible exception of the oil industry), technology transfer and imported expertise and a growing volume of foreign trade.[11] The Soviet state did not build upon these foundations, pursuing instead a policy of trade aversion.[12] From the long-term perspective, Russia appears to have suffered not so much from too great an exposure to the international economy as from a deficiency of contact. In short, internal constraints rather than external conditions appear more likely to account for the persistence of poverty.

Growth recurring

In looking for a suitable framework in which to think about Russia's long-term development I have found the work of Eric Jones especially fruitful. Two of his books deal with the long-run economic history of the world: *The European miracle* and *Growth recurring*. They have attracted surprisingly little attention, except from political historians and sociologists.[13]

In the first of these books, Jones attempted to account for the 'miracle' of development in Europe largely in terms of its location and resource endowment. One striking and largely fortuitous advantage, particularly in northwestern Europe, derived from its relative invulnerability to natural disaster, with the result that there was less depletion of capital: 'the impact of disasters of all kinds, that is including social disasters, was seemingly biassed towards the destruction of human life, the factor of production, labour, away from the destruction of capital'. Where significant environmental shocks were felt, such as the threat from infectious disease, European states came to the rescue by adopting policies to mitigate or manage their impact. By contrast, earthquakes, fires and floods frequently destroyed fixed capital in China, India and Iran, large areas that were prone also to recurrent invasion and cycles of violence. Europe avoided the worst consequences of invasion during the period between AD 1000 to 1500 whereas, during the first half of this period, the Mongols invaded China, at a cost of one-third of the Chinese population; in Iran, carefully constructed systems for irrigating cultivated land were destroyed. The invaders fought amongst themselves to redistribute the spoils of conquest without taking any steps to create additional resources. Europe, to its great fortune, avoided the threat from the Mongols and fought off the challenge from the Ottoman Turks during the sixteenth century. Crudely speaking,

Europe escaped catastrophe, it accumulated capital and it experienced long-run dynamism.

In *Growth recurring*, Jones adopts a somewhat different emphasis. Here, he proposes that all societies demonstrate an inherent capacity for 'extensive growth', that is, a simple addition to the stock of material goods. The record of human progress suggests that this search for additional output has been successful across a range of societies and in different environments. Nonetheless, relatively few societies have been able to generate 'intensive growth', that is, growth in output or real income per head of population. In search of an explanation for this differential experience, Jones now places less emphasis upon environmental advantage or disadvantage, and the cumulative effects thereof, and much more on the appropriate political climate for private sector activity that will stimulate intensive economic growth. Society's capacity to realize intensive growth is limited by the rent-seeking behaviour of government. The most appropriate role for government is to create a legal framework for enterprise and to supply and finance public goods, such as transport infrastructure. Unhappily, governments have often been keener to obtain additional rent rather than to supply the appropriate framework for entrepreneurship. That they frequently did so in an arbitrary and confiscatory manner only compounded the problem.

The historical record shows that some societies outside the miraculous core did demonstrate successful intensive growth, either as a result of improvements in economic organization or investment in new production techniques, leading to a reduction in transaction and transformation costs, respectively. Examples of non-European success include Sung China (between the tenth and thirteenth centuries) and Tokugawa Japan, implying that Judeo-Christian beliefs or 'Western culture' have not been the prime determinants of success. In both instances, growth was a product not of the sudden emergence of some miracle ingredient but of the removal of hitherto existing constraints, by virtue of the relaxation of political obstacles to market-type activity. For instance, the Chinese government encouraged the growth of a land market; peasants who found it difficult to meet the demand for rent moved to towns. In addition, the fixed head tax payable in kind was replaced by an assessment of property, payable in cash, which induced peasants to market their product. In Japan, growth was related to political decentralization, helping to encourage investment in irrigation by local lords.

These exceptional instances of dynamism – which are not, it should be noted, synonymous with industrialization – highlight for Jones the propensity of political institutions to capture by groups or principals who pursue a purely rent-seeking strategy. The frustration of attempts to foster intensive growth is not explained by differences in cultural attitudes (a refusal to take risk, lack of interest in material improvements, a missing Protestant ethic and so forth), nor is the absence of intensive growth the result of the proneness of certain regions to disaster (which can in any case be mitigated by purposive intervention by governments) or the prevalence of invasion (whose effects normally – although not in the case of Iran – proved relatively short-lived). Rather, growth was frustrated by the proclivities of government to appropriate resources for various unproductive ends, hampering the emergence of market-type activity and institutions.[14]

Where do Jones's interpretations leave the economic historian of Russia? Russia did not share in 'the European miracle', except for brief periods of intensive growth. Should we look for evidence of environmental constraints and recurrent disasters, such as those that afflicted the economies of Asia, or should we be satisfied instead with political explanations, such as those advanced in Jones's later work? In what follows I shall consider the usefulness of both kinds of explanation.

Before doing so, however, I wish to raise the fundamental issue of 'East' and 'West', and ask whether this familiar binary opposition is a helpful guide to further thought or whether it is an intellectual trap. In his fine study of eighteenth-century writing on European 'development', Larry Wolff has shown how major Enlightenment thinkers imagined Russia and Poland, pinpointing 'Eastern Europe' as a den of vice, economic backwardness and 'incivilization' which might yet be transformed when the region became 'fully cultivated'.[15] This discourse continued to exert a powerful grip on politicians, generals and academics, including economic historians. Have we simply continued to cement in place a crude and unsatisfactory image of 'backwardness' that then needs to be 'explained'?[16] Jack Goody argues that 'Westerners' have persistently ignored or misunderstood cultural attributes in the East, deeming them dysfunctional for economic success. He demonstrates that the 'spirit of capitalism' was alive and well in the Eurasian continent.[17] I acknowledge the pitfalls inherent in the ascription of essentialized characteristics to an entire region or continent, and one can sympathize with Goody's irritation with social scientists who glibly attribute 'cultural failings' to China or India in order to account for 'backwardness'. I do not assume that Russian culture somehow hindered economic dynamism, but there is nevertheless a problem to address: Russia was not an 'imagined' space, but a real, albeit changing, political and geographical entity, in which the economy failed to flourish over the long run.

Environmental constraints and natural disasters

What, then, of environmental obstacles and disturbances? The Russian historian Kliuchevskii famously considered the Russian natural environment to be 'more difficult and less benevolent than that with which any other nation has had to contend'.[18] The implications for agriculture – until recently the dominant form of economic activity in Russia – have been profound. The impact of climate on crop production has been severe. Four fifths of the Russian sown area suffers from inadequate thermal conditions, compared with less than one fifth in the USA. Historically, this disadvantage has been extremely serious for the Russian economy, helping to explain the pronounced fluctuations in grain yields, with attendant uncertainties for food producers and consumers, as well as for government.[19]

This agricultural lottery was reinforced by other deficiencies of the Russian environment: for example, poor soils in the non-black-earth region gave higher yields if they were fertilized adequately. Unhappily, the stock of animals required to supply organic fertilizer did not come close to being sufficient for this purpose. The reason was that large herds of cattle required protection against the harsh climate (on average, livestock needed to be stalled for 200 days in the year in the non-black-earth region and for 160 days in the black-earth region). Peasants lacked the capacity to invest in barns that would offer protection. Food producers ended up with the worst of all possible worlds: stagnant grain yields (the result of a failure to improve soil fertility); an inadequate stock of animate energy; and no buffer against a shortage of other foodstuffs.[20] Poor and erratic grain yields, apart from their consequences for human nutrition, also implied inadequate fodder for livestock, reinforcing the vicious circle.

Russia also faced recurrent environmental shocks. Of these the most important was the incidence of fire. Medieval chronicles suggest that parts of Kiev and Novgorod, rival city states, suffered widespread destruction. Some 17 major fires struck Moscow between 1330 and 1453. A seventeenth-century visitor observed that 'to make a conflagration remarkable in the country there must be a least seven or eight thousand houses consumed'.[21] According to Turgenev, 'it is well known that every fifth year sees our provincial towns burnt to the ground'.[22] Nor did rural Russia escape lightly. Fires in Tambov province destroyed the equivalent of half all rural property over a 15-year period. Between 1860 and 1887 the value of peasant dwellings in European Russia destroyed by fire may have amounted to the colossal sum of 1.35 billion rubles, equivalent to 150 per cent of the total redemption debt for which former serfs were liable.[23] Deliberate destruction of capital also contributed to the hazardous environment. Churches were destroyed by Mongol invaders, although many were soon replaced. Other forms of violence, such as the internecine conflicts during the Time of Troubles, led to the destruction of fixed capital, notably the saltworks that embodied considerable investment by monasteries and merchants.[24] When we approach the modern era the examples can be multiplied with ease, particularly losses associated with the Russian Civil War and the Second World War.[25]

Cultural attitudes probably reflected the hostile environment. Colin White argues plausibly that 'pioneer risk' – the hallmark of which was the low average expectancy of life – tended to encourage consumption rather than investment. In other words, individuals operated with a short time horizon, preferring to consume any increment in output rather than to invest it. Studies of peasant society refer to the regular festivals and celebrations to which hard-won surpluses were traditionally committed, reinforcing neighbourly solidarity and creating the foundations for reciprocal assistance when next required. But these informal, sophisticated and rational arrangements – a kind of insurance against risk – did not constitute investment in the conventional sense, and they entailed a deferral or abandonment of fixed capital formation.[26]

On this reckoning, the Russian experience bears little resemblance to a 'European miracle'. Much remained to be done to create a larger and more secure stock of capital: sustained investment in livestock and in outbuildings to safeguard the herd; storage facilities to maintain stocks in times of dearth (or to cope with unexpected abundance); and investment in urban and transport infrastructure. Yet the economy did expand; even environmental catastrophe, intermittent wars and invasion did not prevent long-run growth. Despite these dreadful and disruptive moments, total output grew in the long term. But the question remains: why did Russia not manage the transition from extensive to intensive growth? How much explanatory power does Eric Jones's scenario of misgovernment have in the Russian case?

Government: a benign or malignant influence?

Government and environment

Having already established the seriousness of recurrent disasters and the harsh natural environment, to what extent did the imperial regime operate policies to manage these risks? Alternatively, did the government itself promote policies and encourage tendencies that reinforced the hazards of the natural environment? In other words, was the government part of the problem or part of the solution? The latter question can be answered in a very specific fashion. The perceived hostility of the Russian environment was an important consideration in prompting the Soviet government to attempt to master nature. When Stalin proclaimed in April 1928 that 'there are no fortresses the Bolsheviks cannot conquer' he had in mind the enmity of capitalist countries towards the fledgling Soviet state, but he also conveyed the duty of Soviet citizens to subdue the natural world. Nature was conceived as an obstacle to be overcome, something to be transformed into the obedient servant of human society. The disastrous results of this overweening ambition – which was cemented into economic practice by the lack of rental charges for scarce resources – are by now familiar.[27]

Setting this question aside, how did the Russian government deal with the hazards described above? In some respects the pre-Soviet regime may be accused of indifference to environmental damage or disaster. Peter the Great sought to monitor access to state forests, not so much in order to minimize the risk of forest fires but to protect their resources for use by the crown and nobility.[28] Fire insurance only became widespread towards the end of the nineteenth century. It took the combined efforts of the *zemstvos* (local councils) and foreign investors to implement organized fire insurance, and even then it caught on more readily in the towns than in the country-side. Peasants were probably reluctant to commit funds to impersonal agencies, whose activities they could not monitor. But this is an area that requires further research.

On the other hand the tsarist state did seek to mitigate the effects of harvest fluctuations. In the early 1720s and 1740s the tsarist authorities forbade the export of grain, in the midst of domestic harvest failures and rising prices. Landlords were obliged to support serfs in times of dearth. Subsequently, more systematic efforts were made to maintain buffer stocks in order to cushion the population against intermittent shortages. These became more institutionalized after the abolition of serfdom, because the government could no longer count upon serfowners' self-interest to secure peasant survival. In 1868 the government instituted a scheme which required the community to create buffer stocks which would subsequently be loaned to communities in times of dearth, measures that embraced 15 million individuals by 1907. This was undoubtedly relief on an impressive scale. But it came at a price. As an editorial in the journal of the Association of Industry and Trade put it in 1912, 'a healthy state organism cannot . . . progress while having in its budget such a permanent item of expense as famine relief to the population'.[29] The problems remained acute in the Soviet era. At one extreme, state policies during the early 1930s, far from moderating the consequences of food shortages, may actually have amplified them by failing to release stocks of grain, although the latest work in the archives points to the absence of large, secret reserves of grain in 1933.[30]

It thus appears that the Russian government cannot simply be accused of turning a blind eye to disaster. Furthermore, successive regimes have managed to find the means to improve transportation, a *sine qua non* of improved policies of disaster management. This is sometimes thought to have been a particular feature of the modern state. However, well before the great reforms of the 1860s the imperial state actively promoted road and bridge building and the drainage of marshes. As a consequence, the speed of traffic on the main highways trebled between *c.* 1500 and 1850.[31] The Russian state, in its various guises, can take the credit for building an infrastructure.

Government and rent-seeking

All the same, the case that might be made against the imperial regime does not collapse. The charge is frequently levelled against the tsarist state that it (like its Soviet successor) squeezed too much rent out of the system for unproductive ends: defence, internal surveillance and incarceration and, more recently, the space race.[32]

The government's first priority was and remained the need to establish the security of the state. The territorial integrity of the state had been challenged so often, and the length of the Russian borders was so extensive, that this preoccupation is easy to explain. Tsarist Russia had a large army, partly because of extensive borders and great distances, but also because conscripts needed lengthy training. Reforms in military instruction and in defence procurement were introduced belatedly. A large army imposed a heavy burden on the state budget.[33] This may have been necessary expenditure, but was it a productive way to spend scarce funds? As so often, it is difficult to assess the costs and benefits of defence spending. Benefits, such as technological 'spin-off', appear to have been modest.[34] On the other hand, it does not follow that a reduced level of defence expenditure would necessarily have been translated into non-defence investment. More fundamental changes in economic institutions and cultural attitudes would also be required if Russia were to benefit from a lower level of defence spending, supposing this to have been a feasible option.

The budget for administration suggests that the government devoted large sums to internal surveillance, equivalent to one quarter of the budget in 1900. But the large sums spent on administration did not buy as much security as might be thought. The budget for administration conceals a story of underfunding rather than excessive spending.[35] In 1897, the Russian civil service comprised around 150 000 officials, two thirds of them in central government. Numbers grew between 1850 and 1900, but so did the Russian population, and the ratio of officials to population remained constant, at around 1.1 per 1000. Elsewhere in Europe, the ratio was much higher.[36]

The 'undergovernment' of Russia led the tsarist regime to devolve some of the costs of administration on to the peasant community and to other corporate bodies. But relations between state and society were characterized by an absence of mutual trust. The government tended to intervene arbitrarily in village and urban affairs, with disastrous consequences: one thinks of the introduction of the *zemskie nachal'niki* (land captains) and the erosion of *zemstvo* autonomy during the late nineteenth century. Subsequent initiatives to reform local government, for example by creating a *volost zemstvo*, led to bitter confrontation with the forces of conservatism before 1914.[37] Similarly, the Soviet regime was unable to penetrate the Russian countryside except by means of authoritarian and frequently brutal measures that substituted for effective administration. In both instances, the tense relationship between peasantry and state (a function, in part, of modernizing zeal by state and party officials) derived from a failure to fund administrative agencies in the countryside. This left the stranded local agents with two alternatives: to do nothing or to have recourse to *proizvol* (arbitrariness), hardly an ideal breeding ground for entrepreneurship.[38]

Investment in human capital also left a lot to be desired, and this deficiency too should in part be laid at the door of successive governments that identified other priorities. Given that Russia remained an over-whelmingly peasant country until the 1950s, educational provision in rural areas offered immense possibilities for releasing human potential. In pre-emancipation Russia, serfdom offered virtually no educational opportunities. In the post-reform era, peasants were disinclined to take advantage of new opportunities for primary education, because it was costly – in terms of income forgone – to spend time acquiring skills and knowledge that could be learned on the job. Ben Eklof has shown that peasants preferred to devise methods of self-learning; they treated the acquisition of basic literacy skills as a device for placing themselves on more even terms with government officials and landlords. They did not see education as a strategy for upward social mobility or a means of establishing a different kind of command over the natural world.[39] In the Stalinist era, peasants no longer regarded education as a means of preserving village culture but as an escape route out of the collective farm. In neither case did education serve as a means of improving the economic performance of the farm or strengthening economic opportunities in the countryside.[40]

Jones's castigation of capricious and rent-seeking government thus has some element of truth so far as Imperial Russia was concerned, but this has to be set in the context of state formation. The state's need for revenue was not inexplicable, being linked to issues of security. A large territory to police, long borders to defend, vast spaces in which people could evade their obligations – all these considerations dictated the need for close supervision of the population, without which the tax base was likely to disintegrate. However, no amount of imperial rent-seeking could compensate for the fact that Russia was poorly supplied with administrative personnel. Given the vacuum created by a relative lack of administrative density, arbitrariness tended to prevail. The prevalence of *proizvol* was not the result of excessive government but rather a function of Russia's size and consequent undergovernment.[41]

Government and enterprise

There seems little doubt that the arbitrary behaviour of the tsarist state generally inhibited enterprise by imposing increased risks and lowering the potential returns to entrepreneurial activity. As Witte put it, without firm confidence in the security of one's own person and property, without a clear idea of one's right of ownership and of the sure defence of this right by law against an infringement of any kind, there can be no talk about striving for savings and still less about confident investment.[42]

An unfavourable bureaucratic attitude towards private enterprise probably had its roots in patrimonialism, the notion that the tsar had ultimate rights over the use and disposal of land and other assets.[43]

The creation and maintenance of the system of estates (*sosloviia*) also cramped the possibilities of economic progress. For instance, members of the merchant estate (*kupechestvo*) were obliged each year to purchase a certificate of guild membership and to show that they had sufficient capital to belong to the appropriate merchant guild. If they could not do so, they were forced into a lower category of trade, with attendant disruption to established commercial contacts. Should they be unable to sustain their membership of one of the three guilds they lost important privileges, such as the right to exemption from the poll tax. In these circumstances, it made sense to play safe; to take bold decisions was to risk downward social mobility and the loss of crucial *soslovie*-specific privileges. The maintenance of estate-based society fostered conservative attitudes and hindered the creation of a more entrepreneurial culture.[44]

More serious still was the absence of a legal system that protected corporate enterprise in Russia. Thomas Owen argues that Russia never fully developed a legal framework for corporate enterprise. An improved legal system could have reduced the extra element of uncertainty created by capricious and arbitrary government officialdom. Fitful attempts to enable entrepreneurs to register companies for trading purposes – a major source of business despair before 1917 (and one finally introduced in 1990) – foundered on the rock of bureaucratic intransigence. Thus, contrary to the emphasis in the work of Gerschenkron, the state is seen by Owen as a major obstacle to enterprise rather than as an effective and dynamic substitute for private enterprise.[45] The tsarist state broadly upheld the rights of private property; yet its officials associated private enterprise with personal greed and with exploitation of 'the people'.[46]

In similar vein, Annelise Aer finds that patent activity was fitful, largely as a result of official attitudes that failed to conceive of inventions as the property of the individual inventor. By the end of the eighteenth century, 'the inventor's property right as a juridical category was perceived as a special privilege, whose justification came from an ethos of service to the state'. After generations of debate and modest reform, Aer concludes, 'the confidence of inventors in the justice of the system did not increase. The system did not work well in the Russian environment, where the authorities retained their traditionally patronizing and distrustful attitude towards inventors and towards entrepreneurs'.[47]

The consequences of prevailing government attitudes were hardly propitious. Worse still, they permeated large parts of Russian society.[48] The widespread antipathy in tsarist Russia towards private enterprise – the hallmarks of which included a preference for intermittent administrative interference within the factory gates and a long-standing commitment to state enterprise as a counterweight to the private sector (in mining, iron and steel, forestry and lumber as well as armaments) – did not preclude the award of contracts to private entrepreneurs or the imposition of tariff protection for key sectors of industry. But this was bound to create a climate of dependence, turning the businessperson into a supplicant, at the mercy of poorly paid and bribe-taking government officials. Although examples of anti-entrepreneurial attitudes permeated other European societies – allowing one scholar to speak controversially of a declining 'industrial spirit' in England by 1900 – Russia appears to have been distinguished by a peculiar combination of hostile official attitudes and legal obstacles to private enterprise.[49] To be sure, there was a remarkable increase in capital investment during the last two decades of tsarist rule, not least because of the promotion by government of foreign investment. It is also true that the government supported individual firms at times of difficulty and did not stand in the way of the new syndicates formed after 1900 in response to industrial depression. But this tends to support the case being made here: 'it all depended on the administrative decisions of key officials'.[50]

It is hardly necessary to add that popular hostility manifested itself in attacks on capitalist enterprise during 1917 and in the later 1920s, as well as in popular antipathy to fledgling cooperative and private enterprise during the late 1980s.[51] In the post-communist era, many economists agree, 'the most basic need now is for a secure legal foundation' to uphold contracts, and to establish security of titles to land and other property. Only then can uncertainty be minimized and trust be established in commercial transactions. Once trust is secured these transactions will carry a lower premium; in other words, 'windfall profits' will dwindle; popular acceptance of the market economy should increase.[52]

Conclusions

The Russian experience displayed remarkable periods of extensive growth, bought at great cost in terms of the effort required to modify the harsh environment and to open up new territory for resource exploitation. But extensive growth is one thing; why did Russia find it so difficult to go down the road of intensive growth? One answer is that, in pre-revolutionary Russia, governments, merchants, landlords and peasants opted for security in an already hostile world rather than seeking to add to their difficulties by taking the risks involved with innovation. The state's priority was to secure itself against outside attacks on Russia's territorial integrity and to maintain domestic order via an expensive (but diluted) bureaucratic apparatus. Merchants and entrepreneurs sought to maintain their status (and the privileges that went with rank) rather than to take risks; where possible, they demanded direct financial assistance from the state. With few exceptions, they were politically subservient, acquiescing in the surveillance state whilst moaning about its clumsy intervention. In pre-reform Russia, landlords wanted a flow of revenue or of labour service, not to jeopardize established patterns of economic organization. This ethos endured beyond the era of the great reforms; most landlords wanted an easy life. The peasants' priority – again, to generalize – was to preserve community forms and practices, not to abandon themselves to the uncertainties of a market in land. The community was an excellent device to foster cooperation, trust and self-protection, but it was ill-suited to promote differentiation, competition and specialization.

I hope to have done enough to demonstrate that the Imperial regime should not be crudely conceived as a rent-seeking dinosaur. There can be little doubt that over the long run the state stood in the way of intensive economic growth. But although the social system it sustained did not encourage entrepreneurship, the principles by which the state was guided were by no means irrational, given Russia's history, territorial size and resource base. It is in the context of Russia's size, lengthy borders and historical exposure to invasion that one needs to understand the commitment of resources to defence and administration. Yet Russia was not overdefended and overadministered. Given the prevailing political system in Imperial Russia, the state required more civil servants rather than fewer. It was because of undergovernment that we see the emergence of a culture of arbitrariness, which added to the prevailing uncertainties with which entrepreneurs and peasant producers were saddled.

Neither arbitrary behaviour nor the combined impact of environment and natural disaster prevented the growth of capital stock over the long run. Growth – extensive growth – has been achieved in the face of inescapable adversities. However, the attempts that have been engineered to force the pace have ended in disaster. More to the point, intensive growth has been the exception rather than the rule. The legacy of an unbending state – unable or unwilling to provide 'peace, easy taxes and a tolerable administration of justice', the criteria proposed by Adam Smith as the cornerstones for the 'highest degree of opulence' – is one major reason why, at the end of the twentieth century, Russia's participation in the 'European miracle' still seems a long way off.[53]

Notes

1 For a reiteration of the 'experimental' character of the Soviet economic system, see E. Hobsbawm, *Age of extremes: the short twentieth century 1914–1991* (London, 1994), p. 497.

2 L. Graham, *The ghost of the executed engineer: technology and the fall of the Soviet Union* (Cambridge, MA, 1993).

3 Quoted in L. Wolff, *Inventing Eastern Europe: the map of civilization on the mind of the enlightenment* (Stanford, CA, 1994), p. 308.

4 Derived from M.E. Falkus, 'Russia's national income, 1913: a revaluation', *Economica*, 35 (1968), pp. 52–73 (here p. 55); R.N. North, *Transport in Western Siberia: tsarist and Soviet development* (Vancouver, 1979).

5 P. Bairoch, 'Europe's gross national product, 1800–1975', *Journal of European Economic History*, 5 (1976), pp. 273–340 (here p. 307). Bairoch's estimates put Russian GNP per capita at 70 per cent of the European average in 1830, compared with 60 per cent in 1913.

6 See M. Harrison, 'National income', in R.W. Davies, M. Harrison and S.G. Wheatcroft, eds *The economic transformation of the Soviet Union, 1913–1945* (Cambridge, 1994), pp. 38–56; *idem*, 'Soviet economic growth since 1928: the alternative statistics of G.I. Khanin', *Europe-Asia Studies*, 45 (1993), pp. 141–67.

7 G. Vernadsky, *Kievan Russia* (New Haven, 1948), p. 128.

8 I am conscious that much more needs to be said about urbanization. According to Boris Brutskus, the Mongol invasion destroyed the dynamic commercial contacts that Kiev maintained with the Byzantine empire. The centre of gravity shifted to the upper Volga–Oka basin, where agricultural activity was less secure and the scope for division of labour greatly reduced. As a result, urban growth and civic freedom were curtailed. In addition, 'contacts with countries of a higher culture could not be established from this isolated region'. B. Brutskus, 'The historical peculiarities of the social and economic development of Russia', in R. Bendix and S.M. Lipset, eds *Class, status and power* (New York, 1953), p. 530.

9 B.N. Mironov, *Russkii gorod v 1740–1860e gody* (Leningrad, 1990), p. 225. This decline occurred at a time of rapid urban growth in England. See E.A. Wrigley, *Continuity, chance and change: the character of the Industrial Revolution in England* (Cambridge, 1990), pp. 12–17.

10 A. Kahan, *The plow, the hammer, and the knout: an economic history of eighteenth-century Russia* (Chicago, 1985), ch. 4. It should be remembered that only a small fraction of the output of basic products, such as grain, was destined for the external market.

11 Russia, of course, also had to service the accumulated foreign debt as well as to remit profits to foreign-owned corporations, etc. Details are given in P. Gregory, *Russian national income, 1885–1913* (Cambridge, 1982).

12 This is a somewhat exaggerated statement. Soviet planners did purchase selectively from foreign sources of supply, as for example during the first Five-Year Plan, which 'clearly enabled the Soviet economy [to] narrow the technological gap which had opened up since 1914'. R.A. Lewis, 'Foreign economic relations', in Davies *et al.*, eds. *The economic transformation of the Soviet Union, 1913–1945*, p. 214.

13 E. Jones, *The European miracle: environments, economies and geopolitics in the history of Europe and Asia* (Cambridge, 1981, 2nd edn, 1987) and E. Jones, *Growth recurring: economic change in world history* (Oxford, 1988). See also the important work by C. White, *Russia and America: the roots of economic divergence* (London, 1987).

14 C. Wickham, 'The uniqueness of the east', *Journal of Peasant Studies*, 12 (1985), pp. 166–96.

15 Wolff, *Inventing Eastern Europe*, p. 345, quoting the US traveller John Ledyard on 'Incivilization'. The other quotation is from Herder (1769) and appears on pp. 312–13.

16 As in D. Chirot, ed. *The origins of backwardness in Eastern Europe: economics and politics from the Middle Ages until the early twentieth century* (Berkeley, 1989).

17 J. Goody, *The East in the West* (Cambridge, 1997). Note that Goody goes on to say (p. 222) that 'its development was hindered at times by too much political or ecclesiastical interference'.

18 V. Kliuchevskii, *Kurs russkoi istorii* (Moscow, 1956), pp. 46–7.

19 See the discussion in White, *Russia and America*. The fertile black-earth region was especially vulnerable to low rainfall and dry winds from central Asia. Great emphasis is placed by Richard Pipes on environmental obstacles to improved agricultural productivity; R. Pipes, *Russia under the Old Regime* (Harmondsworth, 1977), ch. 1.

20 White, *Russia and America*, pp. 47–9. A key role in the English agricultural revolution was played by intensification of agriculture, the result, in turn, of investment in improved soil fertility. G. Clark, 'Agriculture and the industrial revolution, 1700–1850', in J. Mokyr, ed. *The British industrial revolution: an economic perspective* (Oxford, 1993), pp. 227–66.

21 J.H. Billington, *The icon and the axe: an interpretive history of Russian culture* (1970), p. 24, quoting the Earl of Carlisle in 1663–4.

22 I.S. Turgenev, *Fathers and sons* (Harmondsworth, 1976), p. 140.

23 A.M. Anfimov, *Ekonomicheskoe polozhenie i klassovaia bor'ba krest'ian Evropeiskoi Rossii* (Moscow, 1984), pp. 86–7.

24 C. Halperin, *Russia and the golden horde: the Mongol impact on medieval Russian history* (London, 1985), pp. 78–9; R.E.F. Smith and D. Christian, *Bread and salt: a social history of food and drink in Russia* (Cambridge, 1984), p. 65.

25 P. Gatrell, 'The First World War and war communism, 1914–1920', in Davies *et al.*, eds *Economic transformation*, pp. 224–5; M. Harrison, 'The Second World War', in ibid., pp. 238, 256.

26 E.R. Wolf, *Peasants* (Englewood Cliffs, NJ, 1966).

27 D.R. Weiner, *Models of nature* (Bloomington, 1988), ch. 11. Note that this view also echoed the utterances of the nineteenth-century radical intelligentsia. The oft-quoted remarks of Stalin were first made to the Moscow party organization in 1931.

28 C. Goehrke, 'Geographische Grundlagen der russischen Geschichte', *Jahrbücher für Geschichte Osteuropas*, 18 (1970), pp. 161–204 (here pp. 182–5).

29 For details see Kahan, *Plow, hammer and knout*, p. 12; P.A. Khromov, *Ekonomicheskoe razvitie Rossii v XIX–XX vekakh* (Moscow, 1950), pp. 528–9; S.G. Wheatcroft, 'Crises and the condition of the peasantry in European Russia', in E. Kingston-Mann and T. Mixter, eds *Peasant economy, culture, and politics of European Russia, 1800–1921* (Princeton, 1991), pp. 164–5. The quotation appears in R.A. Roosa, *Russian industrialists in an era of revolution: the Association of Industry and Trade, 1906–1917* (Armonk, NY, 1997), p. 77.

30 R.W. Davies, M. Tauger and S.G. Wheatcroft, 'Stalin, grain stocks, and the famine of 1932–1933', *Slavic Review*, 54 (1995), pp. 642–57.

31 From a range between 20 and 45 kilometres per day in the late fifteenth century to a range of between 45 and 125 kilometres per day by 1850. Dulov, *Geograficheskaia sreda*, pp. 120, 130.

32 For the modern period see the essays in H. Rowen and C. Wolf, eds *The

impoverished superpower: perestroika and the Soviet military burden (San Francisco, 1990).

33 The size of the army grew from 292 000 men in 1750 to 446 000 in 1800. By 1850 it reached 1.12 million men. These figures were equivalent to 1.2, 1.3 and 2.0 per cent, respectively, of the total population. W. Pintner, 'The burden of defense in imperial Russia, 1725–1913', *Russian Review*, 43 (1984), pp. 231–59. For a general survey of some of the determinants of defence spending, see D. Geyer, *Russian Imperialism* (trans Leamington Spa, 1987), ch. 11.

34 J. Coopersmith, *The electrification of Russia, 1880–1926* (1992), pp. 16–21; see also P. Gatrell, *Government, industry and rearmament in Russia, 1900–1914: the last argument of tsarism* (Cambridge, 1994).

35 Pipes, *Russia under the Old Regime*, pp. 281–2. My own view is that Pipes draws too sharp a distinction between tsarist underprovision and the density of the bureaucratic apparatus in Soviet Russia in seeking to account for the origins of the 'police state'. One has only to think of the notoriously weak hold of the Communist Party in the Russian countryside, a point established by Teodor Shanin. T. Shanin, *The awkward class: political sociology of peasantry in a developing country, Russia 1910–1925* (Oxford, 1972), ch. 10; L. Siegelbaum, *Soviet state and society between revolutions, 1918–1929* (Cambridge, 1992), pp. 93–5.

36 S.F. Starr, *Decentralization and self-government in Russia, 1830–1870* (1972), p. 48; J.R. Lampe and M. Jackson, *Balkan economic history: from imperial borderlands to developing nations* (Bloomington, 1982), p. 235.

37 The fact that officials were poorly paid also encouraged them to extort bribes from the population, a point emphasized by Pipes, *Russia under the Old Regime*, pp. 282–6. For an emphasis upon bureaucratic in-fighting and administrative disorder, as well as an overstretched police force, see G. Yaney, *The systematization of Russian government* (Urbana, 1973), pp. 330–8. Yaney modifies the prevailing view of the tsarist police by adding that 'if the "reactionary" MVD [Ministry of the Interior] could not stop the assault of the city and the market on peasant society, at least its police could cushion the blows by preventing a direct confrontation between the villages and the growing horde of uncoordinated functionaries who were striving to bring the blessings of legal-administrative system and economic development to them' (p.336).

38 'All these officials had was power, not control', argues Yaney, *Systematization*, p. 361. Even when the *volost* (sub-district) was recast during the 1920s its officials enjoyed a frosty relationship with the Russian peasantry. N.Weissman, 'Policing the NEP countryside', in S.Fitzpatrick *et al.*, eds *Russia in the era of NEP* (Bloomington, 1991), pp. 174–91.

39 White, *Russia and America*, pp. 110–11; Ben Eklof, *Russian peasant schools: officialdom, village culture, and popular pedagogy, 1861–1914* (Berkeley, 1986).

40 S. Fitzpatrick, *Stalin's peasants: resistance and survival in the Russian village after collectivization* (New York and Oxford, 1994), pp. 99–101.

41 P. Gatrell, 'Economic culture, economic policy and economic growth in Russia, 1861–1914', *Cahiers du Monde Russe*, 36 (1995), pp. 37–52.

42 Quoted in Roosa, *Russian industrialists*, p. 95.

43 This is a major theme in Pipes, *Russia under the Old Regime*, although he suggests that private property acted as a constraint on the 'proto-police state' by the late nineteenth century.

44 A.J. Rieber, *Merchants and entrepreneurs in Imperial Russia* (Chapel Hill, 1982).

45 T.C. Owen, *The corporation under Russian law, 1800–1917: a study in tsarist economic policy* (Cambridge, 1991); *idem, Russian corporate capitalism from Peter the Great to perestroika* (Oxford, 1996).

46 This culture also had important consequences for the conduct of industrial relations. See R.E. Zelnik, *Law and disorder on the Narova River: the Kreenholm strike of 1872* (Berkeley, 1995).

47 A. Aer, *Patents in Imperial Russia: a history of the Russian institution of invention privileges under the Old Regime* (Helsinki, 1995), pp. 199, 207. According to economic historians, patent law generally in Britain and Germany provided a basic incentive for inventive activity.

48 R. Wortman, 'Property rights, populism and Russian political culture', in O. Crisp, ed. *Civil rights in Imperial Russia* (Oxford, 1989), pp. 13–32.

49 M. Wiener, *English culture and the decline of the industrial spirit, 1850–1980* (Cambridge, 1981).

50 J.P. Mckay, *Pioneers for profit: foreign entrepreneurs and Russian industrialization, 1885–1913* (Cambridge, 1970), p. 269.

51 A. Ball, *Russia's last capitalists: the Nepmen, 1921–1929* (Berkeley, 1987).

52 H. Hunter, 'Why were the faulty foundations never repaired?', in J. Cooper *et al.*, eds *Soviet history, 1917–1953* (London, 1995), pp. 243–62.

53 Quoted in P. Burke, *History and social theory* (Cambridge, 1992), p. 147.

|7|

Entrepreneurship, government, and society in Russia

THOMAS C. OWEN

Introduction: entrepreneurship in the era of the great reforms

In his ambitious survey of the causes of poverty in Russia, Peter Gatrell concluded that

> over the long run the state stood in the way of intensive economic growth. But although the social system it sustained did not encourage entrepreneurship, the principles by which the state was guided were by no means irrational, given Russia's history, territorial size and resource base.[1]

Gatrell's insight into the logic of autocratic rule, which both stimulated economic development for the sake of military power and prevented the formation of legal norms conducive to modern capitalism, poses a challenge to historians of the Russian economy. Antipathy towards free markets animated the grand princes of Muscovy, the tsars of Russia, and the Soviet policy-makers who presided over the most complex command economy in the history of the world. At what point, if ever, could Russians have abandoned trade aversion, militarism and autocracy and opted instead for integration into the world economy, constitutional reform, decentralization, respect for the will of the governed and the rule of law? Given the importance of legal and political institutions in fostering or hindering economic development,[2] this question has implications for the understanding of entrepreneurial behaviour, economic policy and social attitudes.

Whatever the deleterious social and environmental consequences of the industrial system and however great the political and economic inequalities that resulted from the predominance of corporations in the modern world, by the mid-nineteenth century it had become clear that countries without a corporate network, as in much of Asia, Africa and Latin America, faced the prospect of direct or indirect control of their economic destinies by Europeans. Entrepreneurs and bureaucrats in Russia perceived this challenge from the West in the 1850s, as the Crimean War made clear the economic backwardness of the Russian Empire. In the next two decades the tsarist government authorized the creation of 568 new corporations, including 50 in railroad construction, 45 in banking, 59 in textiles and 66 in beet sugar production. In per-capita terms, this burst of incorporation was unique in Russian history.[3] However, the collapse of the entire transportation system during the First World War now appears as a strong indictment of tsarist economic policy in the half century following the Crimean War. The spirit of relatively open discussion (glasnost') that pervaded public life in the reign of Alexander II (1855–81) made clear the economic challenge and the weakness of the Russian entrepreneurial tradition, itself the result of centuries of bureaucratic oppression. Still, the tsarist government refused to implement basic reforms.[4]

A comprehensive account of tsarist economic policy would include a quantitative assessment of corporate activity; an examination of rates of successful entrepreneurship among the major social and ethnic groups in the genre known as 'business history', still undeveloped in Slavic studies; and an investigation of the tsarist ministers' rationale for maintaining oppressive legislation. This survey focuses less on the social and cultural determinants of success in the corporate economy than on the contributions of autocracy and social attitudes to the weakness of Russian capitalism.

Government: the military–autocratic mode of rule

From the rise of Muscovy to the late twentieth century, the autocratic system concentrated all available resources on the defence of the largest state in Eurasia. The lack of natural boundaries required the maintenance of relatively large military forces and blurred the distinction between defensive and offensive military action. The concept of the state based on the rule of law (*pravovoe gosudarstvo*, a somewhat artificial translation of the German *Rechtsstaat*) remained a purely theoretical concept, except for the dozen years following the Revolution of 1905, when Nicholas II granted concessions to the principle of constitutionalism in order to break the alliance of the liberal and radical opposition movements.

The essence of the Russian autocracy requires a distinctive theoretical terminology. Max Weber's theory of political legitimacy classified rulers according to three basic ways in which they won the obedience of their subjects. Tradition constituted perhaps the most common in human history, as in most monarchical states and religious organizations. Weber's second principle, charisma, represented the personal influence of an individual, whether a saint, orator or heroic warrior. The third mode founded legitimacy on rational–legal norms of behaviour, as in a bureaucracy in which the rank, power and influence of a given individual depended on objective criteria, including education and demonstrated abilities, apart from ethnic origin, sex, family connections and other attributes deemed irrelevant to the functioning of the organization. Weber recognized that no historical epoch had ever witnessed the emergence of institutions based on only one of these principles, but, relying apparently on Plato, he insisted that these '"pure" types' promoted a scientific analysis of the multitude of specific cases of political power in world history.[5]

None of the Weberian types captures the essence of the Russian Imperial regime or the Soviet system. Ivan the Terrible, Peter the Great and Lenin all despised tradition; Nicholas II, Stalin, and Brezhnev all lacked charisma; and none of the tsars or commissars respected the technical expertise of engineers, scholars and lawyers who strove to uphold the principles of reason, legality and the scientific method.[6] Thus, the so-called 'bureaucracies' of the Imperial and Soviet systems did not constitute genuine bureaucracies in the Weberian sense. Tsarist and Soviet officials remained so imbued with the spirit of red tape and arbitrariness and so unaccountable to the will of their subjects and even, on occasion, to the supreme authority itself, that the administrative machine can best be understood as the opposite of a Weberian bureaucracy, which by definition embodied the principles of rationalism and legality. Despite the formally ramified structure of this system, its functions had nothing in common with the rational–legal behaviour of Weber's ideal type of bureaucratic government. The word 'bureaucracy' is used for the Russian and Soviet administrations only because no other word exists.

The rational–legal type of political and economic organization in the contemporary world promoted the emergence of modern capitalism. The hostility towards capitalism expressed by both tsarist and Soviet officials constituted one of the most significant aspects of continuity between the Imperial and Soviet systems. Although some scholars consider Peter the Great, Catherine the Great, Alexander II, and Sergei Iu. Witte as builders of Russian capitalism,[7] this terminology is imprecise. To be sure, the Russian autocracy fostered the development of heavy industry, primarily to maintain its huge armed forces, but it made only the smallest concessions to the six major features of capitalism, as defined by Weber: rational accounting based on precise calculations of risk and benefit, separate from personal and family funds; a market without restrictions on economic activity based on ethnicity, social status or other subjective factors; the application of modern technology; legal norms associated with a state based on the rule of law, including the defence of private property against arbitrary expropriations by individuals and the state; a free market in labour, meaning the absence of slavery or serfdom; and the public sale of shares in large enterprises, as in the modern stock market.[8] The tsarist regime did authorize some corporations, so that the term 'corporate industrialization' does fit the Russian case, but their tiny numbers demonstrated the strength of autocratic rule and the weakness of Russian capitalism.[9]

It is easy to show the absence of a state based on the rule of law in the tsardom of Muscovy, the Russian Empire and the Soviet Union. More challenging is the effort to define the means by which these autocracies maintained their power and, despite occasional reverses, extended it over the largest land mass in the world. These mechanisms included the largest armed force in Eastern Europe and a variety of administrative measures, including heavy taxation and mandatory state service, to ensure the acquisition of adequate financial and human resources to maintain the system. Any effort to limit the state's absolute power met fierce repression. The Soviet state adopted the familiar autocratic form within a matter of weeks after the Bolshevik seizure of power in October 1917. The creation of the secret police (*Cheka*) in December 1917, the dissolution of the freely elected Constituent Assembly in the following month and the consolidation of power by armed force in the civil war of 1918–20 showed how quickly Lenin and Trotskii learned the art of autocratic rule. Although the Bolsheviks had condemned tsarist rule and Lenin had advocated an almost anarchistic vision of the future socialist society in *State and revolution*, written in the summer of 1917, the Soviet state soon exhibited a striking similarity to Muscovy and the Russian Empire. This dramatic turn apparently occurred spontaneously, as it is doubtful that the Bolsheviks devoted much time to an analysis of the Russian autocracy.

Because this system excluded all three elements of Weber's classic triad – tradition, charisma and legality – the term 'military–autocratic' is appropriate as an analytical term. Weber stressed the function of each ideal type in providing legitimacy for political power. Both as a legitimizing rationale for absolute power and as an explanation of the means by which power was maintained, the term 'military–autocratic' has the advantage of being unambiguous and value-free. The degree to which the Russian and Soviet political systems most nearly achieved this hypothetical state of maintaining autocratic government through military force can be ascertained scientifically, whatever the historian's personal opinion of its most successful exponents, such as Peter the Great, Catherine the Great and Stalin in his last decade, or those that fell short of the goal. Whether the ideal type of military–autocratic rule can fruitfully be employed in the analysis of states outside Russia remains an interesting empirical question. There seem to be at least a dozen promising candidates for the label, from the Assyrian Empire in the Ancient Near East to the Spanish Empire, the Axis powers during the Second World War, North Korea under Kim Il Sung and Iraq under Saddam Hussein.

To be sure, tensions inevitably arose between the military imperative and autocratic power. Autocrats and their advisers did not always succeed in applying the latest military technology, and adherence to absolute power occasionally weakened the capabilities of the Russian armed forces. Ivan the Terrible executed his most capable advisers during the Livonian War; Nicholas I blundered into the Crimean War; and incompetence led to defeat in the Russo–Japanese War and to the collapse of the Russian army in the First World War.[10]

Moreover, military–autocratic rule need not have led to war at every opportunity. Indeed, intelligent practitioners of the policy sought to avoid wars that entailed excessive expenses. Six months before the outbreak of the First World War, the conservative bureaucrat Petr N. Durnovo warned the Emperor that the economic symbiosis of the German and Russian economies, the inadequacy of Russian weapons production and the inability of the railroad network to meet 'the colossal demands which will be made upon them in the event of a European war' made armed conflict with the German Empire an act of economic folly. 'The financial and economic consequences of defeat can be neither calculated nor foreseen, and will undoubtedly spell the total ruin of our entire national economy'; and 'in the event of defeat . . . social revolution in its most extreme form is inevitable'.[11] Indeed, although Russia avoided defeat in 1914–17, its economy collapsed under the strain of war, creating the mood of desperation that allowed the Bolsheviks to sweep into power on the strength of their crude but effective slogan: 'Peace! Bread! Land!' In the Soviet period, two episodes of such tension between autocratic rule and military strength occurred in Stalin's failure to anticipate the Nazi invasion in June 1941 and Brezhnev's clumsy campaign in Afghanistan.

Despite their disagreements on particular strategic and diplomatic issues, to say nothing of their different ideologies, tsarist and Soviet policy-makers demonstrated their common faith in maintaining the military priority by autocratic means and strengthening autocracy by the use of armed force. That is, except for occasional aberrations caused by incompetence at the centre or the need to accommodate demands for reform, both the Russian and Soviet systems stood close to the military–autocratic ideal type over the centuries and accordingly far from the others, based on tradition, charisma and respect for rational–legal norms.

Mikhail Kh. Reutern and military–autocratic rule under Alexander II

To what extent did the tsarist government share responsibility for the failure of corporate entrepreneurs to create a modern transportation network and heavy industry in the era of the great reforms? Historians have stressed the stifling effects of the autocratic form of government on entrepreneurship in Russia in the sixteenth and seventeenth centuries and state-sponsored discrimination against Jewish entrepreneurs, but the persistence of the state's generally deleterious role into the late nineteenth century has been explored only recently. Arcadius Kahan's important essay on the stultifying effects of bureaucratic tutelage pointed in this direction, but it lacked statistical evidence and encountered resistance from scholars who held to the notion of the Russian Empire as a 'Pax Russica' conducive to entrepreneurial success.[12] This concept reiterated earlier notions, linked to modernization theory, that credited the tsarist and Soviet regimes with successful mobilization for economic development in the absence of a bourgeoisie worthy of the name.[13] A more fruitful line of inquiry would explore the harsh economic environment of the Russian Empire, including bureaucratic arbitrariness, that continued to hinder economic innovation in the age of steam and electricity. The role of autocracy in limiting economic enterprise and technological development has recently received attention in studies of tsarist corporate law and economic policy in the last century of imperial Russia.[14]

As for the bureaucrats who managed the tsarist system, the historian requires considerable empathy to understand their motives, priorities and decisions in economic policy. True to the long tradition of military–autocratic rule, Alexander and his ministers repressed internal dissent by force of arms, as in Poland in 1863, and expanded the power of the Russian state by major military campaigns in Central Asia. At the cost of the failure to put the Russian currency on the gold standard, the emperor undertook an expensive and indecisive war with the Ottoman Empire in 1877–8. Equally important, however, is the resistance to fundamental reform manifested by the tsarist minister who is generally considered, by contemporaries and historians, as a supporter of modern capitalism: finance minister Mikhail Kh. Reutern (1862–78).

A member of the group of 'liberal' reformers brought to prominence by Grand Duke Konstantin Nikolaevich after the Crimean War,[15] Reutern served the emperor capably, if not brilliantly, in pursuit of financial stability and economic development. In comparison with bureaucrats of the previous reign, he appeared reformist. However, in at least three ways his policies remained opposed to Weber's definition of modern capitalism.

First, Reutern's encouragement of corporations, primarily railroads, banks and steamship companies, was only partially successful, and he constantly stressed the military benefits of economic development. After the Crimean War, Grand Duke Konstantin Nikolaevich recruited several individuals to harness what one tsarist source called 'private enterprise' for the benefit of the Russian navy. Jacob Kipp called Nikolai I. Putilov the Grand Duke's 'plenipotentiary', 'a man of extraordinary energy and managerial talents' who undertook even before the end of the war the task of coordinating the production of 32 gunboats in state and private plants with the aid of a special loan of 640 000 rubles.[16]

The use of the term 'private enterprise' appears somewhat misleading, however, in view of Putilov's managerial career in the following quarter century. Jonathan Grant, who examined Putilov's business ventures in rail and machinery production, reached a very different conclusion:

> The Putilov factory became the most important rail producer in Russia through a combination of state indulgence, private initiative, and luck. The state aided N.I. Putilov's rise, but ultimately could not prevent his fall, although state officials did try to cushion the blow as much as possible. Therefore, Putilov's story reveals both the extent and the limits of state involvement on the Petersburg industrial scene, as well as the importance of the individual entrepreneur.
>
> N.I. Putilov harbored a grandiose entrepreneurial vision [that included] rail production, a railroad, and a huge commercial port. These rather frenetic plans called for large amounts of capital and ultimately resulted in bankruptcy by the time of Putilov's death in 1880.[17]

Reutern granted special financial aid to Putilov amounting to a million rubles and a favourable change in his contract to deliver rails to the state in 1875, as well as permission to deliver railcars, rather than locomotives, which were far more expensive to build, under a contract with the Ministry of Transportation. 'Putilov was taking advantage of the fact that Reutern generally placed military and political considerations above economic ones when it came to railroad construction'.[18]

The finance minister believed that the enormous state subsidies required by inefficient steamship and railroad companies[19] were entirely justified. In a memorandum of 16 September 1866, Reutern argued that railroads, in particular, would facilitate exports, thereby strengthening the ruble in international currency markets, forging links between Russian grain producers and foreign consumers and increasing the income of the agricultural population. Equally important was the military benefit. 'Finally, with respect to politics, the possibility of moving troops quickly from the center to the border regions will necessarily increase the power of Russia'.[20]

Reutern took special pride in the second aspect of his maintenance of military–autocratic rule: consultation with merchants on questions of economic policy. Obsequious petitions from merchants, a regular feature of economic life under Nicholas I, remained common in the 1860s and 1870s. Early in his term as finance minister, Reutern sought to strengthen existing commercial–industrial organizations while maintaining their non-democratic essence. On 13 May 1866, he submitted to the emperor a memorandum devoted to the 'inclusion of public, nongovernmental elements in participation of financial affairs'. Public discussion, he stated, would be useful to the tsarist bureaucracy as it tackled such issues as taxes, import tariffs and the regulation of trade and manufacturing. He admitted that soliciting written petitions and encouraging debate in the press entailed delays. However, he perceived a greater threat in the power of elective legislative bodies to limit the executive power of the monarch under a constitutional regime. He therefore warned against establishing an advisory body composed of elected representatives because such an institution might easily claim the right to speak for the nation: 'the most pernicious and dangerous of all'. Although he made no explicit reference to a specific historical case, the successful campaign of the elected representatives of the Third Estate in France to establish a National Assembly instead of a merely advisory body in 1789 represented the nightmare to be avoided in Russia at all costs. In contrast, *zemstvos* – institutions of rural self-government created in 1864 – appeared useful precisely because they addressed purely local matters and thereby promoted healthy political and cultural development: 'a school of civic life'. Given what he considered the low level of civic responsibility in Russia, Reutern preferred to meet with representatives nominated by the ministries on the basis of their commercial and industrial expertise, not elected delegates.[21]

In the conclusion of his memorandum of 13 May 1866, Reutern justified his policy of consultation with commercial and industrial experts in explicitly military–autocratic terms. His ministry strove, he wrote, to involve experts in discussions of economic issues because 'this participation is always useful and does not encroach upon the principles of state organization on which the political and civic life of Russia rests, under the protection of a powerful monarchical authority'.[22]

Third, Reutern raised no objection to the use of military power in the repression of the Polish rebellion of 1863 or the expansion of Russian rule into Central Asia. His memorandum to the emperor in opposition to war with the Ottoman Empire, dated 3 October 1876, argued that a long and costly military campaign would hurt the empire by weakening the ruble and depriving Russian merchants of their usual credits from European bankers, investors, suppliers and customers, to the detriment of small producers, 'who are for the most part peasants'. He never renounced his devotion to the maintenance of Russian military might, however. In this memorandum, too, he stressed the connection between economic development and military power:

> The establishment of improved transportation facilities and the newly created [system of] private credit exerted considerable influence on the development of commerce and industry, gradually mitigated the difficulties caused by the peasant reform, and permitted the revenues of the state to rise to such an extent that expenses in all categories have been covered without deficits or loans, although many reforms and improvements, such as the legal reform, the education reform, the improvements in police services, and especially the huge

expenditures for the military, demanded considerable means, the provision of which was formerly out of the question.[23]

In sum, Reutern sought to balance the benefits of foreign technology and free trade against the imperatives of military–autocratic rule. His use of non-democratic consultations to aid in the formulation of economic policy and his support of limited military campaigns demonstrated his skill in pursuing this balance. However, his attempt to harness corporations for the improvement of Russia's transportation network met with only partial success. The weakness of capitalist institutions in the era of the great reforms owed much to the ultimate incongruity between the ideal type of military–autocratic rule and Weber's concept of rational–legal administration, an essential component of modern capitalism.

Russian society under military–autocratic rule

The tsarist government's power rested on its ability to prevent political challenges from below. The complex web of obligations, rewards and punishments that evolved over the centuries persisted into the early twentieth century. These included the universal duty of state service and communal responsibility for taxes. Of special interest to the historian of Russian capitalism are the attitudes of various groups in Russian society toward the rational–legal principle. Although a handful of aristocrats and gentry learned the rudiments of European legality and sought to apply it in the new corporate economy, the tradition of disdain for money making in trade and industry remained strong into the twentieth century. For example, in emigration after the Russian Revolution, Grand Duke Aleksandr Mikhailovich remained thoroughly devoted to autocracy and contemptuous of the very idea of liberalism, which he correctly associated with the free market:

> The throne of the Romanoffs was destroyed not by the future leaders of the soviets and not by bomb-throwing youngsters, but by the titled persons who wore resplendent court uniforms and by the bankers, editors, lawyers, and university professors who lived off the bounty of the empire.

He described with typical aristocratic horror the alleged immorality of financial wizards: Iaroshinskii, Batolin, Putilov and Paramonov.[24]

Members of less educated social groups left few commentaries on modern capitalism, but the attitudes of the clergy, petty townspeople (*meshchane*), artisans (*remeslenniki*) and peasantry appear to have been generally hostile. Barrington Moore, Jr helped to reorientate the debate over the Russian Revolution by stressing that it was not only revolutionary workers who brought the Bolsheviks to power. Russian peasants, angered by the failure of the tsarist government to solve the agrarian crisis, carried out in 1917 the greatest peasant rebellion the world had ever seen,[25] one that swept away both the old regime and the provisional government and permitted the Bolsheviks to take power in the cities. Recently, Edward L. Keenan and Boris N. Mironov have stressed the anti-individualist and communal ethos of village life. In Keenan's words, Russian peasants exhibited

> a strong tendency to maintain stability and a kind of closed equilibrium; risk-avoidance; suppression of individual initiatives; informality of political power; the considerable freedom of action and expression 'within the group'; [and] the striving for unanimous final resolution of potentially divisive issues.[26]

These attitudes conserved the meagre resources available for subsistence in the harsh world of Russian agriculture, but they proved detrimental to the emergence of a bourgeoisie worthy of the name. Recent scholarship has also noted that the violence of the Russian working class reflected the traditional peasant values that many workers brought from the village to the factory after the Emancipation Decree of 1861.[27]

Unlike the social elements that coalesced to form a bourgeoisie in Western Europe, professional men and the commercial–industrial elite in Russia continued to view one another with antagonism.[28] Signs of the fragmentation of the corporate elite along social, ethnic and regional lines emerge from an analysis of the 3285 individuals named in the 568 corporate charters that were confirmed in 1856–75.[29] The positive correlation between Russians and gentry (0.2890) reflected the prominence of bureaucrats, former military men and landlords of Russian ethnicity, especially in St. Petersburg, among corporate founders. The somewhat lower but still significant positive correlations between Jews, Germans and foreigners on the one hand and men from commercial backgrounds on the other testified to the perennial identification of capitalist institutions in Russia with foreigners, a fact that eventually fuelled the revolutionary upheaval of 1917 and continues to weaken the appeal of capitalism in Russia today.[30]

Negative correlations were also significant.[31] The largest negative coefficient, between gentry and commercial men (−0.7724), highlighted the distance that separated the two most important social categories of corporate founders. In some cities and sectors, negative correlations between gentry and commercial entrepreneurs stood even higher than the Empirewide statistic, ranging between −0.8053 and −0.8505 in Moscow and Odessa and in banking, beet sugar, and textiles. Negative coefficients between Russians and Germans (−0.4933) and between Russians and foreigners (−0.4079) likewise showed how rarely individuals from these pairs of ethnic groups cooperated in the founding of new corporations.

Thus, the two largest social groups among founders of corporations – gentry (34.5 per cent) and commercial (50.7 per cent) – and the two most important ethnic groups – Russians (49.1 per cent) and Germans (16.7 per cent) – cooperated very little with one another in the Empire, in many leading cities and in key sectors of the Russian corporate economy from 1856 to 1875. Although modest, the negative correlation between commercial and professional entrepreneurs (-0.2794) suggested that considerable aversion separated them as well.

These patterns confirm the impression, given in the memoir literature, of a small degree of economic cooperation across the most important social and ethnic fissures in Russian society at mid-century. Debates in the consultative institutions fostered by Reutern often revealed serious rifts among merchants in the major cities of the Empire. In his memoirs, a leading Moscow merchant described in unflattering terms several members of the tariff commission of 1867–8: from St Petersburg, the merchant Egor E. Brandt, 'a dried-up, arrogant German'; an Odessa trader, 'one Goldenberg, a clever Jew and former smuggler'; and, from Warsaw, the Jewish banker 'Iulii Vertgeim [Juliusz Wertheim], who knew no Russian and expressed his opinions in French'.[32]

The notion of a 'Russian bourgeoisie', reiterated as an axiom of Soviet historiography, therefore has little basis in fact if the term is taken to imply the existence of a social class conscious of its economic interests and unified by capitalist institutions such as corporations, chambers of commerce, commercial–industrial publications and political parties. The tsarist government permitted the creation of only a tiny number of business groups, mainly local exchange committees (*birzhevye komitety*) and, from 1870s onward, industrial organizations (called 'trade associations' in the USA) in the major mining and manufacturing regions. Preliminary surveys of the history of these groups have stressed the constant quarrels among them to the end of the tsarist period. Even after 1905, when political parties became legal, commercial–industrial parties remained locally based and mutually antagonistic.[33] Although Reutern's policy of consultations did not constitute the only reason for the Russian merchants' antipathy to liberal politics in the half-century before 1905, he won their gratitude because it gave them considerable prestige in an agricultural society largely hostile to commerce.[34]

The legacy of the great reforms

In discussions of potential turning points in Russian history, the reigns of the last two emperors, Alexander III (1881–94) and Nicholas II (1894–1917) continue to receive much attention. Liberal scholars between the two world wars generally held that Bolshevik rule represented an aberration in Russian history. This interpretation rested on impressive statistics of industrial output, agrarian reform and educational improvements. The Constitution of 23 April 1906 appeared to promote the gradual emergence of parliamentary government. In the words of Nicholas Timasheff, son of a tsarist bureaucrat and spokesman for major industrial interests:

Pre-Revolutionary Russia needed [only] a few decades more of peace to be transformed into a society no longer conspicuously backward as compared with the West, and no longer endowed with dangerous tensions. Russia was well on the way towards entering the family of nations enjoying the advantages of modern civilization.[35]

This optimistic assessment has lost its explanatory power. Between the Crimean War and the Russo–Turkish War, Russian policy-makers borrowed from Europe, however slowly and reluctantly, a series of innovations that might have forestalled the social cataclysm of 1917, but they did not move away from the military–autocratic mode of rule towards the rational–legal mode. Despite their considerable abilities as statesmen, Witte and Petr A. Stolypin (prime minister and minister of internal affairs from 1906 to 1911) failed to overcome problems of economic backwardness, massive social protests among peasants and workers and intermittent ethnic conflicts. According to Avenir P. Korelin, 'the ossification of the Russian autocracy and the social egoism and conservatism of the landed gentry' combined to delay reform. After 1861, 'half a century was lost, a period of time long enough for Germany to reform its agrarian system and to give a capitalist impulse to the development of agriculture'.[36] Notwithstanding impressive rates of economic growth in the last business cycle before the First World War, which stood in marked contrast to the modest pace of development in the period of the New Economic Policy and the chaos of Stalin's command economy in the decade before the Second World War,[37] the Russian economy remained firmly under autocratic control in 1914.[38]

Indeed, military spending grew from 37.6 per cent of the total Imperial budget in 1866 to 51.1 per cent in 1885, 53.0 per cent in 1900 and 56.8 per cent in 1913.[39] Table 7.1 illustrates the resilience of the military–autocratic system under the last two emperors.

Table 7.1 Selected categories of net investment and governmental spending in the Russian Empire in 1885 and 1913 (rubles per capita, 1913 prices)

Category of investment or imperial government spending	1885	1913	Percentage change, 1885–1913
Net investment	6.36	13.53	112.7
Net investment in transportation and communication	0.63	1.22	93.7
Total Imperial government spending	5.19	9.98	92.3
Defence spending	2.65	5.67	114.0
Health and education spending	0.26	0.90	246.2

Source: P.R. Gregory, *Before command: an economic history of Russia from emancipation to the first Five-year plan* (Princeton, NJ, 1994), Table A.1, in per-capita terms.

Nearly a quarter century ago, Leopold Haimson argued that the Bolshevik revolution reflected a breakdown of the Imperial system of politics, economics and social organization. Whether or not the Bolsheviks would have triumphed in the absence of the economic chaos caused by the First World War remains an open question. In any case, Geoffrey Hosking and others have demonstrated the failure of the weak liberal parties in the State Duma to wrest power from the tsarist regime in the crucial decade before the war.[40] Thus, the era of the great reforms represented the last chance for the tsarist government to sweep away impediments to modern capitalist enterprise in time to meet the crises of 1914–17. The positive developments that Timasheff observed after 1905 lacked adequate time to mature into a political and social system capable of peaceful change.

It is not yet clear whether Boris N. Yeltsin's decision to repeat the horrors of the Afghan war in a vain attempt to annul Chechen independence marked the final episode of military–autocratic rule in Russian history. If not, then post-Soviet constitutionalism, which grants extraordinary power to the executive branch of government at the expense of the legislative, may well join Marxism, Panslavism, Official Nationality, enlightened absolutism, and Christianity in being stripped of its humanitarian qualities for the sake of militarism in the largest country in the world.

Conclusions

The time has come for historical analyses of the Russian economy that focus not only on legal institutions and corporate statistics[41] but also on economic strategies and policies. It is essential to grasp the interaction between the ministries and the new capitalist institutions as well as the motivations and capabilities of entrepreneurs from all major sectors, cities and social and ethnic groups.

Comparisons and contrasts between Russian corporations and those in Germany and Japan between 1851 and 1900 appear especially promising. Like the Russian Empire, Germany and Japan entered the age of corporate capitalism without constitutional government or free markets but, unlike it, they created formidable economic systems based on long traditions of native entrepreneurship and state support for commerce and industry that were incompatible with the military–autocratic mode of rule. An econometric study of railroad companies throughout the world from the 1820s to 1914 might reveal key determinants of success and failure in all possible social and political contexts.

Finally, we must ask why the several thousand founders of corporations in the era of the great reforms failed to maintain the momentum of entrepreneurship into the late 1870s and 1880s and to convince the tsarist bureaucracy of the need for thoroughgoing economic reforms. The RUSCORP database identifies a handful of landlords and bureaucrats whose careers demonstrated an evolution from the traditional military and pro-autocratic outlook to that of a self-confident corporate elite. A more subtle issue is that of variations in the cultural significance of gentry or merchant status, or even German or Jewish ethnicity, from one city to another and from one decade to another. The ultimate explanation of these complexities lies in a series of meticulous biographical studies, the lack of which has crippled research in Russian business history. The identities of these men are now known,[42] but the task of reconstructing their careers and attitudes promises to be slow and complex, owing largely to decades of neglect by Soviet historians and archivists.

The few detailed studies of corporations now available[43] suggest the cultural complexities of Russian capitalism. For example, in their reluctance to venture out of textile manufacturing and into heavy industry and in their appeals to economic nationalism many Russian merchants exemplified traditional values and an emotional attachment to the military–autocratic ideal, which sometimes served their immediate interests. Echoes of the Moscow merchants' ethnic exclusiveness of the 1860s and 1870s resounded in the militarism and economic xenophobia of Russian entrepreneurs shortly before the revolution of 1917 and in the early 1990s.[44] Conversely, the rational–legal impulse sometimes came out of the gentry side of the equation, as in the early phases of the English and French revolutions and in the entire history of the Russian liberal movement before 1905. Fortunately, the opening of the archives, new expressions of interest by Russians in the history of their own capitalist institutions,[45] and the recent development of inexpensive techniques for the analysis of statistical materials that have languished in obscurity[46] present numerous opportunities for research in Russian economic and business history.

Like the analysis of Russia's perennial poverty by Gatrell, this discussion of entrepreneurship, government and society has stressed the importance of political and cultural impediments to the emergence of capitalism and the rule of law. Although the future of Russia is not entirely constrained by geographical determinism and the historical weight of the military–autocratic principle, the tasks of economic reform in the post-Soviet era remain great because of the historical experience of the Russian Empire. The effort to understand the peculiarities of the history of capitalism in Russia – including entrepreneurial activity among various social and ethnic groups, the effects of bureaucratic tutelage and the nationalist agenda underlying much entrepreneurship – is essential now that Russia has begun its slow and painful reintegration into the international economy.

Acknowledgements

For constructive criticism, thanks are due to John J. Beggs, Stephen J. Bensman, Olga Crisp, Leonard Hochberg, Geoffrey Hosking, Lindsey Hughes, John Klier and Paul F. Paskoff, none of whom, however, bears responsibility for errors of fact or interpretation.

Notes

1 P. Gatrell, 'Poor Russia: environment and government in the long-run economic history of Russia', working papers in economic and social history, University of Manchester, Manchester, no. 36 (December 1996), p. 22.

2 D.C. North, *Institutions, institutional change, and economic performance* (Cambridge, 1990).

3 On the uniqueness of the era of the great reforms in Russian corporate history, see T.C. Owen, *Russian corporate capitalism from Peter the Great to perestroika* (Oxford, 1995), pp. 20, 52, Figure 2.3 on new corporate capital per capita, and Figure 2.10 on railroads and banks. In that monograph I analysed corporate data in Owen, 'RUSCORP: a database of corporations in the Russian Empire, 1700–1914,' revised edn, distributed by the Inter-University Consortium for Political and Social Research, Ann Arbor, MI, 1992. The present discussion focuses on data extracted from 568 corporate charters granted by the tsarist government in the two decades from 1856 to 1875 and the 3285 persons named as founders in those charters.

4 See B. Eklof, J. Bushnell and L. Zakharova, eds *Russia's great reforms, 1855–1881* (Bloomington, IN, 1994); T. Taranovski and P. McInerny, eds *Reform in modern Russian history* (New York, 1995), part one, on the reforms of Alexander II, containing articles by T. Emmons, V.G. Chernukha and B.V. Anan'ich, and L.G. Zakharova, followed by commentary by D. Field; and a recent Russian account of political reforms from the fifteenth century to 1921: B.V. Anan'ich, R. Sh. Ganelin and V.M. Paneiakh, eds *Vlast' i reformy: Ot samoderzhaviia k sovetskoi Rossii* (St. Petersburg, 1996), including a survey of the era of the great reforms (pp. 283–367) by V.G. Chernukha.

5 'Politics as a Vocation' (1919), in H.H. Gerth and C. Wright Mills, eds *From Max Weber* (New York, 1958), pp. 77–128; quotation from p. 79.

6 On the tribulations of a Russian engineer who suffered political persecution under the tsarist regime and was executed in 1929 during the antispecialist hysteria of the first Five-Year Plan, see L.R. Graham, *The ghost of the executed engineer: Technology and the fall of the Soviet Union* (Cambridge, MA, 1993).

7 'A middle class that in the West European sense unified the propertied, educated society never materialized in Russia. A capitalist economy under state tutelage did'. A.J. Rieber, 'The sedimentary society', in E.W. Clowes, S.D. Kassow and J.L. West, eds *Between tsar and people: educated society and the quest for public identity in late Imperial Russia*, (Princeton, NJ, 1991), pp. 353–4. In the preceding sentence, on p. 353, Rieber correctly noted the anticapitalist essence of tsarist economic policy: 'the state economic bureaucracy was unwilling to surrender the economy into private hands'. The problem lies with an imprecise definition of 'capitalist economy'. The concept of capitalist economic development before Peter the Great, advanced in J.T. Fuhrman, *The origins of capitalism in Russia* (Chicago, IL, 1972), is even more dubious.

8 M. Weber, *General economic history*, translated by F.H. Knight (New York, 1927), pp. 276–8.

9 For a statistical analysis of corporate development under the tsarist regime, see Owen, *Russian corporate capitalism*, ch. 2.

10 See W.C. Fuller, *Strategy and power in Russia, 1600–1914* (New York, 1992), p. 376 (on the Russo–Japanese War) and p. 445 (on 1914).

11 P.N. Durnovo, 'Memorandum to Nicholas II', in T. Riha, ed. *Readings in Russian civilization*, revised edn (Chicago, IL, 1969), vol. 2, pp. 465–78; quotations from pp. 471, 476, 478.

12 S.H. Baron, 'Entrepreneurs and entrepreneurship in sixteenth/seventeenth-century Russia', in G. Guroff and F.V. Carstensen, eds *Entrepreneurship in Imperial Russia and the Soviet Union*, (Princeton, NJ, 1983), pp. 27–58; A. Kahan, 'Notes on Jewish entrepreneurship in tsarist Russia', in *Entrepreneurship*, pp. 104–24; Kahan, 'Government policies and the industrialization of Russia', *Journal of Economic History*, 27 (1967), pp. 460–77; and J.A. Armstrong, 'Socializing for modernization in a multiethnic elite', in *Entrepreneurship*, pp. 84–103.

13 A. Gerschenkron, 'Economic backwardness in historical perspective', in *Economic backwardness in historical perspective: a book of essays* (Cambridge, 1966), pp. 5–30, an influential essay that first appeared in 1952; T.H. Von Laue, *Sergei Witte and the industrialization of Russia* (New York, 1963); and Von Laue, *Why Lenin? Why Stalin? Why Gorbachёv? The rise and fall of the Soviet system*, 3rd edn (New York, 1993), first published in 1964 as *Why Lenin? Why Stalin?*.

14 T.C. Owen, *The corporation under Russian law, 1800–1917: a study in tsarist economic policy* (New York, 1991); J. Coopersmith, *The electrification of Russia, 1880–1926* (Ithaca, NY, 1992); P. Gatrell, *Government, industry, and rearmament in Russia, 1900–1914: the last argument of tsarism* (New York, 1994); and T.C. Owen, 'Autocracy and the rule of law in Russian economic history', in J.D. Sachs and K. Pistor, eds *The rule of law and economic reform in Russia*, (Boulder, CO, 1997), pp. 23–39.

15 J. Kipp, 'M. Kh. Reutern on the Russian state and economy: a liberal bureaucrat during the Crimean era, 1854–60', *Journal of Modern History* 47, 3 (September 1975), pp. 437–59; and Kipp, 'The Russian navy and the problems of technological transfer: technological backwardness and military–industrial development, 1853–1876', in Eklof *et al.*, eds *Russia's great reforms*, pp. 115–38. On Reutern's economic policies, see O.S. Hayward, *Official Russian policies concerning industrialization during the finance ministry of M. Kh. Reutern, 1862–1878*, doctoral dissertation, University of Wisconsin, WI, 1973; L.E. Shepelev, *Tsarizm i burzhuaziia vo vtoroi polovine XIX veka: Problemy torgovo-promyshlennoi politiki* (Leningrad, 1981), pp. 71–7, 100–33; and the positive assessment of his career by his loyal aide, Anatolii N. Kulomzin, in *Die finanzielle Sanierung Rußlands nach der Katastrophe des Krimkriegs 1862 bis 1878 durch den Finanzminister Michael von Reutern*, edited by W. Reutern-Nolcken (Berlin, 1914), pp. 174–224. The Russian edition of this work appeared four years earlier; M. Kh. Reitern: *biograficheskii ocherk, s prilozheniem iz posmertnykh zapisok M. Kh. Reiterna*, edited by A. Kulomzin and V.G. Reitern-Nol'ken (St. Petersburg, 1910).

16 Kipp, 'The Russian Navy', p. 123; quotation from the official source on p. 122.

17 J. Grant, 'Private enterprise and the state in Russia: a comparative study of the Putilov Company (1868–1917) and the Kirovsky factory today', paper presented at the Economic History Association, Berkeley, CA, 7 September 1996, pp. 6–7. Grant's account in *Big business in Russia: a history of the Putilov company in late Imperial Russia, 1868–1917* (Pittsburgh, PA, forth-

coming), chapter 1, is the first comprehensive analysis of Putilov's career. The biographical sketch in *Russkii biograficheskii slovar'* praises his innovations excessively and ignores his dishonesty and ultimate financial failure.

18 Grant, 'Private enterprise and the state in Russia', pp. 9–10, with reference to Hayward, *Official Russian policies*, p. 309.

19 Kipp, 'The Russian navy', p. 125, stressed the failure of massive subsidies to 'overcome the tremendous economic and social barriers that confronted the Russian merchant marine'. He referred especially to the Russian Steamship Company, known by its initials in Russian as ROPIT (*Rossiiskoe obshchestvo parokhodstva i torgovli*), founded in 1856 on the initiative of Grand Duke Konstantin Nikolaevich himself. On this company, see W.E. Mosse, 'Russia and the Levant, 1856–1862: Grand Duke Constantine and the Russian Steam Navigation Company', *Journal of Modern History* 24 (1954), pp. 39–48; and Owen, *The corporation under Russian law*, pp. 36–7, and the sources cited there. On railroad finances, see the anonymous pamphlet *The insolvency of Russia and of Russian railways, by a functionary attached to the Russian Ministry of Finance during twenty-five years* (London, 1876).

20 W. Reutern-Nolcken, ed. *Die finanzielle Sanierung*, pp. 55–7; quotation from p. 56.

21 W. Reutern-Nolcken, ed. *Die finanzielle Sanierung*, pp. 9, 6, 10.

22 W. Reutern-Nolcken, ed. *Die finanzielle Sanierung*, p. 15.

23 W. Reutern-Nolcken, ed. *Die finanzielle Sanierung*, pp. 127, 125.

24 Alexander Mikhailovich, *Once a grand duke*, p. 197 (quoted); on financiers, pp. 246–53, apparently referring to Karl I. Iaroshinskii (Jaroszyński), Prokopii P. Batolin, Aleksei I. Putilov, and Petr E. Paramonov. No objective assessment of the business ethics of these four men exists. On the activities of Iaroshinskii in 1916–18, see A.A. Fursenko, 'Russkii Vanderbil't', *Voprosy istorii*, no. 10 (October 1987), pp. 183–8.

25 B. Moore Jr, *Social origins of dictatorship and democracy: lord and peasant in the making of the modern world* (Boston, MA, 1966), ch. 9. On the contribution of a social group largely ignored by Marxists, the radical white-collar employees, to the Bolsheviks' victory, see D. Orlovsky, 'The lower middle strata in revolutionary Russia', in E.W. Clowes *et al.*, eds *Between tsar and people*, pp. 248–68.

26 E.L. Keenan, 'Muscovite political folkways', *The Russian Review* 45, 2 (April 1986), pp. 115–81, especially section 4: 'The political culture of the Russian village', quotation from p. 128; and B.N. Mironov, 'Peasant popular culture and the origins of Soviet authoritarianism', in S.P. Frank and M.D. Steinberg, eds *Cultures in flux: lower-class values, practices, and resistance in late imperial Russia* (Princeton, NJ, 1994), pp. 54–73.

27 See the bibliography in Frank and Steinberg, eds *Cultures in flux*.

28 On the lack of a vigorous 'middle class' or 'bourgeoisie' in Russia, see T.C. Owen, *Capitalism and politics in Russia: a social history of the Moscow merchants, 1855–1905* (Cambridge, 1981); *idem, Between tsar and people*; and H.D. Balzer, ed. *Russia's missing middle class: the professions in Russian history* (Armonk, NY, 1996).

29 Statistics discussed here are from Owen, 'RUSCORP', except that status identifications are improved in two ways: first, by borrowing missing identifications for a given individual from another charter in which he was correctly identified; and, second, by amalgamating various status and occupational categories, including those of organizations, into four groups: gentry (including bureaucratic and military), commercial (including honorary citizens, manufacturers, bankers and representatives of trading firms), professional, and unknown. Ethnic identifications remain the same as in 'RUSCORP' and *Russian corporate capitalism*. Russians, Poles, Jews and Germans are subjects

of the Russian Empire, while subjects of all other states fall into a single category, foreigners, regardless of their ethnicity. All cited coefficients of correlation are significant at the 0.0001 level.

30 Owen, *Russian corporate capitalism*, ch. 5, on 'Capitalism and xenophobia in Russia'.

31 In the calculation of percentages of founders belonging to various ethnic and social groups, all correlations among the five ethnic categories and all correlations among the four status categories are negative, as would be expected because all groups together had a combined total of 100 per cent in a given corporation.

32 N.A. Naidenov, *Vospominaniia o vidennom, slyshannom i ispytannom*, 2 vols (Moscow, 1903–5; reprinted Newtonville, MA, Oriental Research Partners, 1976), vol. 2, p. 76. Naidenov's opinions carried enormous significance because he founded the Moscow Trading Bank and served as the president of the Moscow Exchange Committee from 1876 until his death in 1905.

33 A.J. Rieber, *Merchants and entrepreneurs in Imperial Russia* (Chapel Hill, NC, 1982); Shepelev, *Tsarizm i burzhuaziia vo vtoroi polovine XIX veka*; idem, *Tsarizm i burzhuaziia v 1904–1914 gg.: problemy torgovo-promyshlennoi politiki* (Leningrad, 1987), excerpted in English in Shepelev, 'Business organizations in the Russian Empire, 1906–1914', *Russian Studies in History* 34, 1 (Summer 1995), pp. 40–88; and T.C. Owen, 'Impediments to a bourgeois consciousness in Russia, 1880–1905: the estate structure, ethnic diversity, and economic regionalism', in E.W. Clowes *et al.*, eds *Between tsar and people*, pp. 75–89. The best analysis of a regional organization is S.P. McCaffray, *The politics of industrialization in tsarist Russia: the Association of Southern Coal and Steel Producers, 1874–1914* (DeKalb, IL, 1996). On the failure of the liberal bourgeoisie in Moscow to unify commercial–industrial interests after 1905, see J.L. West, 'Visions of Russia's entrepreneurial future: Pavel Riabushinsky's utopian capitalism', in J.L. West and I.A. Petrov, eds *Merchant Moscow: images of Russia's vanished bourgeoisie*, (Princeton, NJ, 1998), pp. 161–70, and West, 'The fate of merchant Moscow', in the same volume, pp. 173–8. On the most influential business organization in the empire, see R.A. Roosa, *Russian industrialists in an era of revolution: the Association of Industry and Trade, 1906–1917*, edited by T.C. Owen (Armonk, NY, 1997). Also useful are J.H. Hartl, *Die Interessenvertretungen der Industriellen in Rußland 1905–1914* (Vienna, 1978) and H. Haumann, *Kapitalismus im zaristischen Staat 1906–1917: Organisationsformen, Machtverhältnisse und Leistungsbilanz im Industrialisierungsprozeß* (Königstein/Ts., 1980).

34 Despite the Moscow merchants' anger at the government's refusal to establish high protective tariffs for the benefit of Russian industry in 1867–8, Naidenov regarded Reutern highly and considered relations with the Ministry of Finance entirely satisfactory in the 1870s. Naidenov, *Vospominaniia*, 2, pp. 140, 142; on 1870s, see p. 153. On the Moscow merchants' reactionary nationalism before 1905, including its non-economic sources, see Owen, *Capitalism and politics in Russia*.

35 N.S. Timasheff, *The great retreat: the growth and decline of communism in Russia* (New York, 1946), pp. 33–40; quotation from p. 40. Timasheff's father, Sergei I. Timashev, served as the minister of trade and industry in 1909–15 and as the head of the Association of Industry and Trade. See R.A. Roosa, 'Russian industrialists during World War I: the interaction of economics and politics', in Guroff and Carstensen, eds *Entrepreneurship*, p. 167. This optimistic interpretation received its most comprehensive elaboration in J. Walkin, *The rise of democracy in prerevolutionary Russia: political and social institutions under the last three tsars* (New York, 1962).

36 A.P. Korelin, 'The social problem in Russia, 1906–1914: Stolypin's agrarian reform', in T. Taranovski and P. McInerny, eds *Reform in modern Russian history*, p. 161.

37 R.W. Davies, ed. *From tsarism to the new economic policy: continuity and change in the economy of the USSR* (Ithaca, NY, 1991); H. Hunter and J.M. Szyrmer, *Faulty foundations: Soviet economic policies, 1928–1940* (Princeton, NJ, 1992); and P. Gregory, *Before command: an economic history of Russia from the emancipation to the first Five-year plan* (Princeton, NJ, 1994).

38 T. McDaniel, *Autocracy, capitalism, and revolution in Russia* (Berkeley, CA, 1988); Gatrell, *Government, industry and rearmament in Russia*.

39 Figures for 1866 from W. Reutern-Nolcken, ed. *Die finanzielle Sanierung*, p. 89; figures for 1885, 1990 and 1913 from Gregory, *Before command*, Table A.1.

40 L. Haimson, 'The problem of social stability in urban Russia, 1905–1917', *Slavic Review* 23, 4 (December 1964), pp. 619–42, and 24, 1 (March 1965), pp. 1–22; and G.A. Hosking, *The Russian constitutional experiment: government and Duma, 1907–1914* (Cambridge, 1973).

41 As in N. Horn and J. Kocka, eds *Recht und Entwicklung der Grossunternehmen 1860–1920* (Göttingen, 1979); A. Mosser, *Die Industrieaktiengesellschaft in Österreich 1880–1913: Versuch einer historischen Bilanz- und Betriebsanalyse* (Vienna, 1980); and North, *Institutions*. No comparable studies exist in Russian economic history.

42 Owen, *Russian corporate capitalism*, Table 3.5, lists the 32 most active corporate founders in the five cycles of incorporation from 1851 to 1913. None is the subject of a biography or a monograph in business history.

43 Mosse, 'Russia and the Levant'; A.J. Rieber, 'The Formation of La Grande Société des Chemins de Fer Russes', *Jahrbücher für Geschichte Osteuropas*, New Series, 21 (1973), pp. 375–91; F.V. Carstensen, *American enterprise in foreign markets: studies of Singer and International Harvester in Imperial Russia* (Chapel Hill, NC, 1984); C.A. Ruud, *Russian entrepreneur: publisher Ivan Sytin of Moscow, 1851–1934* (Montreal, 1990); and B.V. Anan'ich, *Bankirskie doma v Rossii* (Leningrad, 1991). In the sparse memoir literature dealing with Russian business history, three outstanding examples are Naidenov, *Vospominaniia*; S.I. Chetverikov, *Bezvozvratno ushedshaia Rossiia: neskol'ko stranits iz knigi moei zhizni* (Berlin, undated, 1920s), on woollen textiles in Moscow and sheep breeding in Siberia; and J. Lied, *Siberian Arctic: the story of the Siberian Company* (London, 1960), on the Siberian Steamship, Manufacturing, and Trading Company, formed by Norwegian and British entrepreneurs in Oslo in January 1912.

44 V.P. Riabushinskii, ed. *Velikaia Rossiia: sbornik statei po voennym i obshchestvennym voprosam*, 2 vols (Moscow, 1910–11), a critique of the tsarist government's alleged failure to prepare Russian armed forces for victory in recent and future wars; W. Laqueur, *Black Hundred: the rise of the extreme right in Russia* (New York, 1993), ch. 15; and O.A. Platonov, *1000 let russkogo predprinimatel'stva: iz istorii kupecheskikh rodov* (Moscow, 1995).

45 See V.I. Bovykin and I.A. Petrov, *Kommercheskie banki Rossiiskoi imperii* (Moscow, 1994), a lavishly illustrated survey of banks in the Russian Empire that summarizes the findings of Soviet and Western scholarship.

46 Komitet s"ezdov predstavitelei aktsionernykh kommercheskikh bankov, *O zhelatel'nykh izmeneniiakh v postanovke aktsionernogo bankovogo dela v Rossii* (Petrograd, 1917), containing a mass of financial and economic statistics; and S.A. Pervushin, *Khoziaistvennaia kon"iunktura: vvedenie v izuchenie dinamiki russkogo narodnogo khoziaistva za polveka* (Moscow, 1925), the most sophisticated statistical analysis of the late tsarist and early Soviet economies ever published.

8

The static society: patterns of work in the later Russian Empire

DAVID SAUNDERS

Among the most interesting analyses of the later Russian Empire was that of the school of historical thought headed by the late Pavel Volobuev. In a posthumously published interview, Volobuev held that the principal ideas of the school could be boiled down to the following propositions:

1 'it was impossible to derive the October revolution directly from the maturity of Russian capitalism';
2 'in studying the history of the Russian revolutions it was also impossible to escape the problem of the relationship between spontaneity and consciousness';
3 the nature of 'capitalist development' in the late Russian Empire may have differed from the nature of capitalist development in other countries;
4 the absolutist state may not have played the part in the history of the late Russian Empire that it played in the history of other countries at comparable points in their development;
5 the origins of the October Revolution lay 'not in the level of the development of capitalism in Russia (which was clearly inadequate)', but in the fact that the Russian Empire was 'on the brink of national catastrophe' by virtue of 'the war and . . . the unproductive policies of the tsarist and Provisional governments';
6 there was more than one way in which the society of the Russian Empire could have developed from the starting point represented by its condition at the beginning of the twentieth century;
7 between the October Revolution and the introduction of the Committees of Poor Peasants in June 1918 'a union existed in Russia between the proletariat and the entire peasantry', with the consequence that in its early stages the Revolution possessed a 'pan-democratic potential' which it subsequently lost.[1]

The first, third and fifth of these propositions imply a relatively low level of dynamism in the later Russian Empire. Since dynamism is the opposite of stasis, they give me the courage to refer to the later Empire as a 'static society'. The description is too bold, of course, but its boldness may serve as a reminder that the revolutions of 1917 may not have been the inevitable product of the way in which the society of the later Russian Empire was developing.

Because the careers of Volobuev and his reform-communist associates were interrupted at the beginning of the 1970s, their views still await thorough exploration in Russian-language historical writing. Even when glasnost' was at its height at the end of the 1980s, Vladimir Bovykin, the principal beneficiary of the Volobuevites' demise, made clear that he was not going to give way to his former opponents without a fight.[2] Bovykin was still active in scholarship in the year of Volobuev's death.[3] Although Volobuev himself succeeded in elaborating on the sixth of the above propositions in a book on 'alternativism' in history in 1987,[4] important studies by two of his friends, Konstantin Tarnovskii (on cottage industry at the turn of the twentieth century) and Andrei Anfimov (on Stolypin's agrarian reforms), found their way into print only in 1995 and 1997.[5] In Russia, the pusuit of the hypotheses of Volobuev and his circle has remained difficult.

Because Anglophone historical writing on Russia tends to depend, at least up to a point, on the models that obtain in Russia, the beliefs of Volobuev and those associated with him may not have been properly explored in English either. I shall return to this issue at the end of this chapter.

In what follows I shall look only at what Volobuev's propositions may imply for the study of work patterns in industry and agriculture. I feel that they could be illustrated just as well with reference to things such as the lack of regional coalescence in the later Russian Empire, the slow extension of education, the non-emergence of the concept of individuality, the limited development of geographical and social mobility and the inefficacy of most attempts to alter the Empire's social order from the top down; but I must explore these additional illustrations elsewhere.

Industry

A 'non-dynamic' presentation of work patterns in the industry of nineteenth-century and early-twentieth-century Russian Empire turns first on the perennially small size of the factory labour force (relative to the size of the population as a whole). One authority gives a figure of 95 200 factory workers in the European part of the Empire in 1804.[6] Another concluded that the same part of the empire contained some 660 000 factory workers in about 1860.[7] A third held that at the end of the nineteenth century there were 1 621 188 'real' factory workers in the European part of the Empire, including the Caucasus and Transcaucasus but excluding the Kingdom of Poland.[8] In 1913 the factory labour force of the empire as a whole appears to have been 2 467 200.[9] Since the population of the relevant parts of the Empire at these points in time was probably about 40 million, 60 million, 94 million, and 166 million, factory workers constituted, respectively, about 0.24 per cent, 1.1 per cent, 1.72 per cent, and 1.88 per cent of the totals. None of these estimates is reliable, but none gives the impression that, even at the outbreak of the First World War, employment in factories was commonplace. Factory employment was increasing more rapidly than the size of the population, but it was nowhere near overtaking employment in other spheres.

In addition, factories in the Russian Empire were probably not as advanced as factories in other countries. The greatest (and most contro-versial) student of Russian industrialization, Alexander Gerschenkron, used to speak of the 'advantages of backwardness', by which he meant that because late industrializers did not have to re-invent the machines devised by their competitors, they could catch up with them quickly by moving straight to the most recent technology. It is by no means clear, however, that when the Russian Empire moved in the direction of mechan-ization it moved either quickly or wholeheartedly. Evidence from the reign of Alexander I indicates that at the beginning of the nineteenth century the tsarist authorities had difficulty persuading entrepreneurs to adopt mod-ern technology even when, from the point of view of the government, the need to do so was urgent on account of the unavailability of manufactured goods from abroad.[10] To judge by the fact that in 1860 about 300 000 of the Empire's 660 000 factory workers worked in factories that made use of steam power,[11] mechanization had by then made some headway. At the end of the 1860s, however, the Russian Empire's use of artifically generated motive power was still small by comparison with that of West European countries.[12] In 1894 the Governor of Nizhnii Novgorod refused to ascribe the new phenomenon of mass peasant migration to Siberia to the 'extra-ordinary development of all kinds of mechanized production' which was said by some to be making it difficult for peasants to find non-agricultural work in the European part of the Empire.[13] Although, in terms of number of spindles, the Russian Empire 'had the world's fourth-largest cotton-spinning industry' by 1913 (after Britain, the USA, and Germany),[14] mechanization had not even then made great strides in the economy as a whole. The textile and metal-working parts of Russian industry had benefited, but other parts had not.[15]

Perhaps it may be argued that mechanization in the Russian Empire 'punched above its weight' because it was highly concentrated – that sectors of the economy in which it was absent did particularly badly, but sectors in which it was present did particularly well. Although the Russian Empire contained relatively few cotton mills in 1860, the ones it did contain were comparable to those in contemporary Britain.[16] Some 43.1 per cent of the total of 1 621 188 factory workers in the Russian Empire at the end of the nineteenth century worked in enterprises which employed more than a thousand people.[17] The Kreenholm works outside Narva on the border between Russia and Estonia was 'believed to be the world's largest cotton-spinning enterprise' at the beginning of the twentieth century.[18] The Putilov works in St Petersburg 'employed over 10,000 workers' in 1914.[19] Soviet 'gigantomania' appears to have had tsarist precedents.

Despite appearances to the contrary, however, it does not seem to be the case that the Russian Empire was compensating for the small size of its factory labour force and the small number of its factories by concentrating its efforts. Large factories were not necessarily highly mechanized. Far from attesting to a high degree of modernity, indeed, the enormous average size of factories in late imperial St Petersburg probably indicated how antediluvian they were, for large factories seem to have been constructed mainly for the purpose of bringing large numbers of people together so that they could conduct their work in a highly labour-intensive rather than a highly mechanized manner; 'large size denoted . . . comparative backwardness'.[20]

In another sense – geographical location – mechanized Russian factories were indeed concentrated. In the early twentieth century they were to be found, chiefly, in the Moscow region, St Petersburg, the Urals, the basin of the river Donets, the southwest Ukraine, the Kingdom of Poland and on the Baltic littoral. The industrialized character of these regions is undeniable, but it is important to bear in mind that large tracts of the tsars' domains were affected by industrialization only indirectly.

The growth of industry certainly did not generate a large measure of urbanization. According to Boris Mironov, towns were actually in decline between the 1740s and the 1860s.[21] The census of January 1897 held that only 13.4 per cent of the total population of the Empire (excluding Finland) were town dwellers.[22] The census-takers employed an administrative rather than a socio-economic definition of towns, but a recalculation of their results by a scholar who defined towns economically rather than administratively lifted the urban population of the European part of the empire only to about 15 per cent of the total population.[23] Figures provided by another scholar (again derived from the dubious administrative criterion for towns) make the urban population of the European part of the empire 15.27 per cent on the eve of the First World War.[24] Urban agglomerations grew at an accelerating rate between 1914 and 1917,[25] but they never contained anything like a majority of the Russian Empire's population and they declined precipitately when the Empire fell victim to revolution and civil war.[26]

In talking of such towns as there were, moreover, one has to be careful not to exaggerate their modernity. Take the example of St Petersburg. The population of more than 500 000 in 1852 included only 19 671 factory workers. By 1869 these had increased in number to about 35 000, but they still represented fewer than 5 per cent of the city's population. Although, by 1913, the city's factories employed around 200 000 people, as many as 500 000 people in the total population of 2.2 million worked in non-industrial forms of employment. In 1914 manufactured goods were still not the capital's principal export commodity. It is risky to argue that Russian towns grew because of the growth of factory-based industry.[27]

The truly distinctive feature of Russian industry was not the extent to which it transformed the towns but the extent to which it remained rooted in the countryside. 'Rooted in the countryside' means several things: first, and most important, it means that cottage industry survived much longer in the countryside of the Russian Empire than it did in most other industrializing societies; second, it means that many goods manufactured in towns were manufactured in small workshops rather than in factories (that is, that the working practices which gave rise to them had more in common with those to be observed in a rural cottage industry than they did with those of mechanized factories); third, it means that mechanized factories were to be found in the countryside as well as in towns (that is, that the social outlook of the undoubtedly 'industrial' workers who were employed in factories of this kind tended to be more 'peasant' than 'proletarian'); and fourth, it means that most workers even in the most advanced factories of the Russian Empire's cities retained their links with the countryside and went back there for the haymaking and the harvest.

I shall dwell briefly on the first of these four subpropositions in order to strengthen the case for the view that it may be sounder to speak of a rural capture of incipient industry than of industry edging out agriculture.

The scale and longevity of the Russian cottage industry were very great. Edgar Melton has emphasized that the phenomenon first became significant in the second half of the eighteenth century: 'the rapid expansion of rural trade and industry in the Russian heartland after 1750', he writes, 'was one of the most important developments in the peasant village'.[28] In the first half of the nineteenth century cottage-industry activities were such an important feature of the lives of serfs in the north-central zone of the European part of the Russian Empire that a Soviet scholar felt they deserved nearly half his space in a general account of the lives of these serfs.[29] None of the many attempts to count the Empire's cottage-industry workers in the generation after the abolition of serfdom in 1861 makes out that they were fewer in number than workers in contemporary mechanized factories.[30] If one accepts that there were about four million cottage-industry workers in the countryside of the European part of the Russian Empire on the eve of the First World War,[31] even then they outnumbered workers in mechanized factories.

When measured by value, of course, what cottage-industry workers produced was much less significant than the goods that came out of factories. But a social historian is more interested in mindset. Once cottage-industry workers are taken into account, the mindset of the majority of the Russian Empire's industrial workers at the point of the Empire's demise must be said to have been that of the village rather than that of the factory.

It has always been tempting to see cottage industry as a transient phenomenon, the harbinger of industrialization proper. One of the most perspicacious foreign analysts of the nineteenth-century Russian Empire, Sir Donald MacKenzie Wallace, concluded after spending nearly six years in the European part of the Empire in the 1870s that the many villages he came across in which the inhabitants devoted themselves to the wholesale production of cutlery, axes, nails and icons 'cannot in the long run compete with the big factories and workshops, organised on the European model with steam-power and complicated machinery'.[32] A century later Franklin Mendels briefly persuaded scholars that what he called 'proto-industrialization' was a definable Europewide phenomenon whose presence or absence could be taken to indicate whether or not a society was on the verge of a full-blown 'industrial revolution'.[33] But just as no one now thinks Mendels was right,[34] neither was MacKenzie Wallace. Modern scholarship has vindicated him in respect of the nailmakers of the province of Tver',[35] but he underestimated the resilience of cottage-industry workers in general. To judge, indeed, by the scale of Russian peasants' devotion to the formation of cooperatives at the beginning of the twentieth century,[36] Russian industrial workers who did not work in factories may even have been getting better rather than worse at resisting the 'factory imperative' in the last years of the Russian Empire. If Russian cottage industry was no more than a stage on the road to full-blown industrialization, it was a very lengthy one. Richard Rudolph has demonstrated that the society in which it emerged differed fundamentally from 'proto-industrializing' societies in other parts of Europe.[37] Perhaps it was a society which could sustain cottage industry almost indefinitely. It does not seem unreasonable to say of industrial patterns of work in the later Russian Empire that the really remarkable thing about them was how 'agricultural' they remained.

Agriculture

Agriculture in the later Russian Empire continued to develop mainly by virtue of the extension of the sown area. About 15 per cent of the European part of the Empire was under the plough in 1796, 20 per cent in 1861, 26 per cent in 1881 and 29 per cent in 1912.[38] 'Intensification' (the introduction of advanced agricultural techniques) made little headway. Crop selection, for example, changed very slowly. Historians have been keen to point to the introduction in the nineteenth-century Russian Empire of the potato, sugar beet and, to a lesser extent, flax, herbs, tobacco, tea and cotton; but none of these took up much of the agricultural community's time or space.

Heroic contemporary accounts of the adoption of new crops – flax on an estate in the province of Smolensk, clover in a village to the west of Moscow[39] – have to be set in the context of an overwhelming continuity. Andrei Anfimov (one of the Volobuevites) claimed in a 1980 book that in the last 20 years of the nineteenth century Russian peasants were making a quantifiable shift in the direction of crops grown principally for the market.[40] But his 1980 study was the one in which he was obliged, after the fall of his historiographical coterie, to renege on his view that the post-1861 Russian countryside retained many of the features of serfdom,[41] and even in the 1980 study figures in another part of the book make clear that, relative to the extent of the peasants' agricultural activities as a whole, their shift in the direction of crops grown for the market was marginal.[42] A scholar has estimated that in the European part of the Empire at the start of the twentieth century about nine-tenths of the agricultural area was under grain.[43] Elsewhere, he has estimated that in 1913 non-grain cultures took up only 6 per cent of the agricultural area of the European part of the Empire.[44] Since potatoes accounted for two thirds of the space devoted to non-grain cultures, all other non-grain cultures occupied only about a fiftieth of the cultivated land. Types of grain did not change very much either. Although, at the end of the Imperial period, rye was giving ground to wheat as a percentage of the total grain harvest, it remained very much the staple.[45]

Crop rotation was no more innovative than crop selection. The three-field system, necessitating the permanent fallow of around a third of the agricultural land, showed only a few signs of attenuation. One of the Russian Empire's first notable agronomists, Andrei Bolotov, greatly regretted the failure of his attempt to move from a three-field to a seven-field rotation when managing an estate for Catherine the Great in the province of Tula in the mid-1770s.[46] Although the Ministry of Finance responded with interest to Senator Lev Mechnikov's proposal for the introduction of a seven-field crop rotation on the lands of the state peasants in 1833, and although the private landowner N.A. Bunin actually succeeded in introducing a five-field rotation on his estate of Marfino in Tambov in the 1840s and 1850s, more than three-quarters of Russian peasant households were still working the three-field system at the end of the Imperial period.[47] In the decade prior to 1917 the ultra-innovative peasant Sergei Semenov thought of the seven-field rotation as a 'dream'.[48]

Other standard indicators of agricultural improvement do little to relieve the picture. As meadows and pastures came under the plough, feed for animals declined. As feed declined, the ratio of horses to peasants went down.[49] Apart from less pulling power, a diminution in the number of horses entailed a reduction in the availability of natural fertilizer.[50] The picture in respect of other sorts of artificial assistance was no more encouraging. Agricultural machines were employed in significant numbers only on the peripheries of the Empire (where labour was short). Among farmers in the more highly populated regions, only those on the Baltic littoral used them to any great extent. In the 1980 book which marked his formal repudiation of 'Volobuevism', Anfimov claimed that wooden and iron ploughs were in the ratio of 1.63:1 among peasants in 1910,[51] which gives the impression that metal tools were making headway; but again, in tabulating elsewhere in the book the elements that made up the cost of grain in the late 1880s and just prior to the First World War, he made plain 'the enormous preponderance of living human labour' among the various factors at both points in time.[52]

Unsurprisingly, in view of the above, grain yields tended to be low. A government enquiry of the early 1870s estimated that the return on a single seed had been 3.17 in the years 1802–13, 3.5 in the years 1840–7, 3.4 in the years 1857–63 and 3.6 in the years 1870–1. The wholesale grain yield per person, the commission believed, had been 3.9 *chetverts* in the 1840s, 3.4 *chetverts* around 1860, and 3.5 *chetverts* at the start of the 1870s.[53] Steven Hoch's case for much higher figures remains controversial.[54] It is true that by 1913 the grain-to-seed ratio was considerably higher than it had been in the middle of the nineteenth century,[55] but even then the agricultural productivity of the Russian Empire lagged way behind that of most of its competitors. Between 1911 and 1914, for example, the Russian Empire's grain-to-seed ratio was not much more than a third of that of the German Empire, and its potato-to-seed ratio only about a half.[56] A table comparing the return on rye plantings in 12 countries between 1895 and 1904 has the Russian Empire ahead of only Portugal and Greece.[57] Whereas the average spring wheat yield per acre in the European part of the Russian Empire was 8.9 bushels between 1899 and 1903 (and of winter wheat 15 bushels), in Germany the 'general average yield on land of all categories' was 27.5 bushels and in the United Kingdom 35.4 bushels.[58]

Thus whether one looks at crop selection, the rotation of crops, number of horses, use of fertilizer, improvements in tools or crop yields it is hard to divine drastic changes for the better in the way in which the subjects of the tsar practised farming in the nineteenth and early twentieth centuries.

If, moreover, the second most remarkable thing about industrial work in the Russian Empire (after the degree to which it remained 'agricultural') was how few people engaged in it, the second most remarkable thing about agricultural work (after its primitive character) was how many people engaged in it. The proportion of the population that farmed hardly diminished in the nineteenth and early twentieth centuries. Precisely how large a majority of the Empire's population engaged in farming has occasioned much discussion, because although the pan-Imperial census of 1897 recorded that only 69.8 per cent of the population engaged in 'agriculture in general',[59] and although even this figure may have been too high because some peasants were incapable of greater subtlety in self-description or were anxious, for fear of additional taxation, to conceal the fact that they engaged in non-agricultural endeavours,[60] the statistician who introduced the census's figures held that it was not unreasonable to believe, on grounds of lifestyle, that as many as 91.4 per cent of the Empire's inhabitants could be assigned to the 'rural group'.[61] Whatever view one takes of the matter in detail, the Empire's peasantry was enormous.[62] Signs of modernity in the working patterns of most of the inhabitants of the Empire were vestigial.

The way in which peasants organized their agricultural activities, finally, tended to prevent them from maximizing their agricultural potential. Most peasants in the nineteenth-century Russian Empire belonged to peasant-run communes. The part played by the commune in the allocation of land tended to prevent peasants from taking full advantage of the mid-nineteenth-century changes in their legal status. Not all communes, admittedly, involved themselves in land allocation, but 83.4 per cent of land owned by peasants and 77.2 per cent of peasant households were subject to communal tenure in the European part of the empire in 1905.[63] Theoretically, communes need not have subdivided their land. Peasants could have pooled their labour and divided only the produce. But although they sometimes worked the hayfields in this fashion, they seem to have been determined, where the arable was concerned, to retain a sense of household individuality. Perhaps the communal system arose on the back of an earlier system of household tenure whose disappearance peasants regretted. Peasants who worked scattered strips of land which were unlikely to remain in the hands of their families indefinitely could make few economies of scale and had little incentive to improve the quality of the soil. The scattered and shifting character of their land may, indeed, have been a greater obstacle to their prosperity than its extent, for despite the near universal belief at the end of the nineteenth century that Russian peasants had too little land, they had more than peasants in, for example, contemporary France.[64] Consolidating the strips and universalizing the notion of hereditary title might have enabled them to make the most of what they had.

It may not even be going too far to say that the one big change that undoubtedly did take place in Russian agriculture in the nineteenth and early twentieth centuries, the transfer of large tracts of territory from the state and the nobility to peasants, actually had a downward effect on per capita agricultural productivity, for only the state and nobles possessed open fields and the sort of capital that might have made agricultural intensification possible.

From late 1906, of course, it was government policy to restructure the countryside in such a way that, eventually, peasants would be living not in villages but on scattered consolidated holdings. Since the authorities were also at that time making more resources available to the Peasant Land Bank and encouraging peasants to migrate to Siberia in larger numbers than formerly,[65] it ought to be possible to estimate, on the basis of evidence from the last decade of the Empire's existence, the extent to which peasants themselves were responsible for the slow rate of change in the countryside; for if officials were now making it possible for peasants to abandon their traditional patterns of land use it seems logical to suppose that they had only themselves to blame if they went on employing them.

But the evidence relating to peasant take-up of the late Imperial government's agrarian reforms is equivocal. That consolidation of strips proceeded slowly is not at all surprising, for it was fraught with difficulty. To explain the extraordinary degree to which peasants' strips had become intermingled in the province of Chernigov, one official felt the need to go back to the eighteenth century.[66] In Vitebsk, the local division of the Peasant Land Bank waited five years for an answer from head office to the question how peasants were to consolidate land in their possession when some of it belonged to them absolutely, some was being bought from the Bank and some from private individuals. From a financial point of view, the sensible course when creating farmsteads was to construct them only out of land which still had to be paid for (so that every peasant continued to pay his share). But from an agricultural point of view this approach was crazy.[67]

Cases such as the one in Vitebsk seem to make plain that peasants could hardly be blamed for being slow to move in the direction of consolidating their strips. A botched consolidation threatened to be worse than no consolidation at all. Some peasants would benefit, others would suffer. The authorities probably welcomed this prospect of greater social differentiation,[68] but, to judge by the intensity of the resistance which Sergei Semenov encountered when he embarked on the process of separating from his commune to the west of Moscow, many peasants did not.[69] One is tempted to conclude that peasants were willing enough to move from communal to household tenure, but were not, in the main, keen to think of the move as a step on the road to the amalgamation of their strips and the establishment of consolidated farmsteads. Once they had household tenure they could work at improving the quality of the soil at their disposal without fear that the work would benefit other peasants in the wake of a communal reallocation. If times became particularly hard, moreover, they could sell up. Consolidating their strips, however, and, in particular, moving out of the village to live on a newly amalgamated holding, was financially demanding and risky.

The government was aware, on the eve of the First World War, that the agricultural initiative on which it had embarked in 1906 left a great deal to be desired. An official who wrote in 1913 that it was still 'necessary to . . . free the peasants from the fetters of the communal way of life and their lands from the consequences of intermingled strips and a single obligatory crop-rotation' knew that not much had changed.[70] Even in the event of the successful creation of discrete farmsteads, moreover, there remained the problem of partible inheritance. How could the authorities prevent the consolidated holdings to which, up to a point, the reforms of 1906 were giving rise, from being shared out among a householder's children at the point of death?[71] After the collapse of the Empire in 1917 peasants fell back on their communes and broke up the recently consolidated holdings anyway. It can be said of Russian agriculture, therefore, that even if it was a little more dynamic at the point of the Russian Empire's demise than it had been at the beginning of the nineteenth century, the difference was slight.

Conclusions

A caveat needs to be entered. In looking at patterns of work in industry and agriculture, I have wholly omitted the work of professionals, bureaucrats, priests and the many sorts of trader. In respect of industry, the discussion has distinguished between factories and small workshops but failed to examine the difference between, for example, the 'labour aristocrats' to be found in parts of the Putilov plant in St Petersburg and the casual labourers taken on by the day at the Khitrov Market in Moscow. A full discussion of agricultural developments would have to indicate that the rural young were probably more innovative than the old, and that they were certainly very much more numerous (because of the rapid growth in the extent to which births were outnumbering deaths). It would also have to embrace the whole question of peasant off-farm earnings and, in particular, the importance to peasants of temporary migration to the towns (*otkhodnichestvo*); for peasant incomes were not made up wholly of what they could extract from the soil, and peasant mentalities were not entirely the product of rural experience. The notion of stasis or non-dynamism seems to be severely challenged, furthermore, by the likelihood that, in aggregate, standards of living among the common people were rising both in the countryside and in the towns in the last years of the Russian Empire.

But it still seems to me that the historian of working patterns in the Russian Empire whose unit of enquiry is the Empire as a whole and whose interests extend beyond the immediate preliminaries to the collapse of the Romanov dynasty ought not to highlight nascent capitalism and increasing social differentiation at the expense of traditionalism, persistence and underdevelopment. It seems to me blindingly obvious, moreover, that the principal beneficiaries of the years 1917–21 were not the forces that stood for innovation (the Bolsheviks) but the forces that stood for conservation or even regression (the peasantry, who at last got rid of the landlords and briefly restored a world not unlike the one in which they had lived before their sixteenth-century enserfment). The defeated innovators launched a second assault at the time of collectivization, but Andrea Graziosi's recent presentation of the years 1917–1933 in terms of a 'great Soviet peasant war' in which the Soviet authorities lost the first round has much to recommend it.[72]

Has all this been said before? I referred at the start to the Volobuev school of thought in order to make the point that not much of it has been said in Russian. Until fairly recently, however, anglophone students of industry in the later Russian Empire used to make clear that its development was not very extensive.[73] If, moreover, one goes back as far as Geroid Tanquary Robinson's *Rural Russia under the Old Regime* one can argue that anglophone students have also emphasized the plight of agriculture in the later Russian Empire.[74] As recently as 1972 Paul Gregory concluded that the late Russian Empire was not experiencing 'modern economic growth' in the sense of five out of six criteria for the term put forward in the 1960s by Simon Kuznets.[75]

In the 1980s and 1990s, however, the views of anglophone writers appear to have changed. Perhaps James Y. Simms and Barbara Anderson heralded the new course when they questioned whether there had been a crisis in late nineteenth-century Russian agriculture and emphasized the importance of 'modernization' in respect of late nineteenth-century trends in internal migration.[76] A change of direction on the part of Paul Gregory, however, was probably more important. In a monograph on Russian national income between 1885 and 1913 and in a more general account of Russian economic history between the abolition of serfdom and the late 1920s he tended to play up the positive features of the late-imperial economy at the expense of the negative features.[77] He has gone on writing in optimistic vein since the publication of these books.[78] Although he concedes that in per-capita terms the Russian Empire's economic progress was much less startling than it was in absolute terms, he does not put this point at the centre of his analysis. From the point of view of social rather than economic history, however, the point ought to be central, for it relates to the lives of an overwhelming majority of the Russian Empire's population. It seems to me therefore, that recent work in English echoes virtually all post-1917 work in Russian in its tendency to highlight what changed at the expense of what stayed the same. I have been trying to redress the balance.

Notes

1 V.L. Telitsyn, 'Interv'iu s akademikom Pavlom Vasil'evichem Volobuevym', *Otechestvennaia istoriia*, no. 6 (1997), pp. 117–18 (my distillation).
2 See, for example, V. I. Bovykin, 'Problemy perestroiki istoricheskoi nauki i vopros o "novom napravlenii" v izuchenii sotsial'no-ekonomicheskikh predposylok Velikoi Oktiabr'skoi sotsialisticheskoi revoliutsii', *Istoriia SSSR*, no. 5 (1988), pp. 67–100.
3 He was the principal editor, for example, of *Inostrannoe preprinimatel'stvo i zagranichnye investitsii v Rossii: Ocherki* (Moscow, 1997).
4 P.V. Volobuev, *Vybor putei obshchestvennogo razvitiia: teoriia, istoriia, sovremennost'* (Moscow, 1987).

5 K.N. Tarnovskii, *Melkaia promyshlennost' Rossii v kontse XIX – nachale XXv.* (Moscow, 1995); A. M. Anfimov, 'Neokonchennye spory', *Voprosy istorii*, no. 5 (1997), pp. 49–72; no. 6 (1997), pp. 41–67; no. 7 (1997), pp. 81–99; no. 9 (1997), pp. 82–113.

6 P. A. Khromov, *Ekonomicheskoe razvitie Rossii v XIX–XX vekakh: 1800–1917* (Moscow, 1950), p. 27.

7 A.S. Nifontov, 'Novye materialy o promyshlennom proizvodstve v predreformennoi Rossii', *Istoriia SSSR*, no. 5 (1979), p. 33.

8 B.N. Vasil'ev, 'Chislennost', sostav i territorial'noe razmeshchenie fabrichno-zavodskogo proletariata Evropeiskoi Rossii v kontse XIX – nachale XXv.', *Istoriia SSSR*, no. 1 (1976), pp. 101–2.

9 A.M. Anfimov and A. P. Korelin (eds), *Rossiia 1913 god: Statistiko-dokumental'nyi spravochnik* (St Petersburg, 1995), p. 223.

10 Iu. Ia. Rybakov, *Promyshlennoe zakonodatel'stvo Rossii pervoi poloviny XIX veka* (Moscow, 1986), p. 29 (establishment in 1810 of a 'Special Committee for Reviewing the Condition of Manufactories in Russia'); St Petersburg, Rossiiskii gosudarstvennyi istoricheskii arkhiv (RGIA), fond (f.) 18 (Department of Manufactures and Internal Trade of the Ministry of Finance), opis' (op.) 2, dela (d.) 30, 48 (subsequent developments).

11 A.S. Nifontov, 'Fabrichno-zavodskaia promyshlennost' v predreformennoi Rossii', *Istoriia SSSR*, no. 1 (1983), p. 29.

12 J.H. Bater, *St Petersburg: industrialization and change* (Montreal, 1976), pp. 100–2.

13 RGIA, f. 391 (Resettlement Administration of the Ministry of Agriculture), op. 1, d. 47, list (l.) 190.

14 S. Thompstone, 'Ludwig Knoop, "the Arkwright of Russia"', *Textile History* 15 (1984), p. 64.

15 Vasil'ev, 'Chislennost'', p. 105.

16 Thompstone, 'Ludwig Knoop', Table 3, p. 50.

17 Vasil'ev, 'Chislennost'', Table 9, p. 103.

18 Thompstone, 'Ludwig Knoop', p. 52.

19 R.B. McKean, *St Petersburg between the revolutions: workers and revolutionaries, June 1907–February 1917* (New Haven, CT, and London, 1990), p. 238.

20 Bater, *St Petersburg*, pp. 389–90 (and compare p. 227).

21 B. Mironov, *Russkii gorod v 1740–1860-e gody: demograficheskoe, sotsial'noe i ekonomicheskoe razvitie* (Leningrad, 1990), especially pp. 28–9, 249.

22 N.A. Troinitskii, ed. *Obshchii svod po imperii rezul'tatov razrabotki dannykh pervoi vseobshchei perepisi naseleniia, proizvedennoi 28 ianvaria 1897 goda*, 2 vols (St Petersburg, 1905), vol. i, p. 1.

23 V. Semenov-Tian-Shanskii, *Gorod i derevnia v evropeiskoi Rossii: Ocherk po ekonomicheskoi geografii s 16 kartami i kartogrammi* (St Petersburg, 1910), p. 77.

24 A.G. Rashin, *Naselenie Rossii za 100 let (1811–1913 gg.): Statisticheskie ocherki* (Moscow, 1956), pp. 25 (total population in 1913), 87 (urban population on 1 January 1914).

25 The population of St Petersburg, for example, went up by just under 213 000 between December 1910 and January 1914 but by 301 500 in the shorter period between the outbreak of war in 1914 and the February revolution of 1917: McKean, *St Petersburg between the revolutions*, p. 339.

26 For the decline, see D. Koenker, 'Urbanization and Deurbanization in the Russian Revolution and Civil War', *Journal of Modern History* 57 (1985), pp. 424–50.

27 Bater, *St Petersburg between the revolutions*, pp. 54–5, 91–2, 257, 387.

28 E. Melton, 'The Russian peasantries, 1450–1860', in T. Scott, ed. *The peasantries of Europe from the fourteenth to the eighteenth centuries* (London and New York, 1998), p. 257.
29 V.A. Fedorov, *Pomeshchich'i krest'iane tsentral'no-promyshlennogo raiona Rossii kontsa XVIII – pervoi poloviny XIX v.* (Moscow, 1974), pp. 82–197.
30 P.G. Ryndziunskii, *Krest'ianskaia promyshlennost' v poreformennoi Rossii (60–80-e gody XIX v.)* (Moscow, 1966), pp. 78–80.
31 For the figure of four million, see Tarnovskii, *Melkaia promyshlennost'*, p. 11, note 17, and p. 25.
32 Sir Donald MacKenzie Wallace, *Russia* 2nd edn, 2 vols (London, 1905), vol. i, p. 135–7.
33 F.F. Mendels, 'Proto-industrialization: the first phase of the industrialization process', *Journal of Economic History* 32 (1972), pp. 241–61.
34 See, for example, D. C. Coleman, 'Proto-industrialization: a concept too many', *Economic History Review*, 2nd series, 36 (1983), pp. 435–48.
35 P. Sears McKinsey, 'Kustar' metalworking: the Tver' County nailmakers and the Zemstvo cooperative movement', *Canadian Slavonic Papers*, 24 (1985), pp. 365–84.
36 See, for example, Tarnovskii, *Melkaia promyshlennost'*, pp. 115, 251–2.
37 R.L. Rudolph, 'Family structure and proto-industrialization in Russia', *Journal of Economic History*, 40 (1980), pp. 111–18.
38 V.K. Iatsunskii, 'Izmeneniia v razmeshchenii zemledeliia v evropeiskoi Rossii s kontsa XVIII v. do pervoi mirovoi voiny', in V.K. Iatsunskii, ed. *Voprosy istorii sel'skogo khoziaistva, krest'ianstva i revoliutsionnogo dvizheniia v Rossii: Sbornik statei k 75–letiiu akademika Nikolaia Mikhailovicha Druzhinina* (Moscow, 1961), table 2, pp. 125–7 (my extrapolation).
39 Aleksandr Nikolaevich Engelgardt, *Letters from the country, 1872–1887*, translated and edited by C.A. Frierson (New York and Oxford, 1993), pp. 64–71, 81, 113–14, 222; S. T. Semenov, *Dvadtsat' piat' let v derevne* (Petrograd, 1915), pp. 99, 104–5, 107.
40 A.M. Anfimov, *Krest'ianskoe khoziaistvo evropeiskoi Rossii* (Moscow, 1980), p. 227.
41 For Anfimov's apology see *Krest'ianskoe khoziaistvo*, p. 7.
42 Anfimov, *Krest'ianskoe khoziaistvo*, table 52 on pp. 190–1.
43 V.K. Iatsunskii, 'Osnovnye momenty istorii sel'skokhoziaistvennogo proizvodstva v Rossii s XVI veka do 1917 goda', *Ezhegodnik po agrarnoi istorii vostochnoi Evropy: 1964 god* (Kishinev, 1966), p. 63.
44 V.K. Iatsunskii, 'Izmeneniia', p. 114.
45 J. Metzer, 'Railroad development and market integration: the case of tsarist Russia', *Journal of Economic History*, 34 (1974), table 1, p. 534 (harvest figures for all crops, all grains, rye and wheat between 1894 and 1913).
46 A.P. Berdyshev, *Andrei Timofeevich Bolotov – vydaiushchiisia deiatel' nauki i kul'tury 1738–1833* (Moscow, 1988), pp. 142–5; L.V. Milov, 'A.T. Bolotov – avtor krest'ianskoi entsiklopedii', *Voprosy istorii*, no. 7/8 (1991), pp. 20–1 and 25, note 57.
47 RGIA, f. 379 (Department of State Properties of the Ministry of Finance), op. 2, d. 139, ll. 27–47, 59; V.V. Eliseev, 'Marfinskaia ekonomiia N. A. Bunina', *Voprosy istorii*, no. 7 (1997), p. 174; Anfimov, *Krest'ianskoe khoziaistvo*, table 49, p. 177.
48 O. Figes, *A people's tragedy: the Russian Revolution 1891–1924* (London, 1996), p. 235.
49 Anfimov, *Krest'ianskoe khoziaistvo*, pp. 136, 151, 152–3 (table 44), pp. 174–5, 227.
50 Anfimov, *Krest'ianskoe khoziaistvo*, pp. 174–5.

51 Anfimov, *Krest'ianskoe khoziaistvo*, p. 232.

52 Anfimov, *Krest'ianskoe khoziaistvo*, pp. 171–2.

53 A.S. Nifontov, 'Razvitie sel'skogo khoziaistva Rossii v 60–70-kh godakh XIX veka', *Voprosy istorii*, no. 6 (1967), p. 58.

54 S.L. Hoch, *Serfdom and social control in Russia: Petrovskoe, a village in Tambov* (Chicago, IL, and London, 1986), pp. 30–6.

55 Iatsunskii, 'Osnovnye momenty', p. 55.

56 A.M. Anfimov, *Krupnoe pomeshchich'e khoziaistvo Evropeiskoi Rossii (Konets XIX – nachalo XX veka)* (Moscow, 1969), p. 375.

57 Anfimov, *Krest'ianskoe khoziaistvo*, p. 193.

58 G. Tanquary Robinson, *Rural Russia under the Old Regime* (Berkeley and Los Angeles, CA, 1961; 1st published in 1932), pp. 130, 290, note 24.

59 Troinitskii, *Obshchii svod*, vol. i, pp. 2–3, vol. ii, p. 264 (87 693 911 people out of 125 640 021).

60 K.B. Litvak, 'Perepis' naseleniia 1897 goda o krest'ianstve Rossii (Istochniko-vedcheskii aspekt)', *Istoriia SSSR*, no. 1 (1990), p. 120.

61 P. Bechasnov, 'Kratkii obzor tsifrovykh dannykh', in Troinitskii, ed. *Obshchii svod*, vol. i, pp. xiii–xiv.

62 For a full discussion of the size of the peasantry see D. Moon, 'Estimating the peasant population of late imperial Russia from the 1897 census: a research note', *Europe–Asia Studies*, 48 (1996), pp. 141–53.

63 Anfimov, *Krest'ianskoe khoziaistvo*, table 24, p. 88.

64 Robinson, *Rural Russia under the Old Regime*, p. 97.

65 *Polnoe sobranie zakonov rossiiskoi imperii*, 3rd series 33 vols (St Petersburg, 1885–1916), vol. xxv, p. 790 (no. 26 871, 3 November 1905, the law which, in scheduling the abolition of redemption payments, also made more resources available to the Peasant Land Bank); I.I. Popova, 'Pereselenie krest'ian i zemleustroistvo Sibiri', in A.K. Dzhivelegov *et al.*, eds *Velikaia reforma: Russkoe obshchestvo i krest'ianskii vopros v proshlom i nastoiashchem* 6 vols (Moscow, 1911), vol. vi, p. 257 (the change in government policy on migration to Siberia in 1905–6).

66 RGIA, f. 592 (Peasant Land Bank), op. 3, d. 480, ll. 30–1.

67 RGIA, f. 592, op. 3, d. 272, ll. 1–6.

68 For the view that they did, see S. M. Dubrovskii, *Stolypinskaia zemel'naia reforma* (Moscow, 1963), p. 55.

69 Semenov, *Dvadtsat' piat' let v derevne*, especially pp. 261–3, 361, 370–1.

70 RGIA, f. 395 (Department of Rural Economy of the Ministry of Agriculture), op. 2, d. 2965, l. 3.

71 RGIA, f. 395, op. 2, d. 2965, *passim* (a file entitled 'On measures to limit the fragmentation of small landholdings'), and K.A. Krivoshein, *Aleksandr Vasil'evich Krivoshein: Sud'ba rossiiskogo reformatora* (Moscow, 1993; 1st published in 1973), p. 99.

72 A. Graziosi, *The great Soviet peasant war: Bolsheviks and peasants, 1917–1933* (Cambridge, MA, 1996).

73 See, for example, O. Crisp, 'The pattern of industrialisation in Russia, 1700–1914', in O. Crisp, *Studies in the Russian economy before 1914* (London and Basingstoke, Hants, 1976), p. 5: 'By the commonly accepted criteria of industrialisation Russia in 1914 was not yet an industrialised country'.

74 Robinson, *Rural Russia*, especially pp. 94–116 (ch. 6, 'The hungry village').

75 P. Gregory, 'Economic growth and structural change in tsarist Russia: a case of modern economic growth?', *Soviet Studies* 23 (1971–2), pp. 418–34, taking as its point of departure S. Kuznets, *Modern economic growth* (New Haven, CT, 1966).

76 J.Y. Simms Jr, 'The crisis in Russian agriculture at the end of the nineteenth

century: a different view', *Slavic Review*, 36 (1977), pp. 377–98; B.A. Anderson, *Internal migration during modernization in late nineteenth-century Russia* (Princeton, NJ, 1980), especially, 23–68.

77 P.R. Gregory, *Russian national income 1885–1913* (Cambridge, 1982); *idem, Before command: an economic history of Russia from emancipation to the first Five-Year Plan* (Princeton, NJ, 1994).

78 P.R. Gregory, 'Searching for consistency in historical data: alternate estimates of Russia's industrial production, 1887–1913', *Journal of Economic History*, 57 (1997), pp. 196–202.

9

Popular culture and market development in late-Imperial Russia

STEVE A. SMITH

Commentators were not slow to explain the difficulties of the transition to a market economy in post-Soviet Russia in terms of deep-seated hostility to the market within Russian culture. P.I. Smirnov concludes an article on 'market civilization' and Russian national character thus: 'We agree with those researchers who characterise Russian national character as first and foremost non-market'.[1] N.M. Klopyzhnikova claims that 'the great mass of Russian peasants were never commodity producers, had no experience of independent, economic activity, i.e. were not fully oriented to the market'.[2] And, from a non-liberal perspective, L.N. Vdovina states: 'The Russian communal traditions are a poor base for the kind of social egoism and individualism desired by certain politicians today'.[3] In the West the same view has been echoed by eminent commentators. John Keep argues:

> The public looked askance at the profiteers. . . . Elderly people and blue-collar workers objected vociferously to the high earnings of some entrepreneurs, whom they compared invidiously to the 'nep-men' and 'bourgeois' of popular mythology. The prospect of transition to a free market awakened deep-rooted egalitarian sentiments. . . . Envy of those who had 'made good' had been the foundation of mass support for Stalinism.[4]

The argument of this chapter is that there were indeed values and beliefs in the culture of the Russian peasantry which were antipathetic to the development of a market economy, but I go on to argue that from the time of the emancipation of the serfs in 1861 until the First World War peasants were heavily involved in the market and that cultural norms did not seriously impede this involvement. I suggest that popular attitudes to the market were more complex and contradictory than the above-cited authors suggest, and I explore this ambivalence by briefly examining the period of the First World War and 1917 Revolution, when the free market proved inadequate as a mechanism for feeding the Russian army and townspeople. The chapter concludes by entering a caveat about culturally-based explanations of Russia's current economic travails.

It is useful to begin by reminding ourselves that Russians were not always seen as temperamentally ill-disposed to trade and entrepreneurship. In the seventeenth century foreign visitors to Muscovy were impressed by the country's economic performance and potential.[5] The Swedish diplomat Kilburger noted that Russia's inhabitants 'from the highest to the lowest, love to traffic, which is why there are more shops in the city of Moscow than in Amsterdam or some entire kingdoms'.[6] And Olearius, visiting Russia in the 1630s, commented that 'their cleverness and shrewdness are manifest in their commerce among other activities; when buying and selling for profit, they resort to any expedient they can think of to cheat a neighbour'.[7] It is only fair to mention that such visitors invariably commented also on the ways in which the government restricted the activities of merchants. But Samuel Baron, whilst emphasizing the timidity of merchants and the interference of government, concludes of the seventeenth century that 'successive generations of Muscovite entrepreneurs demonstrated considerable resourcefulness and succeeded in advancing the country's commercial development to a respectable extent'.[8] One may make of such observations what one will; they remind us, however, that Russia's economic backwardness in relation to Western Europe emerged only gradually and that the causes of this increasing economic backwardness may relate less to cultural than to structural factors.

Peter the Great created conditions facilitating the growth of a national market, by stimulating mining, metallurgical, armaments and textile industries, by acquiring Baltic ports (Catherine II later acquired Black Sea ports) and by building roads and canals. Yet there can be little doubt that as the eighteenth century progressed, the market in Russia failed to develop at a pace comparable to that in Western Europe. This was, in the first place, a result of geographical factors, including the harsh climate, the huge size of the Empire and poor communications. The uncertain climate, for instance, led to sharp fluctuations in grain yields and consequent insecurity for food producers and consumers; and long distances to market meant high transportation costs, that made certain kinds of trade unprofitable. In the second place, the underdevelopment of the market was a result of the 'rent-seeking' activities of the state. Since the overwhelming priority of the autocracy was to defend the lengthy borders of the Empire, it tended to monopolize and exploit commerce and industry for its own ends, with detrimental consequences for private enterprise. In particular, credit institutions, insurance mechanisms and commercial law were all poorly developed in comparison with those in Western Europe.[9] Thirdly, whilst commodity and monetary relations did develop within the framework of a serf economy, the latter discouraged labour mobility and a land market. Finally, within this structural context a culture developed which was itself a factor braking market development. In particular, the peasant commune, an eminently rational response to a hostile environment and to the fiscal claims of the state, had a strong collective ethos which punished risk-taking, innovation and investment.[10] The communal peasantry tended to regard the entrepreneurial minority as selfish and individualistic and a threat to the collective interest. In ethical terms, they prized values of mutual aid, reciprocity and a certain commitment to redistribution rather than those of individualism, self-reliance and tolerance of inequality.

If we examine this collective ethos we can more closely identify beliefs and values that were antipathetic to the development of a market culture. First of these was the so-called labour principle (*trudovoe nachalo*). For peasants, physical labour, the stuff of their existence, was the source of wealth and value. The value of land, for example, was determined by the labour invested in it rather than by the price it could command on the market. The land was a resource that belonged to those who worked it and made it productive, and there was resistance to seeing it as a commodity, something to be bought and sold. As is well-known, this meant that the peasantry did not consider that the gentry had legitimate title to the land they owned, since they did not work it by the sweat of their brow.[11] In some ultimate sense, the land was no one's property, except possibly the tsar's, but in the immediate term it was the collective property of the *mir*, with individual households having only a provisional right of use of the land. It is not clear how far the labour principle affected attitudes to other social goods apart from land. To some extent, grain was seen, like land, as a means of subsistence to which all had a right. It was thus, for example, abhorrent to hope that grain prices would be high. Yet the rights of the individual household to dispose of grain – once taxes had been paid – were always greater than they were in relation to land. And after 1861 grain seems increasingly to have been seen as a form of money.[12] It is also noteworthy that deeply-rooted resistance to seeing land as a commodity did not prevent the development of a land market once serfdom was abolished and certain demographic and economic processes had come into play.

Secondly, the labour principle conditioned peasant conceptions of property. For centuries the basic function of the family plot and property of the household was to reproduce the *tiaglo*, or tax-bearing capacity, of the household. Property was thus seen as having a twofold aspect, as both a means of family subsistence and a means of fulfilling one's duties to the state. Customary law distinguished vaguely between collective, individual and intermediate property rights, but terms such as *sobstvennost'*, *vladenie* and *pol'zovanie* were ill-defined.[13] The principal distinction in the peasant community was between the property of the *mir* – crimes against which were punished harshly – and property belonging to outsiders – crimes against which were treated relatively leniently.[14] 'Bourgeois' legal distinctions surrounding property were absent.[15] According to Maksimov, 'To steal something in which no labour has been invested, and which thus represents ill-gained capital, is not a sin . . . [But] everything that has been gained by labour, tended safely, formed by human intelligence and skill, becomes inviolable'.[16] At the same time, peasants had a highly proprietorial attitude to the movable property of their own household and jealously guarded it against threats from other peasants in the commune:

> It is well-known that peasants are the most extreme when it comes to owning private property, and not a single peasant will give up a single one of his kopecks, not a single shred of hay. A peasant is merciless if someone tramples his grain; he will pursue the trespassing to the last degree, he will take a poor man's last shirt, he will beat him up if there is nothing to take, but he will not excuse damage done by trespassing.[17]

Use of property as a means of self-enrichment at the expense of others was condemned by peasants.[18] It was precisely the tendency to use property as a means of capital accumulation that distinguished the kulak. Nevertheless, according to Engelgardt, 'every peasant has a bit of the kulak in him. They will exploit one another's need if given the chance'.[19] However, to demand 'dishonorable' conditions for the hire of horses, to exploit the labour of agricultural workers, to charge high rents or rates of interest was to threaten the solidarity of the commune, and those who engaged in such divisive activities were often called *miroedy* – literally, commune-eaters. This term, incidentally, was commonly used by officials – an indication of the extent to which negative attitudes to capitalism extended to the upper reaches of society.[20] Similarly, peasants viewed the storekeeper or trader as a parasite who made an 'extra charge on the labour of others' ('*na chuzhoi trud nadbavku*'), that is, who forced an income from others without producing anything himself. In practice, of course, poor communications, long distances to markets and the underdevelopment of systems of credit and cooperation made dependence on middlemen inevitable.[21] Nevertheless, commercial intermediaries of all types tended to be seen as *spekulianty*, and attitudes towards them were coloured by antisemitism. Again, such attitudes were mirrored in the higher echelons of society. Certain members of the Congress of Mining Industrialists in the Donbass, for instance, expressed mistrust of the 'whole class of small-time peddlar Jews' (*zhidki skupshchiki*) who 'sell coal in the city, at a higher price of course, and gain an unearned profit on the coal producers' labour and capital'.[22]

Finally, one may note the tendency of peasants to put safety first, to avoid activities that might place their families and the commune at risk. The peasant did not look far into the future, and if he made a surplus in a good year he tended to spend rather than save it. Olga Tian-Shanskaia, in seeking to explain the peasant belief that 'it is a sin to pile up money', was unsure whether this was rooted in deep-seated fatalism, in a psychological reluctance to take charge of one's destiny or whether it was a more pragmatic response to the uncertainties of price that agricultural produce could command from year to year.[23] This way of posing the question is suggestive, since it allows us to think of cultural orientations to the market as existing at two levels.

At the deeper level, just described, there were values and norms in Russian peasant culture that were at odds with those prized by a capitalist society. These values and norms may be said to amount to a rejection of the market as a principle of distributive justice. As we have seen, peasants believed in a fundamental right to subsistence which the community should guarantee its members. They did not believe that access to land should be determined by the market, and they considered that the *mir* should step in to override excessive individualism or tendencies to inequality.[24] Even in developed capitalist societies, of course, the extent to which distribution should be based on need or individual achievement and the extent to which government should interfere to correct inequalities brought about by the operations of the market continue to be contentious issues. But in pre-revolutionary Russia there was little support at any level of society for the market as a mechanism for distributing scarce goods and resources. Sections of the bureaucracy continued to feel unease at – even downright hostility towards – private enterprise. This was not merely because private enterprise competed with the state for financial, material and human resources but also because officials associated it with personal greed and exploitation of the people. In the Ministry of Agriculture, for example, right down to the promulgation of the Stolypin reforms, concern continued to be expressed about the activities of *imushchie, zazhitochnye, kulaki*, who were seen as agents of exploitation.[25] For its part, the intelligentsia associated business with egoism and materialism and satirized the greed, vulgarity and philistinism of Russia's merchant class. At the same time, however, cultural orientations to the market existed at a second, more practical, level, where they comprised those social competencies which peasants drew upon to face new economic opportunities and challenges (for example, the ability to drive a hard bargain) and those dispositions which influenced their ability to take risks and to conduct themselves effectively in the market place (such as the famed 'individualism', already alluded to, which commentators always had difficulty reconciling with peasant collectivism). I would suggest that when judged at this more practical level, peasant culture did provide certain resources for entrepreneurship once the structural conditions for market expansion were in place.[26]

For different reasons, historians in the West and in the former Soviet Union tended to minimize the significance of peasant participation in the market after 1861. Yet the intensification of commodity and monetary relations, the broadening of property and civil rights, the growth of population, urbanization and industrialization and the development of the railways brought about rapidly increasing market involvement on the part of the peasantry. Certain caveats, of course, must be entered. By and large, production for the market was not so much a response to the perceived benefits that the market could bring as something forced on peasants by the need to pay taxes and redemption payments. Nor was involvement in the market necessarily associated with increasing prosperity. Even in grain-surplus regions millions of peasants participated in the market principally as buyers, having little surplus of which to dispose. It was a common pattern, for example, for peasants to have to sell grain in the glutted autumn market and then to have to buy rye in the spring at higher prices.[27] Market participation was also highly differentiated by region, with the Baltic, Ukraine, the North-West, South-West and Siberia much more affected than the Central Black-Earth or Middle Volga regions. Finally, and most obviously, the wealthy minority of peasants was able to take much greater advantage of market opportunities than were poor and middle peasants. Nevertheless, by the end of the nineteenth century market relations were a fact of life for most peasants. An average of about 30 per cent of net grain was marketed per annum between 1909 and 1913.[28] And the sale of agricultural produce, together with earnings of handicraft production and money wages, meant that peasants became purchasers of manufactures, buying cotton, sugar, kerosene and other consumer durables. Finally, we may note that after 1905 there was a huge growth in cooperative credit associations, so that by 1915 some 10 million families were members of these.[29]

In seeking to explore how far peasant culture impeded or facilitated this participation in the market, we must recognize that the 'market' did not exist as an abstract concept for Russian peasants in the way that it does for us today. It was essentially a set of small-scale social relations, consisting of particular commercial transactions with particular individuals, such as the kulak, *skupshchik* or *lavochnik*, in particular places, such as the nearby market (*bazar*), periodic market (*iarmarka*) or shop. Local markets bore an 'almost exclusively petty character, an adjunct to church', and even in the twentieth century many commercial transactions were still conducted via barter or in exchange for labour rather than money.[30] What the market meant to a peasant can be inferred from the description sent to Count V.N. Tenishev by a correspondent in Vladimir guberniia in the 1890s:

There are no traditional middlemen [*skupshchiki*], although in spring certain local inhabitants buy up butter and eggs and trade directly with Moscow. Variations in the price of products are not significant. Occasionally, people buy up rags. Peddlars of different wares have passed into legend. There remain only the scythe sellers from Riazan' who come in May or June and sell on credit until the grain has been threshed. There is regular barter between local peasants and market gardeners, who come from Rostovskii uezd, rye being exchanged for onions, cabbages and cucumber seedlings. Lately, commerce in permanent shops has increased markedly. In the village [*selo*] of An'kovo there are 16 shops and four wholescale concerns [*firmy*], three of which buy up flax and the other hops. Forms of trade carried out by peasants in An'kovo, such as trade in meat, in making white wheatmeal loaves [*kalachi*] to sell at market, and in *maiachestvo*, which is the local word for profiteering, i.e. small-scale buying up of goods to resell to the commission agents of the big depots [*firmy*], are being taken up in the village of Il'inskoe, where commercial entrepreneurship is less strongly developed.[31]

The scattered and impressionistic evidence suggests that there were elements in traditional culture which facilitated peasant involvement in such local and personalized markets. Peasant proverbs, for example, suggest that peasants clearly recognized the different interests of buyer and seller: 'The seller has one price, the buyer another'; 'In trade there are two fools: one gives cheaply, the other asks a high price'. There is recognition that prices are not a matter of whim: 'Don't take your price with you when you go to market'; 'If you overcharge, your wares will stick around, if you sell too cheaply, you won't make a profit'. And proverbs suggest that whilst peasants saw that the aim of trade was to make a profit (*barysh*) - 'Never trade at a loss' – they also recognized that prices fluctuate and that one may make an unforeseen loss – 'Profits and losses travel on one sleigh, live in one pocket'. There is also a rudimentary understanding of the laws of supply and demand: 'When there's a lot, it's cheap; when there's little, it's dear'; 'When little is brought, demand will be high'. But this is coloured by a certain fatalism, a sense that the market is ultimately outside anyone's control. 'There is nothing freer than trade and even there unfreedom lives' (*Vol'nee torgu net a i tam nevolya zhivet*); 'In trade money is free, but the buyers and sellers are unfree' (*Na torgu den'gi na vole, a kuptsy i prodavtsy vse pod nevolei*).[32] Other evidence shows that peasants paid minute attention to the prices of different commodities and understood why they fluctuated. In his remarkable diary, A. A. Zamaraev, an industrious peasant from a village near Tot'ma in Vologda, wrote of 1914:

> The weather this summer was thoroughly bad. Grains and grasses were undernourished and because of this, livestock dropped terribly in price in the autumn. Cows were twelve rubles each, horses five or six. Hay cost 20 to 60 kopecks a pud, oats 1 ruble 50 kopecks.[33]

The rapid growth of the market in Imperial Russia was cut short by the First World War. War, revolution and civil war were starkly to demonstrate the capacity of peasants to withdraw from the market, proving that the rural economy remained fundamentally a subsistence one, in which the greater part of food, and to some extent handicrafts, was consumed by the families that produced it. During the first year of war more than seven million men were taken out of agriculture, and these were followed by another eight million during the next two years. This led to a reduction in sown area, especially on landowners' estates. At the same time, the ending of grain exports meant that domestic grain supplies actually increased by some 10 million tons a year.[34] Nevertheless, low grain prices, fixed by the government at the start of the war, together with rapid price inflation and a lack of manufactured goods, meant that peasants became increasingly unwilling to market grain. By 1916 gross yield from peasant farms had fallen by 40 per cent, compared with the average for pre-war years; and only 17.1 per cent was marketed. The volume and ratio of marketed output from peasant farms thus fell with the war, although, curiously, the ratio actually rose between 1914 and 1916 – from an untypical low of 11.6 per cent in 1914, to 17.1 per cent in 1916.[35] With less and less to buy, peasants shifted from cash crops (wheat, barley and sugar beet) to subsistence crops (rye, oats and potatoes). They ate more, fed their livestock better, stocked up their barns and turned their grain into vodka rather than selling it for a derisory profit. Given that large procurements went to the army, this led to severe shortages of food in the city, causing the tsarist government in November 1916 to introduce a monopoly on grain. This presaged the requisitioning of grain at fixed prices that was expanded by the Provisional Government and ruthlessly executed by the Bolsheviks.

As the supply situation worsened in the towns, hostility towards those who made a profit out of shortages of food and subsistence intensified. Much urban opposition to the market took a 'peasant' form – not surprising, given the huge numbers of peasants who flocked to the cities – acquiring its most dramatic and horrible form in the *samosud*. This was essentially a form of mob law imposed by the rural community against those who breached its norms or threatened its well-being, usually inflicted on outsiders. It could take several forms – the most vicious being reserved for horse thieves.[36] As used to describe crowd actions in cities, the term had a looser sense, and the nature of the 'community' in whose name the crowd acted was less clear-cut. According to one report, 'a samosud occurs simply when there is no court and the people has lost its confidence in the force of government and law'.[37] Like the word 'pogrom', which was also used by the press to describe these crowd actions, the term could refer to a number of distinct types of action. Sometimes it referred to food riots; sometimes to the looting of shops; sometimes to the lynching of officers by soldiers and sailors; sometimes to the summary punishment of thieves (something which happened increasingly in 1917, as the militia lost its authority). But there was one type of *samosud* – crowd action against those accused of 'speculation' – that is particularly revealing of popular attitudes to the market. A nasty example occurred in Pereiaslavl' in October 1917. A long line of people was standing outside a shop, waiting to buy galoshes. On being told that the shop had sold out, the queue started to disperse. Then a cart, laden with boxes, was spotted coming out of the building. Some of those who had been waiting stopped the driver and, to their fury, discovered that the boxes contained galoshes. The crowd stormed the shop, killing the owner, and then turned on adjacent shops and stalls, leaving eight proprietors dead and 20 wounded.[38] Another dramatic case took place in September 1917 in Khar'kov, where the local food board was using the Kamennyi Stolb hotel as a storehouse. After 'provocative rumours spread that goods were being taken out for speculative ends', a huge crowd gathered in the hotel yard. Having milled around for some time, members of the crowd burst into the hotel in search of the owner. He managed to escape and summon the cavalry, but just as the latter arrived, a shot rang out in the hotel yard. In the confusion, the cry went up that the owner and a Jew had shot and killed two cavalrymen, whereupon the crowd began frantically to search for the culprit. Someone pointed to a Jew in the crowd, named Moreino, who was seized and beaten up. The mob dragged him to the militia office and ordered the official to interrogate him. However, after 10 minutes, they grew restive and demanded that the official release the prisoner into their custody. As the official was trying to calm them down, Moreino was grabbed and thrown into the air. After he had hit the pavement several times, his throat was cut.[39] These two cases may have been particularly shocking, but when set beside many briefer reports of crowd action against *spekulianty*, one can discern a pattern.[40] Although it is often soldiers and sailors who initiate violence, the role played by women in these *samosudy*, especially by soldiers' wives, is striking. This is not surprising, given that it fell to women to stand for long hours for food and other scarce items. In most cases, *samosudy* occurred after women had queued in vain for bread or meat or uncovered some particularly scandalous example of profiteering. It was not unusual for the militia to step in to try to calm the situation, but they rarely succeeded, whether because they were outnumbered or because they secretly sympathized with the crowd. The victims of *samosudy* were not always killed, yet these actions were often characterized by horrific brutality (in a huge riot at Kazanskaia stanitsa in Kuban' in early 1918 40 presumed speculators were killed, and four had their bodies quartered).[41] Such spectacular violence – in the sense of violence making a spectacle of itself – seems to have been designed *pour encourager les autres*, as a warning to other traders to watch out. There is, of course, nothing peculiarly Russian about hostility to black marketeers – it was a feature of life in all belligerent countries – yet the *samosud* was a specific cultural archetype and it appealed directly to the values discussed above: a strong belief in the right of everyone to subsistence; an objection to those whose livelihood was gained not by honest toil but by exploiting the privation of others; a belief that traders deliberately created shortages in order to rack up profits; and, finally, a belief that Jews were to blame for the misfortunes of the Russian people.

The way peasants saw the market during the war years can be gleaned from the diary of Zamaraev, a peasant of conservative disposition in remote Tot'ma.[42] In March 1915 he records, 'now there are no drunks, there is no wine. But they say that in the towns there is vodka in some places. It means everything is available for the rich'.[43] In January 1916 he contrasts Russia unfavourably to England, 'where all classes of the population from the highest lords to the poor' are forgoing luxuries in aid of the war effort.[44] By 1916 there was nothing in the shops in Tot'ma, and in September he comments with satisfaction that three sugar magnates in Kiev have been jailed for speculation.[45] Although he lived far from any city, Zamaraev was not unsympathetic to the plight of the towns:

Townsfolk complain about the peasantry, that they try to sell dear, and call us all fleecers [*zhivoderami*]. In fact life for townsfolk, if they are not big officials, is very hard. Everything is expensive, both goods in the shops and peasant produce'.[46]

In January 1917 he recorded:

The grain crisis is particularly acute, there is very little in the towns. They distribute it by ration . . . . In some places there is no meat, in others no salt, in others they sit in the dark because there is no kerosene.[47]

Though these are the views of one man, there is evidence that they reflect a willingness on the part of peasants to set up fair exchange relations between town and country, so long as these did not seriously disadvantage them. At the First Congress of Soviets of Peasant Deputies in May 1917, delegates demanded a state monopoly on all products of mass consumption at fixed prices, restitution of order in transport and curtailment of capitalist profits. At the Second Congress on 26 November they demanded strict control of production and distribution by workers, peasants and employees. These demands, of course, were put forward by members of the Socialist-Revolutionary party, not by rank-and-file peasants, yet they appear to have had the backing of their rural constituents. Many district (*uezd*) soviet congresses, for example, including ones in grain-surplus *guberniias* (provinces), expressed support for the state monopoly and for fixed prices, though they were careful to say that such prices should be fixed by local organs and that they wished to deal with cooperatives and credit associations rather than with central procurement agencies. More problematically, these congresses demanded exchange of grain for fabrics, leather, iron goods, tea or sugar rather than for money, a demand that was palpably unrealistic given the collapse of industrial production.[48] At the beginning of March 1918, the congress of soviets of Shuia and Kovrovskii *uezds* in Ivanovo-Voznesensk declared:

the most radical measure of struggle with market speculation . . . is consumer cooperation, along with measures to regulate prices on the private market, without at this serious time disrupting the bringing to market of necessary produce. Allow commodity exchange of manufactures, not stopping at requisition . . . . Draw the cooperatives into direct, intimate work with food procurement and distribution. The principle should be 50% of purchases for the uezd and the guberniia department and 50% for the locality.[49]

Such positions were, of course, derived from (left) Socialist Revolutionary ideology, and it is irrelevant to the purposes of this paper whether or not they constituted a practical alternative to Bolshevik attempts to eliminate the market in favour of a state monopoly on distribution. But their contradictory combination of support for free trade, in the shape of exchange of grain for manufactures, together with recognition of the right of public organs (preferably local and cooperative) to requisition food, may well reflect ambivalences in peasant culture. On the one hand, in spite of blood-curdling threats from the Bolsheviks, peasants proved throughout the civil war that they were determined to uphold their right to trade. On the other, they do not emerge as principled believers in free trade, since they are not deaf to appeals to cooperation and to the subsistence ethic. This would be consistent with the view, articulated above, that at the deepest level peasants had deep reservations about the market as a just mechanism for allocating scarce resources. Yet even during the darkest days of the Civil War peasants never withdrew completely from the market. Above the mistrust of the self-seeking and inequality engendered by the unbridled market lay more adaptive, pragmatic and individualistic dispositions. Peasant culture, in other words, was neither monolithic nor immutable.

In conclusion, we should not deduce that 'market-friendly' elements in peasant culture 'caused' peasants to operate successfully as commodity producers and consumers, since culture does not determine the ends of economic action in this way. Rather economic circumstances present individuals with various choices, and culture serves as a tool kit from which they can select elements to construct an appropriate economic strategy.[50] Conversely, we should be careful about blaming Russia's current woes too readily on deficiencies in its culture. There may indeed, as Vdovina avers, be deep-seated cultural resistances to the 'social egoism and individualism' demanded by economic reformers; yet public opinion surveys show that a substantial majority favours the proposition that a 'free market is essential to [Russia's] economic development'.[51] If there is a decided coolness towards the free market, this derives less from the 'deep structure' of Russian culture than from a pragmatic assessment of the benefits and losses that the market to date has brought to post-Soviet Russia. The history of late-Imperial Russia suggests that if the market starts to work effectively, Russians will not deterred by inherited norms and values from operating in it successfully.

Notes

1 P.I. Smirnov, 'Dvizhenie Rossii k rynochnoi tsivilizatsii i russkii natsional'nyi kharakter', *Vestnik Leningradskogo Universiteta* (1991), p. 104.
2 N.M. Klopyzhnikova, 'Vliianie traditsionnoi krest'ianskoi kul'tury na stanov-lenie rynochnykh otnoshenii na sele', *Problemy perekhoda Rossii k rynochnoi ekonomike*, Sbornik rabot avtorov poluchivshikh granty Moskovskogo otdele-niia Rossiiskogo nauchnogo fonda i Fonda Forda (Moscow, 1996), p. 107.
3 L.N. Vdovina, 'Chto est' "my"? (Russkoe natsional'noe samosoznanie v kontektse istorii ot Srednevekov'e k Novomy vremeni)', in *Russkii narod: istoricheskaia sud'ba v XX veke* (Moscow, 1993), p. 13.
4 J. Keep, *Last of the empires: a history of the Soviet Union, 1945–1991* (Oxford, 1996), pp. 395–6.
5 P. Dukes, *The making of Russian absolutism,1613–1801* (London, 1982), p. 51.
6 B. Kurts, 'Sochineniia Kil'burgera o russkoi torgovle v tsarstvovanie Alekseia Mikhailovicha' (1915). Cited in W. Kirchner, 'Western businessmen in Russia: practices and problems', *Business History Review*, XXXVIII (autumn 1964), pp. 315–27.
7 S.H. Baron (ed. and trans.), *The travels of Olearius in seventeenth-century Russia* (Stanford, CA, 1967), p. 133.
8 S.H. Baron, 'Entrepreneurs and entrepreneurship in sixteenth/seventeenth Russia', in G. Guroff and F.V. Carstensen, eds *Entrepreneurship in Imperial Russia and the Soviet Union* (Princeton, NJ, 1983), p. 56.
9 See P. Gatrell's contribution to this volume (Chapter 6).
10 In an interesting study of different ethnic groups of peasants in Ufa province, Rodnov shows that Russian peasants were more likely than Bashkirs, Tatars, Belorussians and others to be kulaks (that is, to farm more than 15 *desiatins* of sown land). However, such entrepreneurial Russian peasants were drawn chiefly from the ranks of migrants, former state peasants and the peculiar group of Urals peasants with legal title to their land (*korennye sobstvenniki*). The mass of communal Russian peasants, concentrated in the north, west and central areas of the province, were far less likely to engage in entrepreneurial farming. M.I. Rodnev, *Osobennosti vkkhozhdeniia razlichnykh natsional'nykh grupp kres'tianstva v rynochnuiu ekonomiku v nachale XX veka (na primere Ufimskoi gubernii)* (Ufa, 1998), pp. 18–21.
11 For examples of this attitude in the 1905–7 Revolution, see M. Perrie, 'The Russian peasant movement of 1905–7', in B. Eklof and S.P. Frank, eds *The world of the Russian peasant: post-emancipation culture and society* (Boston, MA, 1990), p. 205.
12 I.N. Slepnev, 'Novye rynochnye realii i ikh prelomlenie v mentalite porefor-mennogo krest'ianstva' in V.P. Danilov and L.V. Milov eds *Mentalitet i agrarnoe razvitie Rossii (XIX–XXvv.)* (Moscow, 1996), p. 224; A.N. Engel-gardt, *Letters from the country, 1872–1887*, translated and edited by C.A. Frierson (New York, 1993), p. 208.
13 G.P. Sazonov, *Krest'ianskaia zemel'naia sobstvennost' v Porkhovskom uezde* (St Petersburg, 1890).
14 C. Worobec, 'Horse thieves and peasant justice in post-emancipation Imperial Russia', *Journal of Social History*, 21 (1987), pp. 281–93; M. Perrie, 'Folklore as

evidence of peasant mentalité: social attitudes and values in Russian popular culture', *Russian Review*, 48 (1989), pp. 133–34.

15 O.Iu. Iakshiian, 'Sobstvennost' v mentalitete russkikh krest'ian', in *Mentalitet i agrarnoe razvitie*, p. 103.

16 S. Maksimov, 'Narodnye prestupleniia i neschastiia', *Otechestvennye zapiski*, 183 (1869); Cited in V. Chalidze, *Ugolovnaia Rossiia* (New York, 1977), p. 25.

17 Engelgardt, *Letters from the country*, p. 60.

18 B. Mironov, *Istorik i sotsiologiia* (Leningrad, 1984), p. 22.

19 Engelgardt, *Letters from the country*, p. 223.

20 R.H. McNeal, *Tsar and Cossacks, 1855–1914* (Basingstoke, Hants, 1987), p. 121; P. Gatrell, 'Economic culture, economic policy and economic growth in Russia, 1861–1914', *Cahiers du monde russe*, XXXV, 1–2 (janvier–juin 1995), pp. 37–52.

21 G.P. Sazonov, *Rostovnichestvo-kulachestvo: nabliudeniia i issledovaniia* (St Petersburg, 1894); R. Gvozdev, *Kulachestvo-rostovshchichestvo: ego obshchest-venno-ekonomicheskoe znachenie* (St Petersburg, 1899).

22 T.H. Friedgut, *Iuzovka and revolution: life and work in Russia's Donbass, 1869–1924* (Princeton, NJ, 1989), p. 29.

23 O.S. Tian-Shanskaia, *Village life in late tsarist Russia*, D.L. Ransel, ed. (Bloomington, IN, 1993), p. 144.

24 On the basis of these characteristics one might argue that the Russian communal peasantry subscribed to a moral economy, but I have avoided the term, since my point is that it was no bar to 'rational peasants' taking advantage of the opportunities which the market had to offer. The *locus classicus* of this debate is J. Scott, *The moral economy of the peasant* (New Haven, CT, 1976); S. Popkin, *The rational peasant: the political economy of rural society in Vietnam* (Berkeley, CA, 1979).

25 Y. Kotsonis, *Continuity and change in Russian agrarian history: agricultural cooperatives in the European north, 1900–29*, PhD dissertation, Columbia University, New York, 1991.

26 My general interpretation is broadly in accord with Timothy Mixter's account of peasant involvement in hiring markets. On the one hand, he emphasizes their positive attitude towards the latter:

> Migrant labourers knew that they had some power inside the hiring market and little outside it . . . . They helped to create it by sabotaging the winter hiring system when they learned that through the recruitment fairs they could get higher wages. They perpetuated the market by being reluctant to hire out to estates that were far from it and returned to the *rynok* frequently to hire anew and check on the latest wage rate and information.

On the other hand, he stresses their moral reservations:

> Migrants wanted a free market but one regulated by their definitions of morality. They wanted the security of dependable relations and in the hiring market insisted that employers be moral and not deceitful. For themselves, though, they often rejected the tenets of a moral economy which they had in some ways tried to impose on employers. They wanted freedom of action so that they could use their mobility to play on employer anxieties and possibly garner higher wages by playing the market.

T. Mixter, 'The hiring market as workers' turf: migrant agricultural labourers and the mobilization of collective action in the Steppe grainbelt of European Russia, 1853–1913', in E. Kingston-Mann and T. Mixter, eds *Peasant economy, culture and politics of European Russia, 1800–1921* (Princeton, NJ, 1992), pp. 335, 337.

27 G.T. Robinson, *Rural Russia under the Old Regime* (Berkeley, CA, 1932), p. 103.

28 In 1913 the net grain product has been valued at 3725 million rubles and marketed output at 957 million rubles, a ratio of 26 per cent. P.R. Gregory, 'Grain marketings and peasant consumption, Russia, 1885–1913', *Explorations in Economic History*, 17 (1980), p. 157.

29 Mironov, *Istorik i sotsiologiia*, p. 29.

30 Ia. Iakovlev, *Derevnia kak ona est': ocherki Nikol'skoi volosti, Kurskoi gubernii* (Moscow, 1923), p. 42.

31 B.M. Firsov and I.G. Kiseleva eds *Byt velikorusskikh kresti'an-zemlepashtsev: opisanie materialov etnograficheskogo biuro kniazia V. N. Tenisheva* (St Petersburg, 1993), p. 114.

32 These examples were all collected by V.I. Dal' in the mid-nineteenth century and are cited in Slepnev, 'Novye rynochnye realii', *passim*.

33 V.V. Morozov and N.I. Reshetnikov eds *Dnevnik Totemskogo krest'ianina A. A. Zamaraeva, 1906–1922gg.* (Moscow, 1995), p. 97.

34 T.M. Kitanina, *Voina, khleb i revoliutsiia. Prodovol'stvennyi vopros v Rossii, 1914–oktiabr 1917* (Leningrad, 1985), pp. 22, 26.

35 A.M. Anfimov, *Rossiiskaia derevnia v gody pervoi mirovoi voiny* (Moscow, 1962), p. 280. Anfimov mentions that in the boom years, 1909–13, peasants marketed just under a quarter of their gross grain yield, which represented about three quarters of the total grain marketed. This compares with Gregory's estimate of a ratio of marketed output of *net* grain yield of roughly 30 per cent. Gregory, 'Grain marketings'.

36 S.P. Frank, 'Popular justice, community and culture among the Russian peasantry', in Eklof and Frank, eds *The world of the Russian peasant*, pp. 133–53.

37 *Zemlia*, 16 June 1917, p. 3.

38 *Gazeta Kopeika*, 5 October 1917, p. 4.

39 *Gazeta Kopeika*, 29 September 1917, p. 4.

40 The generalizations that follow are based on my collection of press reports of *samosudy*. For other instances see D.P. Koenker and W.G. Rosenberg, *Strikes and revolution in Russia, 1917* (Princeton, NJ, 1989), pp. 259–60.

41 *Krasnaia Gazeta*, 15 March 1918, p. 2.

42 A. Chaianov described the Tot'ma district as 'one of the remotest corners of our country and one of the most heavily based on the natural economy'. A. Chaianov, *The theory of peasant cooperatives*, D. Wedgwood Benn, trans (London, 1991), p. 92.

43 *Dnevnik Totemskogo krest'ianina*, p. 103.

44 *Dnevnik Totemskogo krest'ianina*, p. 125.

45 *Dnevnik Totemskogo krest'ianina*, p. 146.

46 *Dnevnik Totemskogo krest'ianina*, p. 148.

47 *Dnevnik Totemskogo krest'ianina*, p. 152.

48 Iu.A. Il'in, 'Gosudarstvennoe regulirovanie i rynochnye otnosheniia krest'ianskikh khoziastv tsentra Rossii v gody grazhdanskoi voiny i interventsii (oktiabr' 1917g. – mart 1919g.)', in *Voprosy istorii ekonomicheskikh i politicheskikh otnoshenii v Rossii (XXv.): sbornik rabot avtorov poluchivshikh granty Moskovskogo otdeleniia Rossiiskogo nauchnogo fonda i Fonda Forda* (Moscow, 1996), pp. 9–13.

49 Cited *Voprosy istorii*, p. 8.

50 A. Swidler, 'Culture in action: symbols and strategies', *American Sociological Review*, 51 (1986), pp. 273–286.

51 D.S. Mason, 'Attitudes towards the market and political participation in the postcommunist states', *Slavic Review*, 54, 2 (1995), pp. 385–406.

10

Popular monarchism: the myth of the ruler from Ivan the Terrible to Stalin

MAUREEN PERRIE

Popular faith in the particular benevolence of rulers towards their humblest subjects was not unique to Russia, but popular monarchism has generally been regarded as a distinctive and durable feature of Russian peasant mentality. Some have suggested that it may help to explain the persistence of the autocratic system into the twentieth century; but, paradoxically, popular monarchist ideas played a major part in most of the peasant uprisings in tsarist Russia that constituted the main threat to the stability of the regime before the revolutions of 1905 and 1917.

The phenomenon which Western scholars tend to characterize as 'popular monarchism' or 'the myth of the tsar' was conventionally described by Russian historians in the Soviet period as the 'naive monarchism' or 'monarchist illusions' of the peasant masses. From the 1930s onwards, Soviet scholars' views on peasant political consciousness were influenced by Stalin's assertion (in 1931) that Razin and Pugachev, the leaders of two major popular revolts, were tsarists who acted against the landowners but for the 'good tsar'.[1] From then onwards it became an axiom of Soviet historiography that the four great 'peasant wars' of the seventeenth and eighteenth centuries, led by Bolotnikov, Razin, Bulavin and Pugachev, were dominated by the ideology of naive monarchism.[2]

Manifestations of popular monarchism continued throughout the nineteenth century and into the revolution of 1905. With the end of the Russian monarchy in 1917 – apparently unlamented by the mass of the people – the phenomenon could be assumed to have come to an end. But some scholars have suggested that popular attitudes to Stalin bore more than a passing resemblance to the earlier 'myth of the tsar'; and this chapter will therefore consider popular monarchism in relation to the Stalin period as well as to pre-revolutionary Russia.

The tsarist period

Popular monarchism in the tsarist period assumed three main forms: folklore about 'good' tsars, popular support for royal pretenders and 'rebellions in the name of the tsar'.

Two major historical figures feature as the heroes of folklore cycles about 'good' tsars: Ivan IV ('the Terrible') and Peter I ('the Great'). Ivan the Terrible is depicted in a number of ballads (*istoricheskie pesni*) loosely based on such historical events as the conquest of Kazan' and the *oprich-nina* terror, as well as in a number of folktales (*skazki*) with 'wandering' (universal or international) motifs about benevolent monarchs who act as patrons and protectors of representatives of the lower classes in society. Ivan appears in folklore as a strict but just ruler, whose harshness is directed primarily against the 'traitor boyars' – scheming members of the upper classes who cheat and betray the tsar while also oppressing and exploiting his ordinary subjects.[3] Similar themes appear in the folklore about Peter the Great, who also features in soldiers' and sailors' songs about the capture of Azov, the Great Northern War, and the building of ships and canals.[4]

The folklore about Ivan and Peter as 'good tsars' was not associated with any specific popular movements but it created positive images of benevolent rulers of the past that were used as touchstones for the evaluation of subsequent monarchs. Later tsars who failed to match up to this ideal became the targets of pretenders (royal impostors) claiming to be the 'true tsar'.

Russian history, like the history of many other monarchies, presents a variety of types of pretender. Not all were associated with popular monarchism: some operated only outside Russia and made no attempt to gain popular support (Timofei Akundinov, for example, who claimed to be a son of Tsar Vasilii Shuiskii; and 'Princess Tarakanova', who called herself the daughter of the Empress Elizabeth).[5] Others, who acted within Russia, such as the False Dimitriis of the Time of Troubles of the early seventeenth century, attempted to recruit support from all sectors of society, not just from the peasants and poorer townspeople. (One of the advantages of royal pretence as a mobilizing device was the potentially universal and supraclass appeal of the monarchical principle.) Many pretenders, however, were themselves of lower-class social origin and recruited their support primarily among the 'masses'. Into this category come Cossack pretenders such as 'Tsarevich Peter' in the Time of Troubles, whose orgy of executions of traitor boyars in 1606–7 may have been modelled on the *oprichnina* of his putative grandfather, Ivan the Terrible.[6] Emel'ian Pugachev, the Don Cossack who claimed to be Peter III, the husband whom Catherine II ('the Great') had deposed and murdered in 1762, also appealed primarily to his fellow Cossacks and to enserfed peasants.

Pugachev claimed that the nobles had tried to kill Peter III because of his sympathy for the ordinary people but that he had escaped death and was returning to regain his throne and grant freedom to the peasants and Cossacks.[7]

The Pugachev rising was the only significant Russian revolt to be led by a pretender. Most instances of popular monarchism from the seventeenth to the twentieth centuries fall into the category of 'rebellions in the name of the tsar', in which popular discontent with government policies was directed against the tsar's evil advisers and agents (the traitor boyars) rather than against the monarch himself.[8] Early examples of this phenomenon include the urban revolts of the mid-seventeenth century,[9] one of which has been the subject of a detailed study by the Russian historian N.N. Pokrovskii, who consciously used Daniel Field's term, 'rebels in the name of the tsar' (*buntovshchiki vo imia tsaria*) to describe the insurgents.[10]

In April 1648 the population of the Siberian town of Tomsk rebelled against the oppression, corruption and abuse practised by the town governor (*voevoda*), Prince Osip Shcherbatyi. Shcherbatyi was deposed and imprisoned by the townspeople, who subsequently accused him of treason (*slovo i delo gosudarevo*). A series of petitions addressed to the tsar by the people of Tomsk declared that the governor had acted against the sovereign's interests, since Shcherbatyi's demands on the townspeople had prevented them from fulfilling their obligations to the state. When a response from Moscow to their petitions was eventually received in Tomsk, the townspeople claimed that the tsar's proclamations were false. Rumours spread that the tsar's true proclamation had been altered in Moscow by the boyars and officials; and a new wave of unrest ensued in the town.[11]

Notions typical of 'rebellion in the name of the tsar' also characterized the Cossack-led revolts of Sten'ka Razin in 1669–71 and Kondratii Bulavin in 1707–8. In March 1670 Razin called on his Cossacks to

> go from the Don to the Volga, and from the Volga to go to Russia against the sovereign's enemies and traitors, to remove from the Muscovite state the traitor boyars and the counsellors and governors and officials in the towns.[12]

And Bulavin issued a proclamation in March 1708 beseeching his supporters 'to stand . . . for our pious tsar' and to oppose 'the wicked men – princes and boyars and profiteers and Germans – for their evil deeds'.[13]

Several examples of rebellion in the name of the tsar can also be found in the nineteenth century. David Moon's study of serfs' 'misunderstandings' of tsarist legislation in the 1830s–50s examines a number of cases where peasants claimed to believe that local officials and landowners were concealing or distorting laws that conveyed the tsar's true wishes.[14] The peasant unrest of the 1860s–70s which followed the promulgation of the Emancipation Act of 1861 provides the two classic cases of 'rebels in the name of the tsar' that are considered in Daniel Field's book. The first of these was the Bezdna affair of 1861, when the peasant Anton Petrov interpreted the Emancipation Statutes as granting the serfs 'true' liberty (*volia*), that is, freedom from outside intervention in their affairs and especially from the obligation to continue to work for the landowner. Troops were brought in to disperse the crowds who had gathered to hear Petrov's exposition of the Act, and many peasants were killed when they refused to surrender. The second episode examined by Field is the Chigirin affair of 1876–7, when the revolutionary Populist Iakov Stefanovich forged a false charter in the tsar's name, calling on the peasants to organize themselves into a secret society (*druzhina*) in order to obtain the land and true liberty that had been promised in the Emancipation Act. Many peasants were recruited into the society, but it was discovered by the police, and a wave of arrests ensued.[15]

'Rebellion in the name of the tsar' continued into the early twentieth century. Widespread agrarian unrest in 1902–3 in the Ukrainian provinces of Poltava and Khar'kov was precipitated by the distribution of revolutionary proclamations which the peasants apparently interpreted as manifestos from the tsar granting them land and freedom.[16] In the course of the revolution of 1905–7, too, many peasant disturbances were precipitated by rumours of the appearance of an imperial manifesto granting a general redistribution of the land.[17]

A number of questions have arisen in connection with popular monarchism. How universal was it? Was it really as 'naive' and 'illusory' as Soviet historians claimed? How sincere were peasants' professions of faith in the tsar? Did it underpin or subvert the tsarist system?

It should not be assumed that popular monarchism was a universal phenomenon in tsarist Russia. There is a considerable amount of evidence that some popular attitudes towards the tsar were ambivalent or even hostile from as early as the sixteenth and seventeenth centuries. The popular image of Ivan the Terrible was certainly not unambiguously positive. Some of the folklore depicts his killing of innocent victims from among the common people. Such episodes (for example, the tsar's punitive raid on Novgorod in 1570) are often presented as the result of false denunciations by traitors – or of the hot-tempered tsar himself prematurely jumping to the wrong conclusions. But although his injustice is explained in these ways, it is not excused; at best, in such cases, Ivan is brought to repentance, often as the result of some miraculous intervention.[18]

The phenomenon of pretence also shows that Russians did not have an uncritical reverence for the reigning tsar: the concept of the 'true' tsar or tsarevich, hidden until the time was right for him to claim his inheritance, implied that the tsar on the throne was 'false'. Supporters of the First False Dimitrii in 1604–5 regarded Boris Godunov as a usurper; and when the pretender was himself overthrown in 1606, his murder was justified as the elimination of an impostor, apostate and sorcerer.[19]

Even some episodes that are conventionally depicted as 'rebellions in the name of the tsar' provide ambiguous indicators concerning popular attitudes towards the reigning monarch. In her recent study of the 1648 uprising in Moscow, Valerie Kivelson notes that while much of the evidence suggests that the rebels held the traditional view that the tsar was good and only his advisers were evil, some of the sources can be interpreted as condemning Tsar Aleksei himself. For example, the bondsman Savinka Korepin allegedly said, 'the tsar is young and stupid, and everything [actually] comes from the mouths of the boyars Boris Ivanovich Morozov and Il'ia Danilovich Miloslavskii. They manage everything and the Sovereign knows this and keeps silent. The devil stole his mind'.[20]

With the rise of Old Belief as a protest against the reforms of the Orthodox Church introduced by Patriarch Nikon in the 1650s, hostility towards the reigning tsar assumed a distinctive religious form. Tsar Aleksei Mikhailovich and his son Peter the Great were both identified as Anti-Christ by Old Believers; and, in the case of Peter, rumours were also prevalent that he was a changeling or substitute tsar. By the nineteenth century most of the more extreme and apocalyptic forms of Old Believer protest – such as self-immolation – had disappeared, but many continued to refuse to pray for the reigning tsar in church.[21]

Faith in the tsar, and acceptance of the monarchical principle, were not, of course, peculiar to the peasants: the ideology of monarchism was generally accepted by all strata of Russian society (with the exception of a small handful of radical intellectuals) until the late nineteenth century. The theoretical basis for popular monarchism was thus in many respects identical to that of the monarchism of the elite. Religious ideas, in Russia as elsewhere in Europe, were of paramount importance: the tsar was chosen by God as his representative on earth, and his subjects were required to obey him as a sacred figure.[22]

Patriotic ideas, too, were associated with the figure of the tsar in all parts of Russian society. The monarch was the symbol of the nation and of the state, and undoubtedly the role played by Ivan IV and Peter I in the defence of Russia against foreign foes played a part in their idealization in folklore.[23] Even in the Soviet period some Russian historians recognized that the autocracy attracted a degree of popular support because it was identified with the national interest. In the words of one contributor to a memorable debate on the nature of Russian absolutism, the peasants supported the monarchy partly because 'in reality the feudal state to a certain extent expressed not only the interests of the ruling class but also common national interests (especially in the sphere of foreign policy)' – although he was quick to add that 'in the last resort it also subordinated these to its class aims'.[24]

It was not only Soviet historians, however, who believed that 'in the last resort' popular support for the monarchy was illusory. Daniel Field argued that popular monarchism was a very different phenomenon from the monarchism of the privileged strata of Russian society ('the loyalty or chauvinism of the comfortable, the fortunate, or the suborned'), since the peasants, unlike the elites, were oppressed by the tsar's agents. In defiance of common sense and experience, the peasantry apparently believed that the tsar was their patron and benefactor.[25] 'The myth of the tsar was false', Field asserts flatly.[26]

Many explanations of popular monarchism have stressed its roots in the backwardness, superstition and patriarchalism of Russian peasant society. ('Patriarchalism' was the standard explanation of Soviet historians, buttressed by quotations from Lenin.) Populist revolutionaries such as Stepniak (S.M. Kravchinskii) offered views similar to those of the Marxists:

> For all primitive minds the monarchical idea has a kind of peculiar fascination. The balance of powers, the mutual checks and the control of the various springs of a complicated political machinery, are pure Hebrew to them; whilst they can grasp the idea of a good, benevolent man without an effort. It is difficult for them not to take the empty official phraseology as to their Sovereign's love, and solicitude for their good, literally.[27]

Soviet historians, too, stressed the role of official propaganda, with its 'social demagogy', or rhetoric of paternal benevolence, in creating the naive monarchist illusions of the peasants.[28]

The Soviet concept of 'monarchist illusions' on the part of the peasants, created to some extent by the 'social demagogy' of the tsarist government, implies a relationship between ruler and people based on the manipulation of the latter by the former. Perhaps a more satisfactory, and certainly a more sophisticated, approach to an understanding of popular attitudes is suggested in the work of a US historian of early modern Russia. Noting that 'historians frequently blame the Russian people for their own subordination to tyrants', Valerie Kivelson comments that,

> Instead of attributing the docility of the masses to either false consciousness or spiritual weakness, it seems more fruitful to attempt to understand the compliance (or non-compliance) of the governed within a many-sided relationship between dominant power structures and the subordinate population.[29]

Some recent discussions of popular monarchism have indeed tried to place it in its broader context of interaction between the ruled and their rulers at central and local levels. Several historians have noted that the 'social demagogy' of the tsarist government was not merely empty rhetoric, and that there was some objective basis for popular monarchism, for example in occasional pieces of legislation which genuinely benefitted the peasantry at the expense of the nobility, or in intervention by the central authorities to restrict oppressive actions by local landlords and officials.[30]

The folklore image of Ivan the Terrible and Peter the Great as the scourge of the boyars did have some historical basis in these tsars' persecution of the nobility as a means of strengthening the power of the centralized state; Paul I restricted the labour dues of serfs (*barshchina*) to three days' work for their master per week; and, of course, the Emancipation of the Serfs by Alexander II in 1861 provided the basis for peasant rumours, after the assassination of the 'tsar–liberator' by revolutionary terrorists in 1881, that he had been murdered by nobles in retaliation for the loss of their serfs.[31]

To a certain extent there was a real basis for the popular perception that landlords and officials were the common enemies of the peasants and the tsar, since corruption and local abuses of power damaged the interests of the state as well as those of the ordinary people. N.N. Pokrovskii has noted that it was in the interests of the central authorities to permit petitions from the localities to the tsar, 'rightly seeing this as a serious feedback mechanism, a counter-weight to the inevitable corruption and lack of accountability of the bureaucratic apparatus'.[32] Sometimes corrupt local officials were punished in response to complaints from their subordinates, thereby reinforcing even further the peasants' faith in the justice and benevolence of the tsar.[33]

Daniel Field, in his seminal study, was the first historian to question the sincerity of peasant professions of monarchism (though it must be said that Field's approach to this issue was somewhat oblique, and his discussion rather cryptic). 'The myth of the tsar', he noted,

> was useful to peasants in conflict with the authorities. Naive or not, the peasants professed their faith in the tsar in forms, and only in those forms, that corresponded to their interests. Peasant leaders, finding the myth ready to hand in its folkloric expressions, used it to arouse, galvanize, and unify other peasants. It was a pretext to resistance against heavy odds.[34]

Moreover, Field continued, the peasants' professions of faith in the tsar provided an acceptable excuse, in the eyes of the authorities, for their insubordination; and they could generally be confident that rebellion, as long as it was 'in the name of the tsar', would provoke only token punishment. These considerations led Field to conclude that the peasants of Bezdna and Chigirin were not so much naive as cunning, opportunistic, manipulative and practical. They were not necessarily insincere or hypocritical, but they certainly knew how to make effective use of their own monarchism. The counterpart to the peasants' 'myth of the tsar', in Field's analysis, was the officials' 'myth of the peasant': it was in the interests of the authorities to believe in the naivety of the peasants' monarchism, and to treat their rebellion indulgently, thereby saving themselves the difficulties of punishing large numbers of people. Thus there was a tacit complicity and collusion between peasants and officials in the handling of rural conflicts.[35]

Following Field's lead, other historians, too, have raised the question of the sincerity of popular monarchism. N.N. Pokrovskii, noting that the authors of the Tomsk petitions always stressed the legality of their actions and their devotion to the interests of tsar and state, commented that,

> It would be a mistake not to take into account the entirely under-standable desire of the petitioners to avoid a dreadful punishment for what they had done, but it would be no less erroneous to explain the Tomskans' interpretations of what had happened only in terms of this desire.[36]

Pokrovskii went on to argue that the petitions genuinely expressed the townspeople's own distinctively popular concepts of justice:

> Their appeal to the sovereign was not a ploy, but it reflected the popular concept of how the 'just sovereign' should observe the state interest, in particular by heeding collective complaints against the traitor-governors who were . . . preventing various groups of Siberian society from fulfilling their duty to the state.[37]

In relation to the Tomskans' refusal to accept that the tsar's response to their petitions was genuine, Pokrovskii asked how sincere the rebels' apparent belief in the falseness of the tsar's proclamations really was: but he could only conclude lamely that, 'This question is as difficult as the question of the degree of sincerity of the faith of the followers of the latest peasant–cossack pretender in his true royal origin'.[38] He noted, however, that the Tomskans' refusal to accept the tsar's proclamations as authentic 'helped to reconcile their monarchist illusions with their insubordination to the monarch's decrees' and that this classic feature of popular mentality was to appear many times over the next two centuries.[39]

Amongst later examples of popular belief that the tsar's true wishes had been distorted or concealed by landowners and officials are some of the cases from the second quarter of the nineteenth century, considered by David Moon. Moon, too, tries to answer Field's questions about the sincerity or otherwise of peasants' expressions of popular monarchism – but, while inclining to explanations in terms of the dissimulative, cunning and manipulative nature of peasant behaviour, he has to admit that the evidence is contradictory and inconclusive.[40]

Perhaps in the last analysis such questions are indeed unanswerable, and for that very reason it may not be particularly productive even to raise them. The postmodernists, with their stress on language as the only knowable historical reality, may for once indicate the best way forward, through an analysis of the various 'discourses' used by peasants and non-peasants, and of the relationships between them.

Many historians have viewed popular monarchism as supportive of the tsarist system. Even Daniel Field conceded that, 'Insofar as it encouraged patience and submission, the myth contributed to the stability of the regime'.[41] The notion that 'monarchist illusions' were an expression of the peasant patriarchalism that underpinned the autocratic system was inherent in the views of many of the contributors to the Soviet debate of 1968–72 on the nature of Russian absolutism.[42] Populists such as Stepniak, who regarded peasant faith in the tsar as 'the tragedy of Russian history',[43] saw it as a major impediment to the recruitment of popular support for the revolutionary movement.[44] Indeed, it was partly in reaction to the peasants' lack of response to the Populists' 'movement to the people' of 1874 that Stefanovich and his associates decided to resort to the device of a fraudulent imperial charter at Chigirin in 1876.[45]

In reality, popular monarchism tended to be destabilizing: movements led by pretenders and 'rebellions in the name of the tsar' were directed against the existing order. As Daniel Field pointed out, the myth of the tsar was 'potentially explosive': it involved hostility towards government officials, and to that extent it was subversive.[46] Unlike those Soviet historians who blamed the peasants' tsarist illusions on the demagogy of the autocratic government, Field argued that Russian officials were unable to manipulate the myth of the tsar in their own interests.[47] This may be an exaggeration; but while it is still possible to adduce cases of effective 'social demagogy' (or 'monarchist populism', to use a more neutral term) on the part of the tsarist government in the nineteenth century, it appears to have completely failed by the early twentieth century. Even if the order to open fire on unarmed demonstrators on 'Bloody Sunday' (9 January 1905) did not instantaneously destroy popular monarchism, as Lenin claimed, the government proved unable to capitalize on it subsequently. Nicholas II and his advisers lacked the imagination for a public-relations campaign to 'sell' the monarch to the people,[48] and during the First World War the image of the tsar played only a minor role in patriotic propaganda,[49] thereby prefiguring the absence of any significant popular pro-monarchist backlash after the February revolution of 1917. Paradoxically, it is in relation not to late imperial Russia but to the early Soviet period that historians have spoken of serious attempts by the government to exploit naive peasant monarchism, as part of the creation of the Stalin cult.

The Stalin period

The issue of continuity between tsarist and Stalinist authoritarianism is, of course, much broader than the question of popular monarchism, encompassing as it does the absence in Russia of the tradition and experience of Western-style parliamentary democracy, the lack of a middle class as the focal point of a 'civil society' and the antidemocratic ethos of Leninism. One recent explanation of the continuity has, however, depicted the patriarchalism of Russian peasant society as the basis for the authoritarian political systems that flourished both before and after 1917. The institutions of the peasant family, along with the commune, according to the Russian historian, Boris Mironov, 'fostered citizens who became the most fertile social base for political absolutism . . . It is no wonder that Russian emperors, including Nicholas II, always counted on support for the autocracy from the peasantry and the commune'.[50] The revolutions of 1905–7 and of 1917, in Mironov's view, involved peasant protests 'not against the autocracy in principle, but against a concrete, self-compromising monarch'.[51] He continues: 'Perhaps this is why the new man who reigned in Russia so soon after the overthrow of Nicholas II was a strong, menacing, and cruel figure, in complete accordance with the peasants' idea of the patriarch, the sovereign, the master'.[52] Bolshevism, and particularly Stalinism, according to Mironov, were expressions of 'the peasant understanding of power, which held that a ruler must be authoritarian'.[53]

The notion that Stalin corresponded in many ways to a peasant ideal of the 'strong leader', and that popular attitudes to the Soviet leader resembled popular attitudes to 'good tsars', such as Ivan the Terrible and Peter the Great, is one that has featured prominently in recent discussions of Stalinism and its social base of support. In an article published in 1992, I suggested that two distinct versions of the folk myth of the tsar could be identified in unofficial Soviet attitudes towards Stalin: the tsar as 'hostage of the boyars' and as 'scourge of the boyars'. Into the first category came notions that Stalin either did not know about the Great Terror, or that he had been deceived by 'wicked boyars' such as Ezhov and Beriia into believing that the innocent victims of the purges really were guilty of treason. The second version of the myth presented Stalin as a harsh but just ruler who was not afraid to take all necessary measures against the corrupt officials who were supposedly the main victims of the terror.[54]

A recent book by Sheila Fitzpatrick, however, seems to undermine such parallels. Basing her research on archival sources, Fitzpatrick dismisses any idea that there was a peasant image of Stalin as a 'good tsar' in the 1930s. On the contrary, she cites a considerable amount of evidence of popular antagonism towards Stalin in the countryside.[55] This hostility persisted in spite of attempts by the regime to tap the vein of peasant 'naive monarchism', for example in Stalin's 'Dizzy with success' article of 1 March 1930, which placed the blame for the failures of collectivization on the 'excesses' of local officials.[56] In some regions rumours did spread in the countryside that Stalin had ordered the disbanding of collective farms, but such cases were rare and untypical.[57] Lynne Viola, in her more detailed study of peasant resistance to collectivization, cites several examples of rumours depicting Stalin as the friend of the peasant;[58] but Viola – as did Daniel Field for the nineteenth century – questions just how sincere such peasant attitudes to Stalin really were.[59]

While Viola draws attention to the possibility of peasant manipulation of their own reputation for naive monarchism, Fitzpatrick stresses the extent to which the Stalin regime sought to make use of the 'myth of the tsar' for its own purposes. This happened not only in the 'Dizzy with success' episode of 1930 but also during the rural show trials of 1937, the aim of which was 'presumably to tap a populist vein of envy and hostility towards those with privilege and power: *Stalin is giving the Communist big bosses what they so richly deserve – good for Stalin!*'.[60] The ploy was, however, unsuccessful and the peasants continued to express strong hostility towards Stalin personally.[61] Thus, for Fitzpatrick, the Stalin era was characterized more by the social demagogy or 'monarchist populism' of the regime than by 'popular monarchist' notions spontaneously generated and directed towards Stalin.

Nevertheless, it seems clear that there are definite parallels to pre-revolutionary popular monarchism to be found in peasant appeals to the centre against the abuses of local officials in the Soviet period. Both Fitzpatrick and Viola provide a number of examples of peasant petitions and denunciations addressed not only to Stalin and Kalinin, but also to the Central Committee, the Supreme Soviet, the NKVD and newspapers such as *Krest'ianskaia gazeta*.[62] This often turned out to be an effective strategy on the peasants' part, since the centre was generally responsive to their petitions.[63] Like their pre-revolutionary predecessors, the central authorities in the Soviet period found peasant letters of denunciation and complaint to be a valuable source of information about the situation at grass-roots level and used them 'to compensate for the weakness of the state's administrative presence in the countryside'.[64] The peasants themselves quickly learned what kind of language was likely to provoke a favourable response from the authorities, so that denunciations soon became a popular 'strategy of manipulation' of the state by the peasants in their own interests; interests which – especially in the case of complaints about abusive local bosses – were often identical to the interests of the central authorities.[65]

Finally, we ought to ask whether, in the light of Fitzpatrick's study of the Soviet peasantry in the 1930s, 'popular monarchist' attitudes towards Stalin personally must now be regarded solely as figments of historians' imaginations. A definitive answer to this question may have to await the appearance of further publications based on the archives, but for the moment two plausible hypotheses remain. If a view of Stalin as 'hostage of the boyars' really existed, perhaps it was the preserve not of the peasantry but of the party and state functionaries who fell victim to the purges. And the view of Stalin as the 'scourge of the boyars' may not have been a contemporary but a retrospective image, idealizing him as a harsh but just upholder of order in contrast to the relatively weak rulers who succeeded him.[66]

Conclusion

Many approaches to popular monarchism have treated it as an abstract ideology. Terms such as 'the myth of the tsar' reflect and reinforce a view of the phenomenon as a form of peasant *mentalité*, or an aspect of popular political culture. The fact that popular monarchism proved to be such a durable feature of Russian history, presenting itself in virtually unchanged forms over some four centuries, also suggests that it belonged to a realm of ideas largely independent of mutable socio-economic or political–administrative structures.

But, as Daniel Field has insisted, it is important to examine popular monarchism in the context of its particular historical manifestations:[67] much of our evidence comes from specific incidents in which peasants invoked the name of the tsar in order to legitimize their protests against the actions of his local representatives. And it is perhaps in the context of the perennial problem of centre–local relations in Russia that popular monarchism can most fruitfully be situated. Central government's need for control over provincial authorities inspired various types of appeal to local inhabitants for information concerning abuses by officials; and peasants and members of other subaltern classes were able to take advantage of these appeals in order to pursue their own grievances. To the extent that both central government and the lower classes had a common interest in restraining corruption and maladministration on the part of local authorities there was a real basis both for monarchist populism and for popular monarchism; those at the top of the political hierarchy spoke the same language as those at the bottom when they condemned middle-level officials as 'traitor boyars'. Problematic relations between the centre and the localities are not, of course, a specifically Russian phenomenon, but the particular difficulties of control of a vast empire, in the absence of any democratic mechanisms of feedback, may help to explain why popular monarchism played a greater role in Russia than it did in other European states.

Notes

1 I.V. Stalin, 'Beseda s nemetskim pisatelem Emilem Liudvigom, 13 dekabria 1931 g.', in his *Sochineniia*, vol. 13 (Moscow, 1951), p. 113.
2 For a lively narrative of these revolts, see P. Avrich, *Russian rebels, 1600–1800* (London, 1973).
3 M. Perrie, *The image of Ivan the Terrible in Russian folklore* (Cambridge, 1987).
4 For a brief discussion of positive popular images of Peter, see N.V. Riasanovsky, *The image of Peter the Great in Russian history and thought* (New York, 1985), pp. 82–5.
5 On these 'adventurist' pretenders, see S.M. Troitskii, 'Samozvantsy v Rossii XVII–XVIII vekov', *Voprosy Istorii*, no. 3 (1969), pp. 144–5.

6 M. Perrie, *Pretenders and popular monarchism in early modern Russia: the false tsars of the Time of Troubles* (Cambridge, 1995).

7 For a discussion of Pugachev's claims and promises, in the context of popular rumours about other 'tsar-deliverers', see K.V. Chistov, *Russkie narodnye sotsial'no-utopicheskie legendy XVII–XIX vv.* (Moscow, 1967).

8 D. Field, *Rebels in the name of the tsar* (Boston, MA, 1976). Field identifies popular monarchism with the formula, 'The tsar wants it, but the boyars resist' (p.14).

9 E.V. Chistiakova, *Gorodskie vosstaniia v Rossii v pervoi polovine XVII veka (30–40-e gody)* (Voronezh, 1975).

10 N.N. Pokrovskii, *Tomsk, 1648–1649 gg. Voevodskaia vlast' i zemskie miry* (Novosibirsk, 1989), p. 151.

11 Pokrovskii, *Tomsk*, pp. 90–121, 300–1.

12 *Krest'ianskaia voina pod predvoditel'stvom Stepana Razina. Sbornik dokumentov*, vol. 1 (Moscow, 1954), p. 235.

13 *Bulavinskoe vosstanie (1707–1708 gg.)* (Moscow, 1935), pp. 450–51.

14 D. Moon, *Russian peasants and tsarist legislation on the eve of reform* (Houndmills, 1992), pp. 80, 111–12, 176.

15 Field, *Rebels in the name of the tsar*.

16 M. Perrie, *The agrarian policy of the Russian Socialist-Revolutionary Party, from its origins through the Revolution of 1905–1907* (Cambridge, 1976), pp. 56–7.

17 M. Perrie, 'The Russian peasant movement of 1905–1907', *Past and Present*, no. 57 (November 1972), p. 126.

18 Perrie, *The image of Ivan the Terrible*.

19 Perrie, *Pretenders and popular monarchism*, p. 103.

20 V.A. Kivelson, 'The devil stole his mind: the tsar and the 1648 Moscow uprising', *American Historical Review*, 98, 3 (June 1993), p. 747.

21 Riasanovsky, *The image of Peter the Great*, pp. 74–82; N.S. Gur'ianova, *Krest'ianskii antimonarkhicheskii protest v staroobriadcheskoi eskhatologicheskoi literature perioda pozdnego feodalizma* (Novosibirsk, 1988).

22 The classic study is M. Cherniavsky, *Tsar and people; studies in Russian myths* (New Haven, CT, 1961); see also V.M. Zhivov and B.A. Uspenskii, 'Tsar' i bog. Semioticheskie aspekty sakralizatsii monarkha v Rossii', in *Iazyki kul'tury i problemy perevodimosti* (Moscow, 1987), pp. 47–153.

23 A.V. Buganov, *Russkaia istoriia v pamiati krest'ian XIX veka i natsional'noe samosoznanie* (Moscow, 1992), pp. 82–98.

24 A.N. Sakharov, 'Istoricheskie faktory obrazovaniia russkogo absoliutizma', *Istoriia SSSR*, no. 1 (1971), pp. 116–17.

25 Field, *Rebels in the name of the tsar*, pp. 3–4, 17–18.

26 Field, *Rebels in the name of the tsar*, p. 18.

27 Stepniak [S.M. Kravchinskii], *The Russian peasantry*, new edition (London, 1905), p. 620.

28 See, for example, Sakharov, 'Istoricheskie faktory', p. 116.

29 V.A. Kivelson, *Autocracy in the provinces: the Muscovite gentry and political culture in the seventeenth century* (Stanford, CA, 1996), p. 10.

30 Field, *Rebels in the name of the tsar*, pp. 9–17.

31 Cf. A.N. Engel'gardt, *Iz derevni; 12 pisem 1872–1887* (Moscow, 1987), p. 533: 'the squires did [it] in revenge for [our] freedom'.

32 N.N. Pokrovskii, 'Sibirskie materialy XVII–XVIII vv. po "slovu i delu gosudarevu" kak istochnik po istorii obshchestvennogo soznaniia', in *Istochniki po istorii obshchestvennoi mysli i kul'tury epokhi pozdnego feodalizma* (Novosibirsk, 1988), p. 26.

33 A.A. Preobrazhenskii, *Ural i Zapadnaia Sibir' v kontse XVI – nachale XVIII veka* (Moscow, 1972), pp. 351–2.

34 Field, *Rebels in the name of the tsar*, p. 209.
35 Field, *Rebels in the name of the tsar*, pp. 210–14.
36 Pokrovskii, *Tomsk*, p. 93.
37 Pokrovskii, *Tomsk*, p. 94.
38 Pokrovskii, *Tomsk*, pp. 279–80.
39 Pokrovskii, *Tomsk*, p. 281.
40 Moon, *Russian peasants and tsarist legislation*, pp. 175–6.
41 Field, *Rebels in the name of the tsar*, p. 209.
42 See the journal *Istoriia SSSR*, 1968–72, *passim*.
43 Stepniak, *The Russian peasantry*, p. 614.
44 Stepniak, *The Russian peasantry*, pp. 112–14.
45 Field, *Rebels in the name of the tsar*, p. 169.
46 Field, *Rebels in the name of the tsar*, pp. 16, 22–4.
47 Field, *Rebels in the name of the tsar*, pp. 23, 209.
48 D. Lieven, *Russia's rulers under the Old Regime* (New Haven, CT, 1989), p. 284.
49 H.F. Jahn, *Patriotic culture in Russia during World War I* (Ithaca, NJ, 1995), pp. 173–4.
50 B.N. Mironov, 'Peasant popular culture and the origins of Soviet authoritarianism' in S.P. Frank and M.D. Steinberg, eds *Cultures in flux. Lower-class values, practices and resistance in late imperial Russia* (Princeton, NJ, 1994), p. 68.
51 Mironov, 'Peasant popular culture', pp. 68–9.
52 Mironov, 'Peasant popular culture', p. 69.
53 Mironov, 'Peasant popular culture', p. 72.
54 M. Perrie, 'The tsar, the emperor, the leader: Ivan the Terrible, Peter the Great and Anatolii Rybakov's Stalin', in N. Lampert and G.T. Rittersporn, eds *Stalinism: its nature and aftermath* (Houndmills, 1992), pp. 94–6.
55 S. Fitzpatrick, *Stalin's peasants: resistance and survival in the Russian village after collectivization* (New York, 1994), pp. 17–18, 286–312.
56 Fitzpatrick, *Stalin's peasants*, p. 288.
57 Fitzpatrick, *Stalin's peasants*, p. 289.
58 L. Viola, *Peasant rebels under Stalin: collectivization and the culture of peasant resistance* (New York, 1996), pp. 56, 171–2.
59 Viola, *Peasant rebels under Stalin*, pp. 93, 95, 172.
60 Fitzpatrick, *Stalin's peasants*, p. 312; emphasis in the original.
61 Fitzpatrick, *Stalin's peasants*, p. 313.
62 Fitzpatrick, *Stalin's peasants*, pp. 256–9, 299–300; Viola, *Peasant rebels under Stalin*, pp. 91–8.
63 Fitzpatrick, *Stalin's peasants*, pp. 14–16, 159–61; Viola, *Peasant rebels under Stalin*, pp. 97–8.
64 Fitzpatrick, *Stalin's peasants*, p. 15.
65 Fitzpatrick, *Stalin's peasants*, pp. 13–16; cf. Viola, *Peasant rebels under Stalin*, pp. 95–9.
66 Perrie, 'The tsar, the emperor, the leader', pp. 95–6.
67 Field, *Rebels in the name of the tsar*, pp. 25–6.

|11|

Russian rulers: tsars, commissars and presidents

ROBERT SERVICE

Russia's rulers across the twentieth century are frequently compared with each other. When Boris Yeltsin assumed power after the collapse of the Soviet Union, many looked for connections between his methods of governance and those of his predecessors. Newspapers referred to him as Tsar Boris. The picture has been drawn of a succession of Russian rulers who used by and large the same techniques to govern their country. Boris Yeltsin, it was suggested, had no difficulty in adjusting to power since he needed only to fit himself into an existing framework. Other comparisons had been made earlier. Vladimir Lenin was thought unnervingly akin to the most vigorous Romanov tsars. Joseph Stalin had been seen in the same light, being likened in particular to Ivan the Terrible, and Stalin was also compared to Lenin. Moreover, Stalin's successor Nikita Khrushchëv was juxtaposed alternately to the old tsars, to the more recently deceased Lenin and occasionally to Stalin. Mikhail Gorbachëv was compared to an abundance of rulers: Peter the Great, Alexander II, Alexander Kerenskii, Vladimir Lenin, Nikita Khrushchëv; and it was not unknown for Stalin himself to be proposed as the model for Gorbachëv's methods. Continuity in Russian rulership has been a constant theme of scholars, diplomats and political commentators.

There exists no consolidated theory of continuity. Usually, the comparison is made in a fairly casual fashion, and often the intention is to throw the career of the present ruler into relief rather than to postulate an unbroken political sequence. Nevertheless, the working assumption of most observers is that there is something about the modern Russian tradition of rulership that permits us to stress the recurrence of certain techniques, assumption and objectives.

A number of questions arise from this. First, how are the various aspects of continuity to be explained? It is possible, for example, that they were simply the result of the whim of successive rulers. Thus when Stalin copied Lenin, he might have done so while having the freedom to do the opposite.

Another possibility is that the aspects of continuity were the product not of lengthy deliberation by the rulers but of a sense that something drastic had to be done to deal with a particular emergency facing a specific ruler. Rulers might have reinforced those aspects out of mere opportunism. Thus Nicholas II in 1905–6 and Lenin in 1921–2 had to deal with peasant revolt and could simply have used the instruments of suppression that lay readily to hand. Another possibility is that Russian society – Imperial, Soviet and post-Soviet – has enduring features that have gone on predetermining the fashion in which the country could be ruled. According to such an analysis, Lenin and Stalin had to adjust their revolutionary objectives and their methods of governance to the reality of the society that they came to rule. Nor is it discountable that the various aspects of continuity do not result from a substantial tradition but rather are borrowed from elsewhere in the world. For example, it might be argued that when Khrushchëv represented himself as a Leninist, he was merely using the Leninist past to legitimate the decidedly Western techniques of political image building.

This leads to a basic question about continuity itself. Could it be that we have exaggerated the strength of continuity and that the differences among Russian rulers from Nicholas II to Boris Yeltsin are greater than their similarities? By homogenizing the Russian historical experience, furthermore, we may inadvertently be encouraging the acceptance of notions about the unchangeability of Russia. The implications of such an error are depressing. If Russia is unalterable, the range of policies to be adopted in relation to it is narrower than they might otherwise be.

The case for continuity is as follows. Russian supreme rulers from Nicholas II onwards have had monarchical authority or something very close to it. In other words, it was not only tsars but also communist party leaders – Lenin, Stalin, Khrushchëv, Brezhnev, Andropov, Chernenko and Gorbachëv – who could impose their personal will upon the political system; and in the post-communist period, Yeltsin's authority as defined constitutionally since 1993 has been little inhibited by other political ogans.[1] Naturally there are qualifications to be made. Whereas Nicholas II and, after 1937, Stalin had a monarchical authority that did not require them to refer decisions to their subordinates,[2] this was not true of the other supreme leaders, who to a greater or lesser extent had to consult before policies could definitively be elaborated and announced. Nevertheless, it is true that most Russian supreme leaders from Nicholas II to Yeltsin did not suffer unduly from the importunities of their close associates. Although the system ceased formally to be monarchical after the February 1917 Revolution, it has also borne the imprint of this reality for large portions of the century.

In the same decades, moreover, the supreme leaders have consistently disliked to be regarded as 'politicians'. All have hated what they pejoratively have dubbed *politikanstvo*. Nicholas II despised the political parties and until 1905 prohibited them by law. Lenin's idea of politics left no room for interparty competition, and he too derided the profession of politician even though he was one. He, also, detested political systems of multiparty competition.[3] Unlike Nicholas II, he himself led a party; but his one-party state was an attempt to move beyond the conventional understanding of politics inasmuch as the original definition of 'party' embraced the notion of a plurality of parties. Thus Lenin and his successors were also in their peculiar fashion antiparty despite being spirited advocates of the virtues of their own party. Even President Yeltsin in the years since the fall of communism in Russia has been little different. It is true that he has openly advocated the benefits of multiparty competition for democratization in Russia, but he has never founded or joined a political party. He has stood above party. To this extent there has been a persistent contempt for pluralist politics among the Russian rulers of the century.

What is more, there has been a distinct tendency for them to build up their personally appointed central administrative apparatus separate from the general government of the country. Nicholas II could have influence on appointments to the Council of Ministers even after he gave Pëtr Stolypin the post of chairman of that Council in 1906.[4] Government was in the gift of the tsar. Stalin had his own Special Department, which meant that he was not beholden even to the Party Central Committee Secretariat. Other general secretaries were never so powerful but all of them had considerable latitude for the appointment of personnel. It must be admitted that Lenin had to rely not so much on institutional regularity as upon personal charisma in seeking to get his favoured functionaries selected to office; and that Gorbachëv deliberately ran down his opportunities to exercise political patronage in the late 1980s. But generally the pattern has been remarkably durable. Even Yeltsin has maintained a Presidential Administration, rising to 5000 members by 1998, in order to maintain an executive office separate from interference by the government or the Federal Assembly.

Twentieth-century Russia has a tradition, too, of central appointment of local government officials. Nicholas II chose the provincial governors. Whenever these displeased him, they were sacked and replaced – and such a procedure survived the introduction of the Basic Law in 1906. Under the communists the chief provincial executives from 1920 onwards were the party first secretaries and all of these were put in place by the central party apparatus dominated by the general secretary of the day from Stalin onwards.[5] After 1991, moreover, Yeltsin appointed his plenipotentiaries to the provinces. It must be added that elections have been introduced that allow local people to elect their own councils and their leaders. Nonetheless, the Russian presidency has large residual powers to intervene directly in provinces, regions and republics.

Russia has also had a persistent problem of arbitrary rule. Nicholas II, under the duress of the 1905–6 revolutionary upsurge, granted a Basic Law and agreed to abide by it. Yet the Basic Law allowed him to prorogue the state Duma whenever he liked and to decree any measures that might have been balked by the Duma. Furthermore, a large number of the provinces of the Russian Empire remained under 'state of emergency' governance before the First World War, and the governors in those provinces were a law unto themselves.[6] And so despite the formal constraints upon Nicholas II there were plenty of loopholes that Nicholas II was able to exploit. Thereafter Lenin made a career mocking constitutional and legal proceduralism, and he and his successors were openly contemptuous of even 'Soviet legality' whenever the interests of the communist one-party regime were threatened. The arbitrariness of Joseph Stalin was notorious since he coupled it to mass murder on an extraordinary scale. But other communist party leaders exhibited the same contempt for law; the entire regime was founded upon arbitrary methods. This was true even of Gorbachëv (although, to be fair to him, he used arbitrary methods with the ultimate purpose of establishing a political and judicial order that would terminate arbitrariness).

As for Yeltsin, he came into power promising to end 'totalitarianism'; but in various ways, especially by breaking the existing constitutional order and bombarding the Russian White House in October 1993, he did not put an end to arbitrary rule – and his continuing passivity in the face of corrupt, fraudulent practices has been undeniable.[7] Russia since the fall of communism has not been turned into a country of constitutional and legal order.

It is tempting to add a further category to the tradition of modern Russian rulership: ideocracy. From Lenin to Gorbachëv there was a state-imposed ideology, Marxism–Leninism, which was imposed on all the media of public communication and on schools and recreational facilities. The pattern, however, is not continuous. Nicholas II, however reluctantly, allowed alternative religious and even political ideologies to be expressed in public. Recently, Boris Yeltsin has made it part of his campaign of de-communization to insist on the virtues of cultural pluralism and of religious and political freedom; indeed, this was also Gorbachëv's professed purpose in the final couple of years of his tenure of political power. Russian rulership, then, has not always been an ideocracy, but ideas have certainly had an extraordinary importance for Russian rulers. Gorbachëv fought to the end of his Soviet presidency for his own evolving notion of Leninist socialism. And Yeltsin has given speeches and issued autobiographical sketches that, more than is usual for a Western politician, cover general questions of political, social, economic and cultural life.[8] Russian rulers have sought to provide explicit ideological leadership even when they have not aspired to the imposition of an ideocracy.

Thus there seems to be an impressive continuity about Russian rulership. The factors include the following: single dominant rulers who despise normal political competition and who build up personal administrations at the centre and appoint administrators for the provinces within an environment of highly arbitrary rule – and who seek to convince the rest of society that their own ideology is the most desirable for the country's present and future governance.

But is the continuity so very strong? Two leaders who have not yet been given consideration are the successive premiers of the Provisional Government that was overthrown by Lenin's communist party in the October 1917 Revolution: Prince Georgi Lvov and Alexander Kerenskii. By no stretch of the imagination were they unchallengeable leaders. In Kerenskii's case, the threats from colleagues included a mutiny by his chief military commander Lavr Kornilov. This is not all. Kerenskii belonged to a political party (although it has to be added that he tried to put himself above parties in order to hold his coalition together).[9] And the central administration headed by Lvov and Kerenskii were far from being in their gift and those local representatives they sent to the provinces were often rebuffed by the various elected bodies.[10] Nor did Lvov and Kerenskii resort greatly to arbitrary measures in their techniques of rule. In all these ways they were an important exception to the pattern. On the other hand, it is equally arguable that they confirm the pattern inasmuch as they were so dramatically ineffective in imposing their personal will.

There are other partial disruptions to the pattern. Not only Lvov and Kerenskii but also Gorbachëv and Yeltsin were confronted by huge impediments when attempting to formulate policy. Pressure-group activity, both open and covert, was a mighty force with which they had to contend. In addition, Gorbachëv introduced the beginnings of a multiparty system and therefore his position as communist party leader was something more than a political formality. Yeltsin was tempted to join the party led by his prime minister Yegor Gaidar in 1993. At the last moment, probably because he sensed that Gaidar was not popular in the country at large, he drew back from the brink. But the pattern of rulership is certainly not a monolithic one.

Not only Lvov and Kerenskii but also the later Gorbachëv as well as Yeltsin were without a firm grip on central and local political appointments. In particular, Yeltsin has never dared to propose his favourites to lead the various autonomous republics of the Russian Federation. With regard to arbitrary rule, furthermore, Gorbachëv sincerely aimed to root it out of Russian public life. His minister of the interior Vadim Bakatin pointed out to him that crime and corruption were likely to endure until economic regeneration had taken place.[11] But Gorbachëv and Bakatin agreed on the medium-term objective of creating a 'law-based state' (*pravovoe gosudarstvo*). Furthermore, there can be little doubt that Yeltsin would like to have created such a state even though he has made such a hash of the process. Last, there is a substantial difference between the way that Lenin, Stalin and Khrushchëv purveyed their ideas and the way practised by Nicholas II and Boris Yeltsin. Communist leaders wanted to open a window into people's minds; the tsars did not, and the first post-communist president has not either.

There are further weaknesses in the tradition of rulership. For instance, the method of selection of rulers has varied over the years. Nicholas II was 'chosen' by birth: his father had been tsar, and Nicholas was the next in line to the throne. Lenin, by contrast, selected himself. He led the successful seizure of power and had the authority and charisma to dominate his associates. Stalin emerged from the debris of communist factional disputes, Khrushchëv from disputes among a few communist leaders. Selection by the ascendant party leadership became the norm through to Gorbachëv. Then, as a break in the pattern, Yeltsin was chosen on the basis of a freely contested election and then re-elected. Such were the variations, and they were counterparted by the variations in the modes whereby supreme office was lost. Nicholas II was compelled by the February 1917 Revolution to abdicate, and Gorbachëv was under irresistible pressure to resign his Soviet presidency after the abortive August 1991 *coup d'état*: this too was a revolutionary event of a kind. Lenin, Stalin, Andropov and Chernenko by contrast left office by dying. Khrushchëv was ousted by a conspiracy within the central party leadership. The differing methods of selection and removal indicate considerable turbulence in the mode of leadership.

In their styles of rule, too, the rulers contrasted a lot to each other. Nicholas II appeared in public only rarely, usually for occasions of high ceremony. But he received delegations of peasants and workers as *khodoki*, and went around places of Russian Orthodox Church pilgrimage.[12] Nicholas II was positively gregarious in comparison with Stalin, who revealed himself in the flesh but rarely in the Second World War.[13] His pictures were everywhere, but he kept his personal appearances to the absolute minimum. The occasional speech at (the ever less frequent) party or soviet congresses sufficed for him in the 1930s. The idea that he modelled himself on the tsars has a grain of truth in it, but as usual he did so on his own terms. At the opposite extreme were Khrushchëv, Gorbachëv and – until being incommoded by ill health – Yeltsin. Khrushchëv gave the impression of having visited every factory workshop and kolkhoz dairy in the USSR; Gorbachëv travelled the length and breadth of the USSR, giving large speeches, from Minsk to Vladivostok. To some extent they were adopting the techniques of US presidential campaigns, but they were not just copying others: the factional struggles in the communist party in the 1920s had been accompanied by whistle-stop campaigns by Trotskii, Zinoviev and Lunacharskii. Be that as it may, Yeltsin too maintained a sharply engraved profile in the public media.

There was also quite a difference in sartorial presentation. Tsar Nicholas switched between sumptuous, seventeenth-century garments and a simple contemporary soldier's tunic. Kerenskii, too, wore a tunic sometimes and sported a military crew-cut; at other times he wore the professional man's dark three-piece suit. Lenin was rarely ever seen without such a suit. Stalin usually wore his version of a military tunic, but after 1945 he sometimes used the uniform of Generalissimus of the Soviet Army. When Khrushchëv wanted to show off, he put on a decorated peasant smock. Otherwise he preferred a (tightly fitting and ill cut) dark grey suit and hat. This virtually became a uniform for his successors; for they wanted to avoid wearing clothes that might make obvious the material privileges which were denied to the rest of society. Cautiously, Andropov took to having his suit made by the best available tailor, and Gorbachëv broke with precedent by wearing a pork-pie hat. With Yeltsin there was rarely a hat in sight: no doubt he wished to draw attention to the fact that he still had a shiny, silvery shock of hair whereas the most notable feature of Gorbachëv's cranium was the lightning-shaped red birthmark.

Not only have Russian rulers looked different from each other but also they have aspired to diferent images for themselves. Nicholas II was hoping to be the traditional 'little father' to his people and yet at the same time to be a man of the people, especially the Russian Orthodox Christians. In several ways this has been true, too, of Yeltsin, a populist leader *par excellence*. Nicholas II used the 'holy man' Rasputin to keep him in touch with what the ordinary Russian public were thinking; Yeltsin prides himself on his intuitive grasp of popular wishes as the result of his own lowly social origins. Both Nicholas II and Yeltsin asserted that they were defenders of the interests of all groups in society – and this was also the case for party leaders from Khrushchëv onwards. Gorbachëv particularly aspired to the image of a leader for all the people all of the time. By contrast Lenin identified himself above all with 'the proletariat' and, to a lesser extent, the peasantry. He anathematized the old propertied elites and was none too keen on the country's professional experts. Gradually, Stalin shifted the image of the supreme leader so as to include the promotees (*vydvizhentsy*) and to give them precedence over 'ordinary' workers and *kolkhozniki*.[14]

An even greater contrast is evident in the historical figures to whom each of them rendered homage. Nicholas II looked back to his father Alexander III and back still further to his distant ancestor, Tsar Alexei, who came to the throne in 1645.[15] Lenin eulogized Marx and Engels; if he admired Russians, it was typically the anti-tsarist revolutionaries such as the writer Nikolai Chernyshevskii. The heroes for Stalin were a more contradictory group: Lenin and Marx among the revolutionaries and Ivan the Terrible and Peter the Great among the tsars.[16] Khrushchëv restored simplicity. For him there could be no other idol than Lenin, and this fixation continued down the line of his successors. Gorbachëv, while objectively destroying Leninism, was an intense enthusiast for Lenin. Even so, there were other figures which had an appeal for him, especially the peaceful reforming tsar Alexander II and the late nineteenth-century industrializing minister of finance, Sergei Witte. With Yeltsin there has been a fascination with Peter the Great as the country's first great modernizer. He also expressed admiration for Margaret Thatcher; but later he has emphasized the native heroes at her expense.

Thus there have been frequent switches from leader to leader in terms of height of visibility, dress, group appeal and historical self-identification. With the exception of the dreary similarity of Brezhnev, Andropov and Chernenko, Russian rulers have gone out of their way to impress their own image onto public consciousness in order to reinforce the kind of policies and practices they espouse for the country.

It is clear, too, that the rulers themselves had a role in deciding how they should act and be seen to act. On questions of image this is especially obvious. Nicholas II deliberately chose Tsar Alexei as his *alter ego* as a means of asserting the Romanov dynasty's majesty and longevity. Unlike Stalin, he did not want to emphasize the need for traumas in the country's development and did not draw attention to Peter the Great, far less to Ivan the Terrible. Some rulers have been more active than others in developing their image. Kerenskii was among the most inventive. Scarcely had he entered the Provisional government's first cabinet as minister of justice when he commissioned the printing of thousands of postcards with his face surrounded by a laurel wreath and the Tauride Palace in the background. He had newsreels taken of himself. He appeared, after a domestic accident, with his arm in a sling: he wanted everyone to believe that he had incurred the injury by personal bravery on the Eastern front. And what are we to make of Yeltsin devoting a whole chapter of his second autobiographical volume to the foundation of a presidential tennis club?[17] Surely this was an attempt to represent the Russian president – against the well-founded rumours – as vigorous, self-disciplined and rather Westernized.

There is plenty of evidence that the rulers offered active consideration of the structures through which they ruled the country. Despite the many constants of twentieth-century political Russia, there has hardly been a year when the supreme leader has not tampered with the administrative framework. All have fretted that the framework has inhibited the realization of their personal will.

The prime example is Nicholas II, who never became reconciled to the existence of the State Duma – and the Tsarina Alexandra sharpened his distaste for the semiconstitutional order introduced after 1905. Lenin was even busier in elaborating the state order he desired. The one-party, one-ideology state was largely the product of the discussions held in the communist party – under his direction – in 1917–19. He continued the elaboration thereafter. Organized factions were banned from the party. State political censorship was formalized. The functions at the *Cheka* were redefined. Subsequently, Stalin first elevated the party's authority still higher and then drastically reduced it; he also sought, in the Great Terror of 1937–8, to eradicate the informal cliental groups and the local 'nests' of officials that had sprung up after the October 1917 Revolution.[18] Khrushchëv began by trimming the powers of the political police and re-elevating the party. But thereafter he bifurcated the party organizational structure, decentralized the central ministries and set up regional economic councils; he also tried to stunt opposition in the party by inviting outsiders even to meetings of the Central Committee. Brezhnev was more modest in his institutional rearrangements, but among them was the reassertion of the party's authority.

Moreover, Brezhnev and his successors tinkered with the structures of economic ministries to raise the level of productivity of industry and agriculture; and, initially, Gorbachëv, too, followed in this tradition. But perestroika turned into a maelstrom of reform. The party was internally reformed. The party's monopoly of power was abolished. A Congress of People's Deputies was introduced, and Gorbachëv became USSR President. Other political parties started to spring up.

Gorbachëv did not have an elaborate plan of reform, but at every stage he tried to work out what was needed next. He also tried to adjust his proposals to his own sense of Russian traditions. Thus he was drawn to the idea of a Congress of People's Deputies partly because he felt it to be congruent with the revolutionary practices of Russians in the year 1917. The fact that the Congress would be noisy, smoky and chaotic did not worry him. The point was to foster a spirit of political change the Russian people would feel at ease with. He and his advisers, moreover, looked not only at the apparent lessons of Russia's history but also at the experience of other countries.[19] The lunge towards presidentialist rule from 1989 was premised upon the perceived efficiency and influence of presidents in France and the USA. This esteem for Western presidential experience has been retained under Yeltsin in the post-communist Russian Federation. All through the century, therefore, rulers of Russia have thought about the agencies of their rule and experimented with them. There is no ossified tradition.

Yet the tradition, when the necessary reservations have been acknowledged, has prevailed over contrary influences with only the shortest exceptional periods: the brief months of power of Lvov and Kerenskii and the last year or two of Gorbachëv's rule. For the rest of the twentieth century Russian politics has been characterized by several aspects of continuity. These aspects are individually paralleled in other industrial societies. But as an amalgam they are without counterpart. They form a distinctive Russian tradition.

But why have the rulers accepted the tradition so readily? Several of them have given thought to it and experimented with it; they have not been just passive receptors. The sorry plight of Alexander Kerenskii and Mikhail Gorbachëv, neither of whom left office at all willingly, gives a clue. Both had started to rule in a non-traditional fashion and were brusquely removed. Kerenskii even had to flee abroad. It would seem appropriate to conclude that rulers ruled in a traditional fashion not least because the alternatives would place their hold on power at risk. Even when a ruler stuck to tradition, there was no guarantee that power would be retained. The most striking instance of this was the forced resignation of Khrushchëv in 1964. Yeltsin's career since 1991 displayed a relapse towards more traditional modes of behaviour as his political and economic difficulties mounted. Unlike Gorbachëv, Yeltsin had no intention of being caught out by his enemies' exploitation of the reforms he introduced. In 1993 the storming of the White House and the manipulative holding of a referendum on the proposed presidentialist constitution marked the end of illusions people could have had about his comprehensive commitment to democracy and constitutionality.

Fear of the alternatives is not the only thing to have held the tradition in place; also of importance has been the cultural formation of the leaders themselves. Nicholas II was brought up to respect the concepts of imperial and dynastic honour; it never occurred to him that he might voluntarily build up a constitutional monarchy. Likewise, most of the communist leaders, reared in the customs of Marxism–Leninism, gave no thought to running their societies in any basically different way. Lenin was the great communist inventor inasmuch as he introduced the one-party dictatorship. But his successors tampered, to a greater or lesser extent, with secondary aspects; they were not just uninformed about alternatives: they were uninterested in the question of alternatives. Even Gorbachëv, Russia's greatest ever reformer, did not embark on his reforms with the clear intention of installing changes of a primary significance. All in all, habituation by upbringing, schooling and life experience has also had its influence upon the prolongation of tradition.

Similarly, it must be recognized that only the most exceptional rulers are likely to alter a political system that seems to be working. 'If it ain't broke, don't mend it!' Nicholas II continued to believe, even after the near-revolution of 1905–6, in the efficaciousness of harsh authoritarianism. He went to his death in 1918 still adhering to a tsarist credo of governance. The communist rulers, too, quickly became conservatives of a certain kind. For they appreciated, perhaps not very sophisticatedly, that any substantial alteration of any part of the communist political order would have pernicious effects on the rest of the architecture. It took the egregious Gorbachëv to attempt a reconstruction (perestroika) – and his endeavours brought the edifice tumbling down. He failed to understand the tautness of the architecture. No wall of the building could be pulled out without drastic damage. Furthermore, he underestimated the crucial fact that his reforms undermined his own political base – the party and the economic ministries – without supplying him with a new one. As the economy fell apart and political and national dissent intensified, he was left friendless many months before the August 1991 coup attempt.

The riskiness of Gorbachëv's approach is manifest in the way he dispensed not only with the existing institutional support but also with the informal groupings that had characterized communist and indeed tsarist rule. Successive leaders thought their cliental following to be crucial. Even Stalin, while seeking in 1937–8 to destroy the powers of patronage enjoyed by his subordinates, jealously retained his own cliental group. Khrushchëv replaced Stalin's cronies with his own. Thereupon the 'Dnepropetrovsk mafia' of Brezhnev became notorious as Brezhnev studded the Soviet political establishment with subordinates who had worked with him since his days in Dnepropetrovsk. Gorbachëv planned to construct a new form of politics and refused to bring a patronage network to the Kremlin from Stavropol, where he had worked after graduating from Moscow State University. By contrast, Yeltsin, as soon as he had pressed Gorbachëv into retirement, started – at least for a time – to surround himself with cronies from his own early political base in Sverdlovsk (now Yekaterinburg). Politics can be a grand enterprise for society's good or evil, but it is also a game of survival, and most Russian rulers have understood this.

Yet more basic factors need to be taken into consideration. Rulership in Russia has also been affected by the nature of the situation in the country for most of the century. In most ways Russia has lived through a recurrent state of emergency. There have been endless crises: the 1905–6 near revolution, the First World War, the two revolutions of 1917, the Civil War, the peacetime repression, the forcible mass collectivization of the peasantry, the show trials of the early 1930s, the Great Terror, the Second World War, the post-war repression, the instabilities of de-Stalinization, the Novocherkassk massacre, the repression of national and religious dissent under Brezhnev, the turbulence of the Gorbachëv years. Rulers and the regimes were primarily responsible for producing these crises. But the crises, once produced, had an impact by restricting the scope for change. Authoritarian and arbitrary rule became endemic. A tense relationship between the rulers and the ruled was turned into permanence. The tradition was ceaselessly renewed. Even when tsarism was toppled, the opportunities for moderating the tradition were weak, and the same has been evident since the fall of communism.

The position has been made worse by the fragility of strong contrary pressures. Autonomous civil institutions were kept weak by tsarism and were eliminated by communism; and the gargantuan use of terror by Stalin made potential advocates of change from below extraordinarily wary of raising their objections. The 'dissidents' were extremely few under Khrushchëv and Brezhnev, who systematically imprisoned the most troublesome among them.

It might be suggested that this is too dark a picture of Russian politics and that both the year 1917 and the late 1980s show how effective Russians have been when civic freedoms have been available. But we must beware of overestimating the solidity of soviets, factory workshop committees, trade unions, soldiers' committees and village land communes. The point about early Soviet history is surely that all these popular elective organs were very quickly crushed or emasculated by the communists. Such a process took months in most cases, within a few years by the rest. Furthermore, the period of perestroika witnessed many attempts by Gorbachëv to mobilize an active pro-reform citizenry. The media of public communication explained with much greater efficiency than in 1917 the need for the supporters of change to join and work in the new autonomous bodies. In this there was disappointment for Gorbachëv. Most citizens were keen spectators of the humiliation of communist bullyboys, but were reluctant to become engaged in politics. The culture of individual and collective self-assertion was slow in being created, and this slowness was among the reasons for Gorbachëv's fall.

And so if the weight of tradition rests upon the Russian political present, however is Russia in the future to remove it? In the short term the prospect is bleak. While attempting an economic and social transformation, Yeltsin and his possible successors are unlikely to abandon the traditional political methods for fear of losing control over the process; and in any case the federal constitution practically ensures that things will stay as they are for a longish time. Furthermore, a coalition of politico-criminal and economic interest groups has a practical incentive to support such a *status quo*.

Betterment will come, if ever it does, through the explosion of discontent from the midst of the broader strata of Russian society, a society that continues to be well educated but which, in contrast to past years, has access to alternative sources of information. So long as television, radio and newspapers are not unduly impeded by the rulers, then politics will remain an arena of worthwhile contestation. The result will be the increasing need of politicians to be ready to be held accountable to the electorate. Yeltsin's cabinets' promises of jam tomorrow cannot satisfy people forever. Education and informational pluralism will be a constraint on authoritarianism. It is hard to say whether the emergent market economy will also be a force for democratization. At the moment the economic structures are those of a piratical capitalism. Successful Russian entrepreneurs do little more than export the country's wealth in raw resources such as gas, oil, timber and gold. There can be no certainty that a less piratical capitalism will be developed; but the hope must be that entrepreneurs will not be eternally content with the poor conditions of material and cultural life. And then there is the international factor. Information about how life is lived elsewhere in the world is an unremitting pressure for the alleviation of popular distress. Last, but not least, the price of continued International Monetary Fund loans may one day include the installation of a law-governed state.

Things, of course, can also go the other way. The ruler and their supportive groups may simply opt – as Lenin and Stalin did – to increase the severity of their rule in order to secure their power and privilege; and Russia would not be the only authoritarian state in the world to face down public protest and constrict the channels of public discussion. Nor does the international banking community have an unblemished record of support for anti-authoritarian politics. If that great change for the better is to break the modern political tradition in Russia, it will take time, luck and the emergence of truly popular politics.

Notes

1 *Konstitutsiya Rossiiskoi Federatsii* (Moscow, 1993).
2 E.A. Rees, 'Stalin, the Politburo and rail transport policy', in J. Cooper, M. Perrie and E.A. Rees, eds *Soviet History, 1917–1953* (London, 1995), pp. 107–11.
3 V.I. Lenin, 'Gosudarstvo i revolyutsiya. Uchenie marksizma o gosudarstve i zadachi proletariata v revolyutsii', in *Polnoe Sobranie Sochinenii* (Moscow, 1958–65), vol. 32, chs 5, 6.
4 G.A. Hosking, *The Russian constitutional experiment: government and Duma, 1907–1914* (Cambridge, 1973), pp. 197–205.
5 R. Service, *The Bolshevik Party in revolution: a study in organisational change* (London, 1979), p. 100.
6 P. Waldron, 'States of emergency: autocracy and extraordinary legislation, 1881–1917', *Revolutionary Russia*, no. 1 (1995), p. 4.
7 J. Kampfner, *Inside Yeltsin's Russia: corruption, conflict, capitalism* (London, 1994), chs 3, 7.
8 See especially B. Yeltsin, *The view from the Kremlin* (London, 1994), ch 7.
9 R. Abraham, *Alexander Kerensky, the first love of the Revolution* (London, 1987).
10 H. White, 'The Provisional government and the problem of power in the provinces, March to October 1917', Study Group on the Russian Revolution Annual Conference, Oxford, 1982.
11 V. Bakatin, *Izbavlenie ot KGB* (Moscow, 1992), p. 199.
12 D.C.B. Lieven, *Nicholas II: Emperor of all the Russias* (London, 1994), ch 2.
13 G. Rittersporn, *Simplications staliniens et complications soviétiques: tensions sociales et conflits en URSS, 1933–1953* (Paris, 1988), p. 248.
14 S. Fitzpatrick, 'Stalin and the making of a new elite, 1928–1939', *Slavic Review*, no. 3 (1979).
15 O. Figes, *A people's tragedy: the Russian Revolution, 1891–1924* (London, 1996), pp. 3–14.
16 R. Tucker, *Stalin in power: the Revolution from above, 1928–1941* (London, 1990), pp. 482–3.
17 B. Yeltsin, *The view from the Kremlin*, ch 7.
18 O.V. Khlevnyuk, *1937–I: Stalin, NKVD i sovetskoe obshchestvo* (Moscow, 1992), p. 77.
19 N. Ryzhkov, *Perestroika. Istoriya predatel'stv* (Moscow, 1992), p. 279.

|12|

Russian Jews and
the Soviet agenda

JOHN KLIER

One aspect of twentieth-century Russian history seemingly not in need of reinterpretation is the assumption that neither late tsarism nor most years of the Soviet period was 'good for the Jews'. The new century greeted Russian Jewry with the Kishinev pogrom of 1903, soon to be surpassed by massacres in Odessa (1905) and Bialystok (1906). Antisemitism was an important mobilizing principle for both the reactionary Black Hundreds after 1905, and the counter-revolutionary Whites in 1919–21. Whatever advantages Jews might have originally received from the rise of Soviet power were more than balanced by late Stalinism's mistreatment of the Jews as 'rootless cosmopolitans' and Jewish nationalists, the post-Stalinist imposition of quotas and restrictions and the demonizing of Zionism and the State of Israel. In the era of late communism, the outside world saw Soviet Jewry primarily as something that needed 'saving'.

If the proper end of Soviet Jewry is seen to lie only in *aliyah* (settlement in Israel) or emigration to the West, then there is substance to the claim that the Soviet Jewish experience was bound to end in tears. Yet there is room for reinterpretation. Even keeping in mind the excesses of late Stalinism, a claim can be made that the creation of a New Soviet Jew, 'Soviet in form, Russian in content', was one of the real success stories of the Soviet experiment. It is not entirely facetious to assert that the Soviet experience was good, if not for the Jews, then at least for individual Jews.

A striking aspect of the early revolutionary period was the extent to which many of the aspirations and needs of Russian Jewry corresponded to the agenda of the new Soviet state. This fact was obscured by the rhetorical tendency of Russian Marxism to deny the existence of the so-called Jewish Question, as conceived by the tsarist state. What were the Jews, after all, argued Marxists, but a sort of ethnic debris, prime material for assimilation once external constraints, which imposed an identity upon Jews, were removed. In Lenin's famous quip, if the Jews were a nation, it was one whose language was a jargon, and whose homeland was the Pale of Settlement.[1]

Lenin, of all people, should have seen the error of such a formulation. The emergence of his 'Bolshevik' faction of Social Democracy at the Second Congress of the RSDRP (the Russian Social Democratic Labour Party) in Brussels and London in 1903 was expedited by the schism he provoked over the claim of the Bund to speak 'as the sole representative of the Jewish proletariat'. Only the withdrawal of the Bund, at that time the largest single faction of the RSDRP, made possible Lenin's victory at the Congress. With them departed what Jonathan Frankel has called the 'genius of their movement' – compromise and common sense.[2] The triumphant Bolsheviks after 1917 had to accept the reality that 'the Jewish street', or at least the left side of that street, was dominated by the Bundists.

Demographic factors also came into play. The Jewish population of the late Russian Empire, including the Kingdom of Poland, numbered almost 5.2 million. In a number of Western and Polish provinces Jews constituted between 8 per cent and 12 per cent of the population. A number of major cities, such as Warsaw, Vilna, Lodz and Odessa, had large Jewish minorities. The general trend of the Jewish population in the early twentieth century was towards urbanization, since economic opportunity in the rural areas was poorly developed. The Jewish population was undergoing explosive growth, a phenomenon which the out-migration of over a million persons under late tsarism failed to control.[3]

The First World War and the Civil War had a dramatic impact upon the Jewish population, whose residential centres were criss-crossed by the lines of the Eastern Front. In 1915 the leaders of the Russian Army took the quixotic decision to relocate Jews from the front lines to the Russian interior. At a stroke the Council of Ministers, after anguished discussions, abandoned what had been the key element of Russia's Jewish policies, the Pale of Settlement. Tens of thousands of Jews flooded into the interior, to be followed by thousands more when pogroms became a staple of the Russian Civil War.[4] A substantial number of Jews settled in Petrograd and Moscow, centres of opportunity in post-revolutionary Russia.

The Jewish refugees of wartime not only endured a very ambiguous legal status but also were sundered from their customary economic pursuits. In this, they were typical of Russian and Polish Jewry as a whole. The economic transformation of Russia triggered by the abolition of serfdom in 1861 and the 'Era of the Great Reforms' engendered crisis as well as opportunity. Jews had been an integral part of the semifeudal economy in the Polish provinces which had been acquired by Russia in the partitions of 1772, 1793 and 1795. Their dominant economic role was that of intermediaries between the peasantry and the landowning nobility. Their activities were determined by their personal freedom and mobility (unlike the peasantry) and their access to liquid capital. Jews were a vital component of the rural economy, serving as leaseholders of estates, foremen and agents, petty tradesmen, middlemen, who purchased surplus grain and moved it to the market, and leaseholders of various feudal prerogatives, such as milling, on estates. The archetypal Jewish pursuit was that of *arendator*, the leaser of the noble right to distil and sell alcohol on the estate.[5] Jews played an important role in the liquor tax farming which was a major source of income for the Russian state budget.[6]

The modernization of the Russian state, however slow and gradual, put an end to these economic activities. The abolition of serfdom forced the rationalization of the manorial economy. Prudent landowners dispensed with Jewish agents in order to manage their own estates. The creation of a national rail network made obsolete the services of Jewish teamsters and hauliers, except on local routes. The great regional fairs, in which Jews played a major role, began to lose their singular importance for the regional economy of the southwest. The state continually reorganized the liquor tax monopoly. Contemporaries were well aware of these changes. Writing in 1869, in the aftermath of emancipation, the Jewish publicist Il'ia Orshanskii recognized the immediate negative impact upon Jews. But this would be a transitory phenomenon, he predicted, 'to the degree that Jewry adapts itself to the new structure of life, forgetting old trades and occupations which are now obsolete, and learning new ones'.[7]

Yet this adaptation did not come to pass. It is tempting to place the blame for the Judeophobia on the tsarist regime, as did both contemporaries and later historians. Restrictive legislation, growing from the state's obsessive fear that 'Jews exploited the peasantry', barred Jews from the opportunities offered by economic transformation. Jews were progressively barred from investing in land, as either buyers or leasers. Although the state was willing to rely on Jewish contractors to build part of the national rail network – Slavophile criticism notwithstanding – Jews found few opportunities on lines which were not operated by their co-religionists. The state discouraged Jewish investments in joint-stock companies. Norms and quotas were imposed on Jews in the emergent professional classes, such as in pharmacy and at the bar. An underlying concern of all state reforms of the liquor monopoly, as well as the notorious May Laws of 1882, was to dispense with the services of the Jews, who were the chief culprits of 'intoxicating the peasantry'. Looming over all this was the Pale of Settlement, which kept most Jews from the economic opportunities of the Russian heartland.

These liabilities, even if taken all together, cannot account for growing Jewish poverty in early-twentieth-century Russia. Even had all the new professions, from bank director to railway conductor, been free of restrictions and all occupied by Jews, they would have been insufficient to relieve the economic crisis. The Pale of Settlement and the Kingdom of Poland, far from being a territorial ghetto, contained some of the most dynamic areas of economic growth in the Empire.

The core of the economic dilemma was twofold: the population explosion of Russian Jewry, and the overconcentration of Jews in a narrow band of mercantile activities. Jewish reformers recognized this reality and pursued a strategy of 'productivization', exemplified by the creation of the Society for the Spread of Productive Work among the Jews of Russia (ORT) in 1880 and recurrent dreams of Jewish agricultural colonization, which were also to inspire the first Russian proto-Zionists. Thus, while the Jewish community was indeed poor, its leadership was aware of the economic changes necessary for economic betterment. There was no vested Jewish interest in maintaining the economic *status quo*. After all, asked one Jewish critic sardonically, 'Who would freely choose the degrading and dangerous job of tavern-keeper?' Russian Jewry contained no powerful and entrenched opponents of change as did, for example, the peasantry. Of all categories of the Russian population, Jews, out of simple pragmatism, were conditioned to welcome economic change.

Turning from the materialism of daily life to the rarified atmosphere of *mentalités* reveals another dynamic element in pre-revolutionary Jewry. The traditional religious and cultural values of Jewish communities in Europe were eroded by the impact of social and economic change in the modern period. The numbers and concentration of East European Jewry, as well as the relative backwardness of many of their host societies, delayed but could not prevent an analogous impact upon Russian Jewry. Some change transpired through conscious efforts of groups such as adherents of *Haskalah*, the Jewish variant of the pan-European Enlightenment movement, or supporters of religious reform, orientated to modernist and traditionalist axes. Much more change was unconscious or reactive, and emerged in various shades of acculturation and assimilation. The first all-Russian census of 1897, which famously revealed that over 97 per cent of Jews in the Empire chose Yiddish as their 'native' tongue, is deeply misleading, because it failed to register the high levels of multilingualism which circumstantial evidence suggests existed in the Jewish community.

As in the West, modernization created the possibility of new identities and new forms of self-awareness. Scholars have been aware of these new identities, even as they differ on how best to catalogue them. Yet Russian statesmen, faced with growing diversity within imperial Jewry – of which they were not entirely unaware – clung to the pre-modern identification of a 'Jew' as a member of a specific faith community. A formal act of religious conversion alone moved an individual out of the category of 'Jew', and beyond the corpus of legislation which regulated Jewish life. One could be a Jewish heretic or a freethinker, or completely assimilated, but without a visit to the baptismal font, one remained a Jew. A few Jews attempted to formulate a new identificational rubric, exemplified by the Duma deputy and Christian convert M. Ia. Gertsenshtein when he described himself as 'a Russian of Jewish origin'. Such a course was overtly rejected by most Jewish intellectuals, for whom religious conversion was viewed as a disreputable act, a betrayal of the Jewish people, however backward and obscurantist they might be.[8]

The disinclination of those Jews who might have been most likely to convert – Russian versions of Heine, for whom baptism was the admission ticket to European civilization – ensured that the vast majority of accultu-rated Jewish intellectuals remained technically within the Jewish commu-nity, and imparted a good deal of energy and creativity to it. As a consequence, a bewildering diversity of Jewish identities emerged, going far beyond the European-style 'Russians of the Mosaic persuasion', which, had the laws of the Empire permitted it, might well have become the most popular path of least resistance. Such individuals would have fulfilled the poet Jehuda Leib Gordon's classic, if misunderstood, exhortation to 'be a man on the street and a Jew at home'.

Every identification decision forced another choice. Socialists found themselves obliged to work in, and for, a renewed Yiddish language and culture, as the only way of taking their propaganda to the Jewish masses. Nationalists were forced to choose between Zionism, Autonomism (invol-ving cultural and administrative autonomy) and Territorialism (involving concentrated Jewish settlement, possibly outside Palestine), to select a Yiddish or Hebrew linguistic medium and to locate their activities within a social–political context. The battleground for these movements was the organized Jewish community, the *kehillah*, into which partisan politics were injected in the years of revolution.[10] Even the Orthodox traditional-ists were forced to organize in order to defend their influence over the daily routine of Jewish life.[11] What this presaged was the collapse, politicization and reconstruction of Jewish communal life in both city and *shtetl*.

It was inescapable that the Jews be included on the Soviet agenda of 'ethnic engineering', because of their numbers and the fact that they were being aggressively courted by such immediate political rivals of the Bolsheviks as the Bund. The Leninist response to ethnic questions grew from the same brand of political pragmatism which led the Bolsheviks to plagiarize the land programme of the Social Revolutionaries. In the case of the Jews, the Bolsheviks tacitly accepted an ethnic status for the Jews, reflecting the influence of the *Folkspartei* and the Bund, who both argued for forms of Jewish cultural and political autonomy. Indeed, the shortage of cadres led the Bolsheviks effectively to turn over the Jewish street to collaborationist Bundists. Without them there would have been nobody to staff the Jewish sections of the party and the state. The Bundists were at least socialists, even if spoiled by their un-Leninist willingness to compro-mise (which allowed their co-optation in the first place). The Bund's ethnicized version of Jewishness, which militantly rejected Judaism's reli-gious culture, was one with which the communists were entirely comfor-table. Indeed, Jews subsequently played a visible role as militant atheists in campaigns directed against both Judaism and Christianity. Zionists, with their Hebrew-based culture and unwillingness to participate in the immediate political rough and tumble, were automatically placed in the enemy camp. In short, the granting of ethnic status to Russian Jewry offered numerous avantages to the Soviet regime.

The Jews were a large and dependable source of cadres for the army, the bureaucracy and the security forces. The Jews of late tsarism had affiliated with virtually every political movement except the Right, and, aside from a few Jewish capitalists, were remarkably untainted by associations with the Old Regime, despite efforts by some socialists to depict pre-war tradition-alists as collaborators and class enemies. The reliable status of the Jews was re-enforced when the counter-revolution made antisemitism one of its mobilizing principles.[12] In a kind of ideological shorthand, merely to be a Jew was a form of security clearance. This confidence was fully repaid. Jews, derided in tsarist times as unpatriotic and cowardly draft-dodgers, joined the civil state administration in large numbers, to the extent that Lev Trotsky lamented that they preferred service with the pen to the rigours of the war front. Still the phenomenon of the Jewish Red Army soldier was not such a rarity that such a figure as the Jewish partisan Levinson in A. A. Fadeev's *The rout* did not seem incongruous.[13] The early Soviet regime expressed its gratitude to the Jews in tangible form, by specifically outlawing and prosecuting antisemitism. Those guilty of anti-Jewish utterances in the 1920s could easily find themselves before a 'comrades' court'.

Jews, as a group, were eager for the opportunities provided by the new Soviet government. The pool of trained, or at least loyal, cadres included not only former Bundists, who served out of a sense of loyalty to the socialist revolution, but also a significant number of Jewish professionals who had been denied opportunity and scope by the tsarist regime. The Jews, in Lenin's grateful words, 'sabotaged the saboteurs', the anti-Bolshevik intelligentsia who refused to serve the new regime. A subsequent example of the utility of the Jews occurred at the time of the annexation of eastern Poland by the USSR in 1939. Ben-Cion Pinchuk has shown how the occupying regime used its Jewish cadres to soften the blow of annexation for Polish Jewry, as well as making use of Polish Jews in the administration of Soviet power.[14]

Once the revolution was fought and won, the Jews also provided ample raw material for Soviet social engineering, as a group for whom 'produc-tivization' was a universally agreed desideratum. The dream of settling Jews on the land, for example, provided excellent opportunities to experi-ment with cooperative and collective farms for Jews, even as these forms of organization were being resisted by the peasantry as a whole.[15] The will-ingness of foreign Jewish charitable organizations, such as the American Joint Distribution Committee, to provide financial support, provided an economic lifeline for the regime, eager to attract foreign investment and expertise. These initiatives bore fruit: on the eve of the collectivization of agriculture, 10 per cent of the Jewish population of the Soviet Union was engaged in agriculture.[16] Ideological and economic goals could even be used to advance strategic objectives, as when the regime selected Birobidzhan, on the Soviet–Chinese frontier, as the territory to host a putative Jewish autonomous region.[17]

Representing a pool of underemployed or unproductive workers, demonstratively mobile, devoid of economic power and lacking vested interests, Jews were obvious raw material for the objectives of the Five-Year Plan. Jews were available to serve as common labourers or to be trained as 'red specialists'. Literature offers an example of both. In Valentin Kataev's 1932 industrial novel, *Time, forward!*,[18] the technical specialist in the preparation of concrete foundations, as well as members of the work gangs on a site in Magnitogorsk, are Jews. Statistics make the same point: by the end of the second Five-Year Plan, 30.5 per cent of Jews were classed as labourers, and 40.7 per cent were considered white-collar workers, as compared with the economic profile of Jews in late imperial Russia.[19] There can be no doubt that Soviet power had solved the economic aspects of the so-called Jewish Question.

As the Jews became a normal part of Soviet society, another phenomenon gained prominence. Although the Jews were provided with the framework for life as an ethnic group – Yiddish-language schools, cultural institutions, etc. – the pre-war period witnessed a growing trend toward acculturation and assimilation.[20] On the eve of the war, 54.6 per cent of the Soviet Jewish population declared Russian as their native tongue, a dramatic increase from the 26 per cent who so declared in 1926.[21] At first glance this might indicate that Lenin's prophecy, that Jewish ethnic material would be subsumed in a larger, supranational socialist culture, was coming to pass. Yet just as many more Jews spoke a non-Jewish language than revealed by the imperial census of 1897, so too a lingering sense of Jewish identity, shorn of its religious foundations, hid behind the statistics of Russification. This claim is supported by the response of Jews to the Holocaust, much of which took place on Soviet soil, with Soviet Jews as immediate witnesses.

The Shoah was the predominant agent in the transformation of Soviet Jewry. The pre-war Jewish population was reduced by half, from approximately 5 million to 2.5 million.[22] The communities which were destroyed were those least changed by Soviet culture. In the main Yiddish speaking, they maintained the closest hold on the traditions of Jewish religious culture. Their destruction put a decisive end to centuries-old East European Jewry as a discrete cultural entity.

Even as this terrible destruction enveloped them, Soviet Jewry again fully complied with the needs of the Soviet state. The German attack on the USSR placed the regime in desperate need of allies. Even when the Allied coalition was formed, the Soviets were in dire need of resources to relieve the terrible pressures placed on the Red Army and the Soviet economy. These included food and war materials and, most of all, a military strategy which would deflect German resources away from the Eastern Front. They key to these objectives lay in cooperation and good relations with the USSR's Western allies, and the support of public opinion, especially in the USA.

The Soviet-style definition of Jewish ethnicity was specific to time and place: a 'Jew' (*evrei*) was the descendent of the Yiddish-speaking group, a group bound together by a common culture developed during a centuries-long residence in Eastern Europe. This ethnic group had no ties to people outside Eastern Europe or with so-called 'World Jewry', and it lacked any links to the inhabitants of ancient (or modern) Palestine.

With the outbreak of the Great Patriotic War, this line was abandoned. Rather, links with World Jewry were reasserted and emphasized. Extensive propaganda was disseminated designed to recall the links between Soviet and US Jewry, and to present the Red Army as virtually the only salvation for Jews under the Nazi yoke. Atrocities, including information about the Holocaust, were publicized in the West. A clarion call was issued to World Jewry to support and assist the heroic USSR. This activity was carried out by a specially constituted body, the Jewish Anti-Fascist Committee (JAFC), an agency of the Soviet Information Bureau under the Ministry of Foreign Affairs. The leadership of the JAFC, drawn from prominent Soviet Jewish artists and professionals, and chaired by the actor Solomon Mikhoels, was specifically charged with making links with Jews abroad. In 1943, Mikhoels and Itsik Fefer were sent to North America to build support among Jewish communities for the Soviet war effort.[23]

External activities were mirrored by internal initiatives designed to promote Jewish support for the war effort and, more importantly, to demonstrate Soviet solicitude for the Jewish population. JAFC activities on the national stage included the publication of a Yiddish-language newspaper, *Eynikayt*, which circulated widely throughout the USSR. The JAFC also sponsored a number of rallies in support of the war effort. In the absence of any other national Jewish body, the JAFC evolved as the 'Jewish address' in the Soviet Union. The Jewish population turned to its offices with petitions, queries and declarations. Its activities provide a means of assessing the strength of Jewish national feeling during and immediately after the war.

The very fact that Soviet citizens approached the JAFC as Jews reveals a sense of identity and communality. Many of the approaches were mundane, such as appeals for help with housing, support in dealings with various governmental institutions or requests for information about relatives lost in the chaos of wartime. Yet other communications reflected a real sense of Jewish identity. The theatre critic A. Eydelman, touring the recently liberated territories, sought JAFC assistance for a group of Jewish refugees he had found in Mogilev-Podolsk. The 'last of the Mohicans of Western Jewry', they were survivors of the notorious regional ghetto created by the Romanians in Transdnistria, between the Dnester and the Bug rivers.

Significantly, they were not even Soviet citizens, and did not speak Russian.[24]

There were numerous complaints about antisemitism in liberated areas and urgent calls for the Soviet state to take action.[25] Besides the essentially negative task of fighting antisemitism, many correspondents called for a positive assertion of the role of Jews in the war effort, through the creation of monuments, museums and publications.[26] A sense of self-confident Jewish identity shines through all these requests. One correspondent complained of the growing intermarriage and assimilation of Soviet Jews, and demanded 'the opportunity to socialise with each other, to turn to a leading comrade for advice, help or support'.[27] Ya. Kantor, writing in 1945 in support of the revivification of Jewish autonomous regions, noted that

> however far the process of Jewish assimilation had advanced, and however subjectively Jews relate to it, one thing is clear: under any circumstances the preservation and development of Soviet-Jewish literature, which is national in form and socialist in content, is in the interests not only of the Jewish people, but of the entire Soviet nation.[28]

Boris Goldenberg, writing to Mikhoels in 1946, explicitly linked the victims of the Shoah to past Jewish martyrs killed by the Romans or in the Spanish Inquisition:

> We will not be ashamed of our ancestry. And what is more, in our country we Jews are not poor relations. The conviction is strong at present that Israel lived in the past, lives in the present, and will live eternally in the future.[29]

It is hardly necessary to note how closely the latter words echoed the sacred Soviet slogan that 'Lenin Lives!' The letter of a guards lieutenant to the JAFC urged the preservation

> of a wonderful people which gave the world some of the brightest luminaries; a people which carried throughout centuries of persecution, death and torture the banner of love for mankind and internationalism; a people of unprecedented creative energy, research, discoveries and inventions; a people with the dream of happiness of a united mankind and a deep faith in progress.[30]

Numerous letters to the JAFC demanded the creation of greater cultural–educational activities, especially the publication of a daily newspaper and a monthly literary journal in Yiddish, as well as theatres and houses of culture.[31]

The preservation of Jewish identity and culture was a stated motive underlying requests, including those made by the JAFC leadership to Stalin himself, for the post-war resettlement of Jews in centres such as Crimea.[31]

Similar expressions of national solidarity and self-confidence could be seen in the great collective outpouring of grief at the funeral of Mikhoels, after his 'accidental' death (arranged by the MGB, apparently at Stalin's direct order) in 1948, or the joy and excitement which greeted Soviet support for the creation of the State of Israel and the arrival of its first ambassador, Golda Meir. In retrospect, these actions and initiatives, such as the Crimean project, may be seen to precipitate their authors towards the abyss. But hindsight should not blind us to the reasonable expectations which the Jewish leadership had at this time. After all, high state and party officials, such as Lavrenti Beria and Georgi Malenkov ordered investigation in response to JAFC complaints, for example, of unequal distribution of post-war food aid to Jews.[33]

Post-war reconstruction and resettlement were a prime consideration of the USSR. The USSR played a major role in the creation of the State of Israel, not least by allowing Polish Jews detained on Soviet soil to be repatriated, with the clear understanding that they would be allowed to emigrate to Palestine. The clandestine aid channelled to the Israelis by Czechoslovakia, with Soviet connivance, is well documented. There was a part to be played in all of this by a vigorous and loyal Soviet Jewry, 'national in form, socialist in content'. Finally, no Soviet Jew could ignore the fact that, without the exertions and sacrifices of the Red Army, European Jewry would almost certainly have been exterminated.

So what went wrong? The simple answer is that the Soviet agenda changed, leaving Soviet Jews dramatically exposed. So many of the tasks to which the regime had assigned them were redefined in a way that transformed acts of the greatest loyalty into deeds of the basest treachery. In particular, the response of the Soviet leadership to the changed circumstances of the Cold War had a fatal impact upon many Soviet Jews. For example, the transformation of the wartime alliance into an adversarial relationship meant that foreign links became compromising and dangerous. This was especially the case with officials of the JAFC, because most of their foreign contacts were with private Jewish philanthropic and communal bodies, with whom diplomatic relations could not be suddenly sundered. Both sides were slow to recognize how continuing contacts placed those on the Soviet side in danger.

The post-war period also witnessed a general attack on non-Russian nationalism, such as that stirred up in Ukraine as a result of the German war, or persisting in areas recently annexed to the Soviet Union, such as the Baltic States. In such an atmosphere, the enthusiastic form of Jewish self-assertion, such as that noted above, was easily labelled 'bourgeois nationalism'. Foreign links and Jewish nationalism came together in the Crimean Project, whereby foreign Jewish welfare bodies, such as the American Joint Distribution Committee, proposed to assist the establishment of a Jewish autonomous region in the Crimean Peninsula, which had been depopulated by war and wartime deportations. This project was later portrayed as a foreign effort to detach the Crimea from the USSR and to turn it into a bastion of Western imperialism on the doorstep of the USSR.

The officially sponsored praise for the genius of the Great Russian people – which should not be confused with a genuine resurgence of Russian nationalism – also had a pernicious impact upon other nationalities. At a time when the courage and resiliency of the Great Russians was being praised for winning the Great Patriotic War, and when the Russian genius was being credited with most of the accomplishments of Western civilization, Jewish claims of war heroism or assertions of national genius were an unwelcome intrusion. Since Yiddish culture had sustained some of the greatest losses in the course of the war, it was natural for Jewish spokespeople to make extravagant claims of its importance and the need to give it massive support. These demands were publicized at a time when they were least likely to receive a sympathetic hearing in official circles. In view of the importance that the State of Israel was later to achieve in Soviet demonology, it should be noted that in the late 1940s Jewish 'bourgeois nationalism' at home was judged a greater sin than the 'bourgeoisie nationalism' of Zionism abroad. Those who wanted a 'Soviet Zion' in the Crimea were shot, while those who dreamed of a return to Eretz Israel were dispatched to the labour camps.[34]

The last years of Stalinism have usually been seen as filled with the greatest menace for the Jews, so they are worth examining in detail for what they reveal about the position of Soviet Jewry. This is particularly the case given the conception of 'Stalin's war against the Jews' as a fairly consistent campaign, driven by its own Stalinist logic. According to this scenario, the aged dictator, who had long harboured antisemitic prejudices, gave full vent to them amidst the growing paranoia of his final days. Jews were said to be a central target of the campaign against 'rootless cosmopolitans', launched by the cultural purge known as the Zhdanovshchina. The signal that the Jews were to be more than just one target of a reindoctrination campaign was provided by the MGB murder of Solomon Mikhoels in Minsk on 12 January 1948. Within the year, virtually all of the leadership of the JAFC was under arrest. Their trial and execution for treason, anti-Soviet activities and bourgeoisie nationalism in 1952 pointed the way to the final stage, to be triggered by the discovery of the 'Doctors' Plot'. The trial of the (largely Jewish) doctors would have culminated in a great national pogrom, secretly organized by the MGB, which would have revealed 'the people's wrath'. For their own protection, the Jews of large Soviet cities such as Moscow and Leningrad would have been relocated to protective centres (that is, concentration camps) somewhere in Siberia or Central Asia.[35] There have been consistent rumours that such camps were already under construction in 1952.

As more information has come to light about the last years of Stalin, including the trial transcripts of the leadership of the JAFC, doubts have arisen about the accepted scenario, especially its integral, consistent nature. Benjamin Pinkus has effectively demonstrated that the campaign against 'rootless cosmopolitans' was not initially directed against Jews, although as the campaign widened they became a logical and favoured target.[36] Rather than a signal for a vast crackdown upon the Jews, the murder of Mikhoels may have had a much more banal origin – Stalin's pique about rumours about his family life said to have been passed on to the foreign press by the gossip-loving actor.[37] The arrest of the JAFC is not surprising, once one reads the archival evidence which reveals official dissatisfaction at the way in which it overstepped its brief by becoming a 'Jewish address' and 'ombudsman' for Jews throughout the USSR. Its assertive Jewishness was also a frequent cause for concern. The arrest of the leadership, the records of the investigation suggest, was originally envisioned to produce a case based on grounds of ideological deviations rather than wholesale treason.[38] The original case was transformed into something grander in 1952, when it was heard by a military collegium. The reasons for this transformation require further investigation. A preliminary conclusion is that the treatment of the Jewish cultural leadership was tied to internal politics of the MGB, rather than part of a consistently unfolding campaign. The Doctors' Plot has never been satisfactorily explained, except as the culminating phase of an anti-Jewish campaign, which fed on Stalin's growing paranoia.[39] Here again, it is necessary to investigate the links to internal Soviet politics and infighting within Stalin's retinue.

Could a punitive pogrom ever have been in the planning stage? It would have represented a real innovation by the security organs, which were not known for mobilizing explosions of mass violence. (They had the model of tsarist ineptitude with such tactics to deter them.) If such an initiative was in the planning stage, there must be ample archival evidence which has yet to be brought to light. There is much anecdotal evidence of a growing mood of antisemitism among the general Soviet public, much of it reported by Jews, especially medical personnel, who were on the receiving end. A fruitful area of research would be to measure the scope of this feeling, as expressed in unprinted letters to newspapers, denunciations to the organs, and pro-Jewish or anti-Jewish letters sent to various Soviet institutions.

Could a mass deportation of substantial numbers of Soviet Jews have been carried out under the conditions described above? As John Keep has remarked, 'the security services had given ample proof that they were capable of organising such an operation'.[40] Yet past resettlements had been directed against small, geographically centralized and easily recognizable national minorities.[41] We may recall Khrushchev's quip that Stalin's desire to deport all the Ukrainians was thwarted by the fact that there were too many of them. The problem with Soviet Jews was that they were not instantly recognizable. (Thus the need, in the course of the press campaign against Jewish rootless cosmopolitans, to include their 'Jewish' name in brackets alongside their Russian name.) Jews were also, as noted above, well-integrated into the national economy and were geographically dispersed. The 'liquidation of the kulaks as a class' in 1929–32, as well as the expulsion of Volga Germans, Crimean Tatars, Chechens and others, did indeed reveal the ruthlessness and determination of the regime when engaged in a death struggle with its perceived enemies. One wonders if the same determination and sense of danger prevailed in 1953. A final point which should be emphasized is the ease with which the entire anti-Jewish campaign collapsed within days after the death of Stalin.

Power, like love, means never having to say you're sorry. All the anti-Jewish initiatives of late Stalinism, of whatever origin, were simply dropped after Stalin's death. There were no apologies, rehabilitations (except for the accused Kremlin doctors) or explanations. All pro-Jewish proposals, such as resettlement or the reinvigoration of Soviet Jewish cultural life, in any language, were totally ignored. Soviet Jews were left without a sense of closure or security, and no outlets for a national identity which had been re-enforced by the external attacks described above.

It was left to others to reconceptualize Soviet Jews as the 'Jews of Silence', in need of rescue and support, and to make them a pawn in the 'great game' of the Cold War. The surprising success of Israel in the Six Days War of 1967 created additional complications. Even as the successes of Israeli arms proved a source of pride to Soviet Jews (and reinforced their claim that Jews had played their fair share in the Great Patriotic War), Soviet ideologues were metamorphising the USSR's opposition to Zionism and the state of Israel into an ideology of 'anti-Zionism', envisioning a fantastic international anti-communist conspiracy, with the State of Israel at its centre.[42] Such policies helped transform the vague discontents and resentments of Soviet Jews into a fully-fledged nationalist movement which played directly into the hands of the USSR's international opponents. The Soviet Union, in effect, was a principal architect of the 'Save Soviet Jewry' campaign which caused it so much embarrassment and travail. It is more than symbolic that one of the first steps which Mikhail Gorbachëv took to establish the credentials of perestroika for the outside world was the *de facto* elimination of constraints on the emigration of Soviet Jews.

Gorbachëv's *rapprochement* with Soviet Jewry, like perestroika itself, was too little, too late, but it does provide a hint of how the Soviet Union could have made effective use of its Jewish population. As we have seen, the young Soviet state, committed to the creation of a totally new socio-economic system, and pre-revolutionary Jewry, seeking a modern identity and a stable and secure economic life, shared goals which were substantially the same. The theoretical formulation of the Soviet state envisioned local autonomy and cultural development for national minorities. This was to be underpinned by rational economic planning which was modern and non-discriminatory in its willingness to use all the human raw material at hand. The only area of potential conflict was the survival of a religious-based culture by some Jews, but even this was undermined by the Holocaust and the spread of secularization throughout Soviet society as a whole. A Jewish community, linked by a strong sense of internal ethnic identity and tied by genealogy and culture to the West, yet firmly integrated into the Soviet system, could have been invaluable to Soviet interests. The persistence with which Jews have retained a distinct Russian Jewish identity after leaving the Soviet Union suggests how easily they might have become a great Soviet success story.[43] The failure of the Soviet Union to make effective use of its Jews and the manner in which it turned them instead into tools in the hands of the enemies of the regime is a striking example of the ideological degeneracy which pointed to the wholesale collapse of the Soviet experiment.

Notes

1 B. Pinkus, *The Jews of the Soviet Union: the history of a national minority* (Cambridge, 1988), p. 50.
2 J. Frankel *Prophechy and politics. Socialism, nationalism, and the Russian Jews, 1862–1917* (Cambridge, 1981), p. 246.
3 Evreiskoe Statisticheskoe Obshchesvto (ESO), *Evreiskoe naselenie Rossii po dannym perepisi 1897 g. i po noveishim istochnikam* (Petrograd, 1917); Pinkus, *The Jews of the Soviet Union*, pp. 89–90.
4 H. Rogger, *Jewish policies and right-wing politics in Imperial Russia* (London, 1986), pp. 100–2.
5 J. Klier, *Imperial Russia's Jewish question, 1855–1881* (Cambridge, 1995), pp. 14–15.
6 D. Christian, *'Living water': Vodka and Russian society on the eve of emancipation* (Oxford, 1990), pp. 99–116.
7 Klier, *Imperial Russia's Jewish question*, pp. 288–90.
8 S. Dubnow, *Nationalism and history: essays on old and new Judaism* (Philadelphia, PA, 1958), pp. 93, 366.
9 M. Stanislawski, *Tsar Nicholas I and the Jews. The transformation of Jewish Society in Russia, 1825–1855* (Philadelphia, 1988), p. 5.
10 I. Levitats, *The Jewish community in Russia, 1844–1917* (Jerusalem, 1981).
11 E. Lederhendler, *Jewish responses to modernity: new voices in America and Eastern Europe* (New York, 1994), pp. 67–103.
12 P. Kenez, 'Pogroms and white ideology in the Russian Civil War', in J. Klier and S. Lambroza, eds *Pogroms: anti-Jewish violence in modern Russian history* (Cambridge, 1991), pp. 293–313.
13 A.A. Fadeev, Razgrom. In *Sobranie sochinenii* vol I, Moscow.
14 B.-C. Pinchuk, *Shtetl Jews under Soviet rule: eastern Poland on the eve of the Holocaust* (Oxford, 1990), pp. 22–7, 49–51.
15 M. Lewin, *Russian peasants and Soviet power: a study of collectivization* (New York, 1968), pp. 81–102.
16 Pinkus, *The Jews of the Soviet Union*, p. 96.
17 N. Levin, *The Jews in the Soviet Union since 1917: the paradox of survival*, 2 vols (London and New York, 1988), vol. I, pp. 282–311.
18 V. Kataev, Vremia, Vpered! In *Sobranie sochinenii* vol II, (Moscow, 1932).

19 M. Altshuler, *Soviet Jewry since the Second World War: population and social structure* (New York, 1987), p. 10.
20 A. Greenbaum, *Jewish scholarship and scholarly institutions in Soviet Russia, 1918–1953* (Jerusalem, 1978).
21 Altshuler, *Soviet Jewry since the Second World War*, p. 185.
22 Altshuler, *Soviet Jewry since the Second World War*, p. 4.
23 S. Redlich, *Propaganda and nationalism in wartime Russia: the Jewish Anti-fascist Committee in the USSR* (no publisher stated, 1982), pp. 115–25.
24 S. Redlich, *War, Holocaust and Stalinism: a documented history of the Jewish Anti-Fascist Committee in the USSR* (no publisher stated, 1995), pp. 225–6.
25 Redlich, *War, Holocaust and Stalinism*, pp. 228–32.
26 Redlich, *War, Holocaust and Stalinism*, pp. 236–7.
27 Redlich, *War, Holocaust and Stalinism*, p. 234.
28 Redlich, *War, Holocaust and Stalinism*, p. 269.
29 Redlich, *War, Holocaust and Stalinism*, p. 238.
30 Redlich, *War, Holocaust and Stalinism*, p. 239.
31 Redlich, *War, Holocaust and Stalinism*, p. 276.
32 Redlich, *War, Holocaust and Stalinism*, pp. 264–7.
33 Redlich, *War, Holocaust and Stalinism*, pp. 246, 249–52.
34 B. Pinkus, *The Soviet government and the Jews, 1948–1967 a documented study* (Cambridge, 1984), pp. 194–5.
35 G. Kostyrchenko, *Out of the red shadows* (Amherst, NY, 1995), pp. 294, 305.
36 Pinkus, *The Soviet government and the Jews*, pp. 151–63.
37 Kostyrchenko, *Out of the red shadows*, pp. 80–3.
38 V.P. Naumov, *Nepravednyi sud. Poslednii stalinskii rasstrel* (Moscow, 1994).
39 Kostyrchenko, *Out of the red shadows*, pp. 248–305; A. Vaksberg, *Stalin against the Jews* (New York, 1994), pp. 238–80.
40 J. Keep, *Last of the empires: a history of the Soviet Union, 1945–1991* (Oxford and New York, 1996), p. 37.
41 R. Conquest, *The nation killers* (London, 1972).
42 W. Korey, *Russian antisemitism, Pamyat, and the demonology of Zionism* (Chur, 1995), pp. 13–29; Y. Ro'i, *The struggle for Soviet Jewish emigration, 1948–1967* (Cambridge, 1991), pp. 286–338.
43 F. Markowitz, *A community in spite of itself* (Washington, DC, 1993); N. Shepherd, *The Russians in Israel: the ordeal of freedom* (London, 1993).

|13|

Kul'turnost' *in the Soviet Union: ideal and reality*

CATRIONA KELLY

'History of the book', or *histoire du livre*, is a relatively new branch of Western historiography, and one that has to date made relatively little impact upon the study of Russia.[1] As one of the pioneers of the field, Robert Darnton, has summarized, 'histories of the book' have generally espoused either 'diffusion study' (analysis of the numbers of copies of books in circulation, quantitative readership surveys and studies of reception more broadly) or 'discourse analysis' (the study of ideological and textological features in the texts circulated).[2] Here, I shall apply both methods, but predominantly 'discourse analysis', in order to consider advice literature, a genre of printed ephemera dedicated to the dissemination of concepts of refined behaviour, and including treatises on etiquette, house management, health and fitness and so on.

Advice literature, whatever its defects as a source for investigating behaviour in the real world (which I would not want to underestimate) is of considerable interest as a source for investigating ideals of behaviour. In the Soviet period, centralization of cultural institutions (state control of publishing and the imposition of rigid print censorship) made advice literature a vehicle of official propaganda. It is therefore an excellent index of the administration's anxieties about certain issues (for instance, health and hygiene in the 1920s, the socialization of adolescents in the 1960s and 1970s), whose importance is made evident by the number of editions of particular types of advice literature issued and the print-runs in which these editions are published. (For example, etiquette books, which practically disappeared between 1917 and 1954, began to be published from the late 1950s in enormous quantities, averaging around 50 titles per year between 1960 and 1970, and 80 between 1970 and 1990; print-runs for these books and for treatises on house management were rarely less than 100 000 copies, and sometimes as high as one million.) Advice literature also provides revealing material about official constructions of the mass reader (assumed to be a person who was naive, ignorant and in need of expert guidance). At the same time, printed expressions of official desires to regulate behaviour had, however indirectly, to negotiate needs and wishes coming 'from below', so that these books also supply oblique information about the concerns of their readers. And, though reading advice literature often feels like wading through a treacle of cliché within a labyrinth of plagiarism, the very stability and repetitiveness of the genre is of historical interest. On the one hand, the banality of the advice offered in Soviet advice books demands an interrogation of the idea that *kul'turnost'*, 'cultured behaviour', was a peculiarly 'Soviet' or indeed 'Russian' phenomenon; on the other, the fact that minor deviations from advice literature tradition could take on considerable symbolic significance facilitated the creation of a 'Soviet' behaviour ethos that depended for its persuasiveness upon a sense that 'Soviet man' (or woman) was a unique creature.

This compressed survey of Soviet advice literature as a contribution to constructing the ideology of 'cultured behaviour' falls into three sections. The first deals with interpretations of *kul'turnost'* in the first three decades of Soviet power, and argues that this succeeded in presenting a remarkably unoriginal behaviour ideal so that this emerged as characteristically 'Soviet'. The second section concerns *kul'turnost'* propaganda in the post-Stalin period, and argues that this progressively undermined the sense of a separate 'Soviet' behaviour. In the third, I raise the question of the ways in which the ideal of *kul'turnost'* reflected and constructed the reality of Soviet behaviour.

To date, the only part of the history of *kul'turnost'* that has been investigated with any degree of thoroughness is the period of 'high Stalinism' (1935–53). The propaganda of 'culturedness' at this date has been seen on the one hand as a 'Great Retreat' from socialist ideology and a form of embourgeoisement,[3] and on the other as the accommodation of a new class, 'the new masters of the Soviet state', including party officials and members of the intelligentsia, most particularly the technocracy.[4] Both these two interpretations are called into question by advice literature. First of all, very little propaganda for *kul'turnost'*, at any rate in the form of advice literature, was addressed to 'the masters of the Soviet state'; its implied target was, on the contrary, that nebulous creature, 'the Soviet mass reader', an individual requiring guidance 'from above'. Second, advice literature offers little support for the hypothesis that any 'Great Retreat', or jettisoning of socialist values, would have made itself evident to Soviet mass readers after 1935. So far as conduct guides were concerned, *kul'turnost'* was associated right through the Soviet period first and foremost with hygienic living, efficiency at work and intellectual self-improvement.

These prerequisites of the 'cultured person', far from being specifically 'Soviet' or 'socialist', can be matched in many conduct manuals from pre-revolutionary Russia and the West. It is instructive to compare extracts from Aleksei Gastev's *How to work* with an extract from an advice manual published in 1765, *Friendly advice to the young man beginning his life in society*:

DON'T FORGET!
YOUR FIRST STEP WHEN RE-ORGANISING FACTORIES AND
OFFICES MUST BE TO ESTABLISH CLEANLINESS . . . .
**Usually people 'get cracking' with a piece of work; where possible,
taking things gradually is a better idea . . . .**
**The cultured worker is easy to distinguish from the uncultured
worker because he always has everything to hand . . . .**
You should never eat while working. It is not only bad for your
stomach, but it is very bad for a person's character, since it causes
him to lose all self-restraint, and it is worst of all for the work being
done, since this will certainly be carried out in a sloppy manner
[*neriashlivo*].[5]

Combine cleanliness with order and method in all that you do . . . .
Avoid distractions. It is a very rational rule of life that you should
spend all your time on carrying out your duties . . . . Those who read
only in order to pass the time, and to boast about how many books
they have read, are unworthy to hold a good book in their hands.[6]

Similar was the formulation of the '10 Commandments' of memory
improvement as set out by A. L. Mendel'son: these included working in
an airy room, observing a rational diet, having plenty of sleep, alternating
physical and mental activity, being diligent, avoiding distractions and
working in silence.[7]

Space permitting, one could proliferate examples almost endlessly: the
self-help books of Samuel Smiles, very popular in Russia in the late nineteenth and early twentieth centuries, are another instance. Though the
complex of behaviour values outlined in these diverse sources came to be
known as *kul'turnost'* only in the late nineteenth century, it had been
familiar under other names, such as *vospitannost'*, or 'good breeding',
since the late eighteenth century. Far from being a specifically Russian
phenomenon, *kul'turnost'* is merely the Russian name for one phase in
what Norbert Elias, in a classic study of 1939, named as 'the civilizing
process', that is, the evolution of behaviour patterns which led to a 'growing
division of behaviour into what is and is not publicly permitted', and '[a
transformation of] the personality structure', so that 'the pressure to
restrain . . . impulses and the sociogenetic shame surrounding them . . .
are turned so completely into habits that we cannot resist them even when
alone, in the intimate sphere'.[8] Perhaps the closest English translation
for *kul'turnost'* would be 'cultivation', in use since the early eighteenth
century to express the supposition that appropriate behaviour was the
result of a conscious process of self-control and self-transformation.

Figure 13.1 'Your *nekul'turnost'* is your enemy'. The anti-type of 1930s *kul'turnost'*: a worker sprawls on his bed in his outdoor clothes, smoking, in the middle of muddle and squalor. Poster produced in Komsomol'sk-on-Amur, 1934. (Iu. Zhukov, *Liudi tridtsatykh godov*, Moscow, 1966.)

At the same time, it would be wrong to underestimate the specificity of the Soviet understanding of *kul'turnost'*. To be sure, the sense that the behaviour ethos so named was uniquely 'Soviet' derived in part from the fact that it pretended to be: truisms of post-Enlightenment behaviour literature all over Europe were presented as new and exciting discoveries (just as the aspirations of people in most Western capitalist societies to material self-betterment acquire an illusory specificity when named as 'the American dream'). But there were also some important features that distinguished *kul'turnost'* from concepts of civilized behaviour in other post-Enlightenment societies. Among the most important of these were the unusually strong emphasis on the collective significance of individual behaviour that went with *kul'turnost'*, and the ideology's pretensions to egalitarianism.

To take the collectivism point first: *kul'turnost'* was not to be understood as the idiosyncratic following of personal enthusiasms; train-spotting, pigeon-fancying or 'trivial pursuits' of any kind were not encouraged; reading was for information, not pleasure.[9] It represented the acquisition of a corpus of essential facts that every citizen needed to know: geographical, literary, artistic, musical, historical, and, of course, political. Participation in the *kul'turnost'* drive was, therefore, an act of social solidarity as well as a path to self-betterment; it was an enthusiastic striving for 'the golden mean' in all subjects rather than a search for deep knowledge in any one, a profoundly anti-Socratic form of self-discipline in which it was possible to know *enough* (and therefore, by implication, too much), and in which questions about the purpose of knowledge were not asked. One is reminded of Chernyshevskii's model revolutionary, Rakhmetov, who

> had read Thackeray's *Vanity Fair* with enjoyment, but . . . shut *Pendennis* when he had reached page 20: 'Thackeray said everything he had to say in *Vanity Fair*: one can tell there's nothing new here, so there's no point in reading on'. 'Every book I have read saves me from having to read twenty other books', he said.[10]

Up to a point, this strict denomination of 'useful knowledge' can be matched in post-Enlightenment conduct literature generally. Self-indulgent learning, or 'pedantry', had traditionally been feared as detrimental to harmonious social consensus: as Budgell put it in *The Spectator*, rather than resembling 'the dark lanthorn' of esoteric Egyptian philosophy, it was far preferable to 'be compared to an ordinary lamp, which consumes and wastes itself for the benefit of every passenger'. But Soviet advice literature visualized a whole society of 'useful lamps', in which knowledge was to be transmitted not for its showy effects, but as a gesture of social solidarity. According to Nadezhda Krupskaia in 'How to study: a letter to young people', 'real self-education does not take place in studies but through the process of active participation in collective life'.[12] Accordingly, in manuals such as Kerzhentsev's *Organise yourself!*, and in advisory magazines such as *Pomoshch' samoobrazovaniiu* (Aid for self-education, 1923–31) and *Uchis' sam!* (Teach yourself!, 1926–9), individual self-educating readers were exhorted to band together with their fellows in order to form consciousness-raising groups. Quizzes in popular magazines invited the reader to test his or her knowledge, emphasizing that the information was something to be shared collectively: the procedure was catechistic rather than competitive:

1. Recite by heart at least one poem by Pushkin. 2. Name and describe five plays by Shakespeare. 3. Name at least four rivers in Africa. 4. Name your favourite composer and his three major works. 5. Name five Soviet automobiles. 6. Convert 3/8 into a decimal. 7. Name the three most important sports tournaments of the last year and their results. 8. Describe the three paintings which you liked most at last year's exhibitions. 9. Have you read Stendhal's *Scarlet and black* and Turgenev's *Fathers and children*? 10. Explain why the Stakhanovite movement became possible in our country.[13]

Equally, the 'hygienic' imperative that underpinned *kul'turnost'* was not at all the same as the self-development advocated in pre-revolutionary guides to physical culture. Soviet guides emphasized the collective benefits of fitness. As V. Gorinevskii put it in a pamphlet under the title *The repair and tempering of the human organism*, 'A weak, feeble, intellectually underdeveloped, ideologically and politically indifferent person cannot become a professionally qualified worker of the kind that is needed for Soviet economic construction'.[14] Compare this with the introduction to Boyd Laynard's exercise manual (translated into Russian in 1909), where fitness is seen as a contribution to self-advancement in a competitive sense:

> Just as a steam engine whose furnace has been supplied with bad or insufficient fuel can never drive an express train, so men and women with debilitated constitutions are generally slow and have what is called 'no go' in them. In these days of keen competition such persons stand little chance in the great battle of life. They are pushed aside and others take their place. It is the great law of 'survival of the fittest'.[15]

If an overt and unremitting emphasis on cultivation as a public and collective duty, rather than an individual and private quest, was one distinguishing feature of the Soviet 'civilizing process', another was egalitarianism. Western etiquette books have almost invariably directly addressed the stratification of the society that they regulate (by providing information on how to behave according to the particular rung which one occupies in the social ladder); they have also recognized the stratification of readership (the advice provided in a peerage, dealing with the relative place in the order of precedence of an earl's third daughter and the second wife of a baron is not aimed at the same readership as advice on whether or not it is appropriate to use a fish knife). This overt stratification was also evident in pre-revolutionary Russian conduct guides. Health books and manuals of home management were more opulently produced than were etiquette books; different series were aimed at readers with very different economic resources (compare, for instance, *The lady's world calendar*, which offered advice about organizing 'the tea that is served at five o'clock', with sandwiches and cakes, with '*The Motherland*' *handy library*, whose guide to *bon ton* asserted that roast, salad and compote was a perfectly adequate dinner for guests.[16] As these examples also show, the upmarket kind of literature on house management was obedient to a 'luxury' imperative as well as a 'hygiene' imperative.

Advice on how to negotiate the pitfalls of the class hierarchy was invariably part of the material in turn-of-the-century etiquette books. Authors such as the improbably named Kleopatra Svetozarskaia, who published *Life in society, at home and at court* in 1890, saw etiquette as the vital underpinning of social distinctions, and emphasized that the rules of behaviour were 'not the same for a lady of high society and a bourgeoise [*meshchanka*], for a young man and an old one, for a young man and a young woman'.[17] And letter-writing manuals set out splendidly obsequious examples of the epistolary art, such as the following letter intended for one's departmental head upon promotion (and no doubt delivered upon bended knee):

> *Your Highness F . . . N . . . .!*
> Pray allow me to offer You my sincere felicitations upon the new honour which His Majesty has been pleased to lay upon You. The joy inspired in me — as indeed in all those fortunate enough to serve under Your command — by this auspicious occasion is beyond all measure. My sole and constant desire is to demonstrate to You that I am and always will be
> Your Highness's most obedient servant
> S.K.[18]

By contrast, Soviet conduct manuals never advocated deference of this kind or referred openly to social distinctions. Certainly, stratification of consumption patterns can be inferred from material published in the second half of the 1930s. The famous *Book of tasty and nutritious food*, an opulent culinary manual produced in 1939 as part of Anastas Mikoian's drive to modernize and mechanize the Soviet food industry, contained descriptions of dishes and utensils that were beyond the means of most Soviet citizens. A four-course meal of asparagus with sauce soubise, consommé royale, venison steaks and ice cream served off gilded porcelain and washed down with champagne was not often going to grace the table of the average lathe operator in a Soviet factory. Yet Mikoian's preface stressed that the book was aimed at 'the widest possible public'.[19] Similarly, the campaigns to improve service in Soviet shops and restaurants in the late 1930s and late 1940s, while implicitly favouring consumers over producers and service staff, did not suggest that deference to customers and patrons was a requirement of the 'cultured person'. An illusion of equal opportunity could therefore be preserved. Certainly, the 1930s saw a rehabilitation of the ideas of comfort and elegance (*uiut i iziashchestvo*), that had been lambasted by 1920s radicals such as Maiakovskii; but one should not exaggerate the luxury and esotericism of the material possessions that were labelled as legitimate by Soviet advice literature. Soviet women's magazines of the 1930s and 1940s provide advice on skin care, but not on choosing lipsticks and powders; and, although dress patterns were regularly published, advice was not given on such arcane areas of the 1930s and 1940s dress code as how to match one's handbag to one's shoes, and one's gloves and hat to one's suit (staple fare in Western women's magazines of the time). As Vadim Volkov has argued, *kul'turnost'* depended upon the possession of certain key symbolic items with hygienic associations (curtains, lampshades, tablecloths);[20] and just as in the 1920s, the possession of certain equally totemic, but inessential items (cats, canaries and rubber plants, for instance) was likely to lead to the possessor's being rebuked for 'petit-bourgeois' tastes.[21] Equally stable were the characteristics of *bezkul'tur'e* (unculturedness, a failure to observe hygienic requirements): see Figure 13.1.

If one can speak about a 'Great Retreat', this occurred not in the Stalin era, but in the post-Stalin era. At this point, the crucial features that had identified *kul'turnost'* as a specifically Soviet pattern of behaviour, asceticism, egalitarianism and collectivism, began to come under threat. The quantity of possessions that were deemed appropriate in the Soviet 'cultured person' began to expand out of all recognition. The process is made fascinatingly clear in successive issues of the *Concise encyclopedia of home management*. Between the first edition in 1959, and the second in 1962, 272 new articles were added; the decoration of the 'cultured home', with its

Рисунок Е. ГОРОХОВА.

— Почему такая очередь собралась!
— Сосед акваланг купил.

Figure 13.2 'Why is the queue for the bathroom so long?' 'One of the neighbours has bought an aqualung.' The tensions of combining consumption with living in communal flats. Cartoon from *Krokodil*, 1960.

patterned wallpapers, pot plants, ornaments, showpiece radio sets, rugs and even pedigree cat (an article on cat breeds was included in volume 1 of the second edition) was becoming ever more elaborate.[22] To be sure, some of the new Soviet 'ideal home's' acquisitions were labour-saving devices; 'convenient refrigerators, washing machines, different sorts of electric and gas appliance that make many domestic tasks significantly easier'.[23] This was in tune with the commitment expressed at the Twenty-second Party Congress in 1961, to lightening women's domestic burdens so that their representation in prestigious forms of employment could be improved.[24] But the liberation of women from housework was by no means the only message in house-management literature; indeed, this message was largely undercut by an emphasis on acquisitions that could only add to the burden of domestic existence (such as carpets and display cabinets requiring dusting, or pets needing to be fed, watered and kept clean).

The ideological anxieties that were created by the Party's decision to encourage consumerism (in fact if not in name) is indicated by the large numbers of denunciations of *meshchanstvo*, self-serving materialism, that began flooding from the Soviet presses in the 1960s. B.N. Agapov's book *You're not the only one in the world!*, for example, presented as a signal instance of bad manners the 'china doll in furs' who allowed a long queue to build up in a food shop while ordering the constituents of a holiday banquet.[25] And a 1960 cartoon in *Krokodil* lambasted the owner of a luxury sporting item who behaved inconsiderately towards neighbours in a communal flat (see Figure 13.2). It was also made clear by the fact that post-Stalinist advice literature expressed highly contradictory attitudes to class and status difference. On the one hand, material on conduct insisted that proper Soviet citizens should behave in exactly the same way to everyone. In an instruction manual of 1962 devoted to 'service culture' in Soviet shops, shop assistants were ordered not to discriminate between customers on grounds of dress or appearance: 'In the circumstances of our Soviet society it is imperative that a salesperson should not treat a customer according to external appearance, but be equally polite to everyone'. On the other hand, the same shop assistants were also exhorted to observe rules of behaviour which, in the early Soviet period, would have been considered servile and bourgeois. Not only were they to display 'an attentive, considerate attitude to every customer, a concern for his individual peculiarities' as opposed to the generalized 'care for others' advocated in the 1940s, but they were also to use such forms of speech as 'May I help you to choose your purchase?' and 'Please tell me what you would like', and all this while standing up straight, not 'lolling on the shop fittings'.[26] Similarly, the growth industry of books on *kul'tura rechi*, or correct speech, unabashedly propagandized intelligentsia norms of usage (lexis, pronunciation and stress) and lambasted 'vulgar popular speech' (*gruboe prostorech'e*).[27]

With the egalitarian nature of Soviet culture under severe stress, and the term *intelligentnost'* increasingly used as a synonym for *kul'turnost'*, it is scarcely surprising that collectivism had also become a problematic concept. Soviet guides to *kul'tura povedeniia* published after 1960 display a good deal of anxiety about the question of how far one should actively monitor the behaviour of other citizens. In the 1930s and 1940s, when *bditel'nost'* (vigilance) was propagandized by the Soviet press, and *nedonesenie* (failure to denounce) was a crime, the fact that Soviet citizens had a duty to call wrongdoers to order had been clear and unambiguous. In the post-Stalin era, however, the issue had become confused. Some conduct guides impressed on their readers that interference was unwarranted unless a serious violation of public order was in progress. Criticism of minor faults in public now counted as improper. Particular indignation was inspired by those who criticized others' dress:

If I pretend to the name of a cultured person, then I must treat others with respect. Many people who are essentially very worthy individuals create a good deal of offence to their fellow-citizens by not knowing this rule, by making all sorts of crude observations about their taste and attempting to impose their own taste upon others. If gaffes of this kind are quite excusable in people who occupy the lowest steps of cultural development – for savage tribesmen, who think it is absurd for men to wear trousers – then they are totally unforgivable in those of our fellow-citizens who think that it is absurd for women to wear trousers.[28]

Yet at the same time, 'indifference' was also a vice. The Moral Code of the Builder of Communism, instituted at the Twenty-second Party Congress in 1961, emphasized the collective nature of socialist society, supposedly chracterized by 'a high consciousness of social duty' and 'intolerance towards disruptions of social interests; collectivism and comradely mutual aid'.[29] Liudmila Aleshina, whose *On politeness, tact and delicacy* went through several editions in the late 1970s and early 1980s, cited the case of Vadim, generally considered 'cultured' but in fact failing in signal respects: 'He keeps his workplace tidy, fulfils his quota, gives flowers to all the girls, goes to exhibitions and new plays. But he couldn't care less about anything that doesn't concern him personally. For instance, when he hears people swearing on the street, with little children right next to them'.[30] Urged both to take issue with *bezkul'tur'e* and to ignore it, Soviet citizens were torn between conflicting imperatives; just so, those who were corrected now had the mandate to tell their critics to mind their own business, rather than silently falling into line.

The confusion was not helped by erosion of the former sense of the exclusivity of 'Soviet' behaviour. Authors of conduct guides now sometimes approvingly referred to Western models, and urged readers to emulate them (as, for example, in an admiring evocation of Londoners, politely halting their cars at zebra crossings and waiting on pavements so as not to spoil a tourist's photograph).[31] In the 1920s, 1930s and 1940s Soviet citizens had been told they were proudly self-denying (albeit aspiring to acquire certain essentials of information and props of a hygienic existence) and confidently assured that they lived in a unique society. From the late 1950s, a silent incursion of what in the 1940s had been called *nizkopoklonstvo* (kow-towing to foreigners) was accompanied by a significant and ideologically risky dilution of the egalitarianism and collectivism that had been the identifying features of Soviet *kul'turnost'*.

What, though, of the realities of behaviour? In a final sense, the polarization of 'ideals' and 'reality' is an uncomfortable one, given that 'ideals' were part of Soviet reality and also that normative behaviour guides have – even if only in the most distant sense – to reflect reality. For example, the gradual expansion of the *kul'turnost'* ethos to include concerns that would have been branded in the 1920s as 'bourgeois' was (*pace* Dunham)[32] not simply a case of officials manipulating popular taste from above: it was also a recognition of workers' own desires to acquire certain types of goods, including luxury goods. The literature of the 1920s makes this abundantly clear, with its portraits of characters such as Maiakovskii's Prisypkin, the acquisitive factory worker antihero of *The bed-bug*, or (to take a text not characterized by satirical exaggeration), the women workers in Ekaterina Strogova's story, 'The Womenfolk', of whom we are told 'You'll see our girls wearing stylish checked caps, and coquettish yellow shoes, and beige stockings', while the older women ('old ladies') 'even come into the workshop in curls and powder'.[33] Before the Revolution too, workers' and peasants' accommodation and dress often reflected the desire for what Russian radicals would have seen as fripperies: crocheted hangings, china statuettes, oleographic prints, lace curtains, brass samovars.[34] Like their counterparts in other countries, many Russian workers understood a decent life in terms of *uiut* and *elegantnost'* as well as better education and political participation. Ascetic denunciations of *meshchanstvo*, or petty-bourgeois vulgarity, celebrated a heritage of poverty and deprivation that workers and peasants were themselves keen to escape.

Besides licensing acquisitive ambitions that actually existed, another, and more direct, way in which conduct guides registered reality was in offering advice about inappropriate behaviour. A striking example here is Khodakov's *How not to behave*, a depressing catalogue of time theft and rudeness in the workplace, intoxicated and boorish behaviour at home and out visiting, jostling, staring and ogling on the street.[35] Conversely, where a positive image of reality was attempted, the modesty of the achievements recorded could be revealing: so, for example, in *The culture of passenger service*, a collection of essays aimed at railway workers dealing with the public, has the manager of a provincial station in the Smolensk district boasting that 'there are no queues or pushing and shoving by our ticket offices', and that 'luggage always goes off on the train on which a reservation has been made'.[36] On occasion, too, guides inadvertently recorded the contradictions and drawbacks of official policy. For example, G.Ia. Bruk's

What a peasant going to town to find work should know, a pamphlet of 1930 aimed at *sezonniki*, temporary migrants from the village who dwelt in the city while undertaking work as labourers on construction sites, represented the worker hostel (*obshchezhitie*) as an ideal community which not only indoctrinated incomers in urban values but also turned them into missionaries for *kul'turnost'* once they reached the village. However, the suggestion that a hostel existence in itself offered the opportunity to lead a civilized life was unwittingly undermined by the writer when he emphasized the necessity of hygienic behaviour on the part of the hostel's inhabitants: 'If the lavatories in *obshchezhitiia* are kept in an untidy condition, if *sezonniki* 'relieve themselves' during the night not in the lavatories, but just anywhere, then flies will start breeding in unbelievable numbers'.[37]

A second question concerning the relationship between 'ideal' and 'reality' is that of reception: how far did the conduct manuals succeed in their mission of constructing reality? The answer is clearly far from always, since some of the books themselves take the public to task for their failure to heed the advice provided. A particularly interesting case is that of advice literature aimed at the 'worker correspondents' (*rabkory*) who were responsible for coordinating *stengazety*, or 'wall newspapers', the home-made displays of verbal and visual commentary displayed in every Soviet workplace and educational institution up to the collapse of the regime in 1991. These guides not only reflect confusion about whether *stengazety* were supposed merely to disseminate party decrees downwards or also to reflect 'signals from below'; they also lay bare the fact that the kind of whistleblowing desired by the party authorities – responsible and well in line with party directives – was often not the sort that actually took place. The party ideal is represented rather effectively in Lidiia Chukovskaia's novel of the Ezhov purges, *Sof'ia Petrovna*, the hero of which gets to the publishers where she works one day to find herself denounced in the wall newspaper for defending an 'enemy of the people' at a meeting called to reprimand her friend Natasha.[38] But judging by the strictures published in guides for the 'worker correspondents' responsible for coordinating wall newspapers, the content of the *zametki*, or 'notes', published in them was often far less respectable, consisting of bitchy gossip that gave vent to petty tiffs and to the politics of envy rather than measured and politically literate condemnation. As the authors of one guide complained in 1928,

> A cashier who gave someone the wrong chit is drawn with ass's ears on, a typist who uses face-powder is shown as a prostitute, a worker who has been found drunk is unhesitatingly placed behind bars. This, of course, is quite out of order.[39]

Even as late as the mid-1930s, *stengazety*, to the despair of regulators, continued to be used for equally trivial and scurrilous material. One poison-pen item from *The instrument-maker* (*Instrumental'shchik*), the wall newspaper of the instrument workshop of the Moscow Car Factory, read as follows:

> In our shop, in foreman Shulman's group, there's a certain workman called Semen Katz. He's a clever one if you like. Thinks the world of himself and has nothing to do with anyone else. I should say straight out that Katz has got very lax about his work. After dinner he wiped down his lathe and went off to the dance hall. We must incite public opinion about him and call him to order.[40]

Such material made the hiatus between 'work discipline', as it was understood by the party authorities and conduct regulation, as actually happened at the grass roots, embarrassingly evident.

Yet the assumption that normative behaviour guides could only be misunderstood and subverted by those who read them would be as much an oversimplification as the attempt to trace a direct link between the ideas expressed in these texts and real behaviour. The fact that there is a sturdy tradition of parody advice literature in Russia going back nearly two centuries goes to prove rather than disprove the appeal of the original genre to consumers. And, while publication data, such as print-runs and numbers of editions, provide only suspect evidence of popularity in a culture where printing is controlled by the state, the frequent reprinting of some titles, such as material on physical culture in the 1920s, or on house management in the 1960s (*The book of tasty and nutritious food* and *House management* were reprinted nearly every year in some form or another between 1957 and 1991) was certainly a reflection of popular demand, as was the inclusion of material about house management and etiquette in mass-market magazines such as *Ogonek*. To be sure, the widest audience has always been for cookbooks, which appeal to readers who would treat etiquette books, if they read them at all, as light entertainment, but that there was an audience for etiquette books too is indicated by the fact that titles such as Aleshina's *On politeness, tact and delicacy* and Khodakov's *How not to behave* had runs of around half a million copies in their various editions, that surviving library copies are often ornamented by earnest underlinings, and that the authors of such books cite letters from readers (perhaps invented, but more likely not) expressing their gratitude that the subject of manners had been broached. And the treatise on etiquette remains one of the most widely available genres of non-fiction in post-Soviet Russia as well, a clear indication of the size and enthusiasm of the readership for material of this kind.

Tracing the actual *influence* of the *kul'turnost'* ideal is far harder. It is possible to speculate that Soviet behaviour ideology in the post-Stalin years contributed indirectly to the break-up of the Soviet Union, on the one hand by increasing demand for consumer goods that the state was incapable of providing and, on the other by confusing readers by presenting them with conflicting moral imperatives. At the same time, the abiding element in the Soviet concept of *kul'turnost'*, the celebration of hygiene, order and self-improvement, also had its effects, this time positive rather than negative. The workers who complained in their wall newspapers that workmates were failing to clean up after themselves properly, or indicted the factory management for redeploying funds that had been collected in order to plant flowerbeds in the factory yard, were subscribing to the ideal,[41] as were the visitors to new metro stations in the 1950s who enthused on the beauty of the 'snow-white' tiles and entrance halls.[42] The viability of *kul'turnost'* as ideal is suggested by the fact that the Soviet variant, with its emphasis upon self-education, retains a curious hold even today, when Russians are bombarded with bewilderingly heterogeneous material on behaviour. For instance, a 1997 article in *Ogonek* revealed that Russian tourists in Mediterranean seaside resorts such as Malta, in between downing formidable amounts of alcohol, nude sunbathing, ogling topless women and partaking in oratorios of swearing, still consider it obligatory to pay their tribute to the requirements of *kul'turnost'* by means of cultural excursions: 'If a visit to a museum is part of the package, then on no account can this be missed'.[43]

To a Western reader, such behaviour may seem not only incongruous, but also unlikely: it is, after all, rather difficult to imagine the participants in a 'Club 18–30' holiday in Mykonos demanding a visit to the local museum. Certainly, the self-education ethic still exists in Western Europe, as represented for example by the Open University in Britain, but it occupies a more muted place than it does in Russia, being primarily the occupation of a determined minority rather than of a vocal majority. What is more, it is seen as a contribution to individual rather than collective self-improvement: the idea of visiting a museum *only* because, and if, a group excursion is laid on might strike most Western Europeans as extremely curious. That self-education, albeit in diluted form, is still the ambition of most Russian citizens, that a nodding acquaintance with high culture is still considered requisite for all, and regarded as a contribution to social cohesion, is surely a belated and unexpected tribute to the success of the Soviet system in constructing symbolic reality, whatever its failures in achieving practical goals.

Acknowledgements

This chapter draws on chapters 4 and 5 of my large-scale study of concepts of refinement in Russia, *Refining Russia: gender and the regulation of behaviour from 1760*, research for which has been generously supported by the British Academy via a BA/HRB Personal Research Grant in 1996 and by places on the Academic Exchange with Rossiiskaia Akademiia Nauk in 1997 and 1998.

Notes

1 Though contrast J. Brooks, *When Russia learned to read: literacy and popular literature 1861–1917* (Princeton, NJ, 1984), and F. Wigzell, *Reading Russian fortunes* (Cambridge, 1998).

2 R. Darnton, *The forbidden best-sellers of pre-revolutionary France* (London, 1996), pp. 169–80.

3 N. Timasheff, *The Great Retreat: the growth and decline in Communism in Russia* (New York, 1946); V. Dunham, *In Stalin's time: middleclass values in Soviet fiction* (Cambridge, 1976).

4 S. Fitzpatrick, 'Becoming cultured: socialist realism and the representation of privilege and taste', in *The cultural front: power and culture in revolutionary Russia* (Ithaca, NY, 1992), p. 218.

5 A. Gastev, *Kak nado rabotat'* (Moscow, 1966), pp. 112, 117, 119, 128–9.

6 Anon., *Druzheskie sovety molodomu cheloveku, nachinaiushchemu zhit' v svete*, 2nd edn (Moscow, 1765), pp. 52, 63.

7 A.L. Mendel'son, *Ob ukreplenii pamiati* (Leningrad, 1929), pp. 33–7.

8 N. Elias, *The civilizing process*, translated by E. Jephcott (Oxford, 1994), p. 136.

9 P. Kerzhentsev, *Organizui samogo sebia!* (Moscow, 1925); *Samoobrazovanie putem chitki belletristiki: Chto chitat' vo vremia otpuska* (Leningrad, 1929).

10 N. Chernyshevskii, *Izbrannye proizvediniia v 3 tomakh* (Leningrad, 1978), vol. 1, p. 286.

11 E. Budgell, *The Spectator*, no. 379 (1712). See *The Spectator*, edited by D. Bond (Oxford, 1965), vol. 3, p. 424.

12 N.K. Krupskaia, *O samoobrazovanii. Sbornik stat'ei* (Moscow, 1936), p. 6.

13 *Ogonek* (1936), quoted in V. Volkov, 'Consumption as a way to culture: *kul'turnost'* and the creation of a new middle class', in C. Kelly and D. Shepherd, eds *Constructing Russian culture in the age of revolutions* (Oxford, 1998), p. 301.

14 V.V. Gorinevskii, *Remont i zakalivanie organizma* (Moscow, 1925), p. 5.

15 B. Laynard, *Secrets of beauty, health and long life* (London, 1900), p. 5; the Russian edition was published as *Sekrety krasoty, zdorov'ia i dolgovechnosti* (St Petersburg, 1909).

16 *Kalendar' 'Damskii Mir' na 1917 god* (St Petersburg, 1916), pp. 94–7; Anon., *Obshepoleznaia biblioteka 'Rodiny': Khoroshii ton* (St Petersburg, 1907), p. 15.

17 K. Svetozarskaia, *Zhizn' v svete, doma i pri dvore* (St Petersburg, 1890), p. 3.

18 'Savonov and Bel'skii' (compilers), *Russkii pis'movnik: sbornik obraztosovykh pisem . . .* (St Petersburg, 1910), pp. 32–3.

19 *Kniga o vkusnoi i zdorovoi pishche* (Moscow, 1939), p. 3.

20 Volkov, 'Consumption as a way to culture', pp. 298–9.

21 On canaries and rubber plants, see S. Boym, *Common places: mythologies of everyday life in Russia* (Cambridge, MA, 1994), pp. 5–7, 34, 39. Domestic pets are notably absent from fantasy homes in socialist realist novels, whose standard accoutrements include grand pianos, book cases and sofas as well as orange lampshades and white tablecloths.

22 *Kratkaia entsiklopediia domashnego khoziaistva (KEDK)*, 1st edn, 2 vols (Moscow, 1959); *KEDK*, 2nd edn, 2 vols (Moscow, 1962).

23 *KEDK*, 2nd edn, p. 8.

24 M. Buckley *Women and ideology in the Soviet Union* (London, 1989), p. 146.

25 B.N. Agapov, *Ty ne odin na svete! Zametki publitsista* (Moscow, 1961), p. 11; compare with I.S. Runova, *S meshchanstvom nado borot'sia* (Leningrad, 1962).

26 N.I. Strogov, *Kul'tura obsluzhivaniia pokupatelei* (Moscow, 1962), pp. 11, 18.

27 L.V. Uspenskii, *Kul'tura rechi* (Moscow, 1976); compare with B. Timofeev, *Pravil'no li my govorim? Zapiski pisatelia* (Leningrad, 1963).
28 N.P. Akimova, quoted in M. Khodakov, *Kak ne nado sebia vesti* (Moscow, 1975), p. 89.
29 I. Aasamaa, *Kak sebia vesti* (Tallinn, 1974), p. 81.
30 L. Aleshina, *O vezhlivosti, o takte i delikatnosti* (Leningrad, 1986), p. 9.
31 Agapov, *Ty ne odin na svete!* p. 9.
32 Dunham, *In Stalin's time.*
33 V. Maiakovskii, *The bedbug* (Moscow, 1929); E. Strogova, 'The womenfolk', in C. Kelly, ed. *An anthology of Russian women's writing* (Oxford, 1994), p. 282.
34 V.Iu. Krupianskaia and N.S. Polishchuk, *Kul'tura i byt rabochikh gornozavodskogo Urala konets XIX–nachalo XX v.* (Moscow, 1971), pp. 125–6.
35 Khodakov, *Kak ne nado sebia vesti.*
36 *Kul'tura obsluzhivaniia passazhirov* (Smolensk, 1950), p. 48.
37 G.Ia. Bruk, *Chto nado znat' sezonniku, otpravliaiushchemusia na rabotu v gorod* (Moscow and Leningrad, 1930), p. 11.
38 L. Chukovskaia, *Sof'ia Petrovna* (Moscow, 1988).
39 N. Polotskaia and V. Dokunin, *Redkollegiia stennoi gazety i kruzhok rabkorov* (Moscow, 1928), p. 57.
40 *V pomoshch' stengazete: Lektsii opublikovannye v zhurnale 'Rabochekrest'ianskii korrespondent' za 1935 i 1936 gg.* (Piatigorsk, 1937), p. 81.
41 *V pomoshch' stengazete*, p. 36.
42 S. Garniuk, A. Kats and A. Sonichev, 'Kusok kommunizma: Moskovskoe metro glazami sovremennikov', *Moskovskii arkhiv*, 1 (1996), p. 360. From this perspective, one could see the conflicts expressed in 'wall newspapers' as a sign of workers' internalization of some aspects of the *kul'turnost'* ethos. Workers now knew that they were supposed to 'call wrongdoers to justice', even if they sometimes classified those 'wrongdoers' in ways not sanctioned by the regime. See S. Kotkin, *The magnetic mountain: Stalinism as a civilization* (Berkeley, 1995), p. 217: 'The very fact that [in their memoirs] workers sometimes "erred", and had to be corrected, both for grammar and content, shows how they were implicated in a process of adopting the official method of speaking about themselves'.
43 Iu. Kolesova, I. Petrova and A. Barni, 'Russkie edut!', *Ogonek*, 24 (June 1997), p. 23.

14

The Russian people and the Soviet Union

GEOFFREY HOSKING

When, after the First World War the Ottoman Empire broke up, it was replaced not by a pan-Islamic state, as some of its politicians had wished, but by a Turkish nation-state, committed under Kemal Ataturk to emulating the successful nation-building programmes of Western Europe. The Russian Empire, by contrast, under the leadership of Lenin, went in completely the opposite direction: it reconstituted itself as a multi-ethnic empire, even more universal in doctrine and ambition than its predecessor the tsarist empire, as was indicated by the fact that it did not even bear the name of Russia – or indeed any ethnic or geographic marker.

In other respects, too, the Soviet Union can easily be seen as an enterprise designed to undermine Russian national identity, or at best dissolve it in a multi-ethnic conglomerate. The communists did a great deal, especially in the early years, to encourage the flowering of non-Russian national consciousness on the territory they ruled. They created ethnically-named territorial administrative units: The Ukrainian Soviet Socialist Republic, the Bashkir Autonomous Soviet Socialist Republic and so on. To provide content for these entities, they carried out a programme of what Valerii Tishkov has called 'ethnic engineering'. Ethnographers were sent into the regions to collect data on language, religion, customs, economy, tribal allegiance and so on, and to fashion these data into the raw materials of nationhood, in some cases synthetically 'engineering' nationalities into existence in place of previous tribal conglomerates.[1]

In all ethnically-named republics the party launched primary education and the liquidation of illiteracy in the local languages, sometimes in the process improvising a written and printed language where none had previously existed. By the late 1920s 192 languages had been identified, most of which had to be made as different from one another as possible and be provided with grammars, dictionaries and so on.[2] At the same time the policy of *korenizatsiia* or 'indigenization' selected and trained indigenous cadres to take positions of responsibility in their own republics.

The Russian Republic existed as well, of course, alongside the others; indeed it was much the largest both in extent and population, but it lacked its own communist party, its own capital city, its own radio and later television, its own Academy of Sciences – attributes possessed by all the other union republics and in some cases the autonomous ones too.

The Russians in fact were in the situation wittily outlined recently in an article by Yury Slezkine. He likens the Soviet Union to a communal apartment, in which each nationality had its own room where it got on with its own life. The Russians, for their part, occupied the hallway, the corridor, the kitchen and the bathroom: they ran the place and got in everyone else's way, but they had no room of their own.[3]

The Russians, then, were a kind of homeless ruling class, in danger of losing their identity. In the course of massive social change inspired from above, many of the most characteristic features of Russian culture and tradition were destroyed or undermined. The names of streets and whole cities were changed, expunging familiar Russian designations and replacing them with the emblems and heroes of proletarian international-ism. The peasant community (*mir*) was turned into the caricature of the kolkhoz. The Russian Orthodox Church saw most of its clergy arrested and most of its parishes closed down. The best of Russian literature, art and music was either suppressed or driven into emigration. Millions of Russians were uprooted and relocated in raw new 'melting-pot' industrial towns, where different ethnic groups lived elbow-to-elbow. And that is to say nothing of the Gulag Archipelago, where, according to Solzhenitsyn, a whole new 'nation' of *zeks* (prisoners) was created, a travesty of 'proletarian internationalism'.

To all appearances, then, the Soviet authorities did their best to relativize and downgrade Russian national identity. But this is only part of the story. I shall argue that the Soviet Union also did a great deal, in spite of everything, both to perpetuate Russian traditions and to strengthen Russian national feeling.

In fact, as I have argued in a previous work,[4] the tsarist empire had also in many respects obstructed the growth of Russian national consciousness. The difficulty lay in the way in which empire reinforced a fundamental polarity running through Russian history, at least from the time when Muscovy began to become a great Eurasian empire. That is the polarity between state and local community, *gosudarstvo* and *zemlia* in the medieval Russian terminology. Both have tended to be very strong, each in their own way; the state in the means of coercion, the local community in solidarity and mutual responsibility. But there have been few intermediary institutions to provide links between them. The extent of the institutional and cultural divide between *gosudarstvo* and *zemlia* has had fateful con-sequences. Over the centuries the state repeatedly endeavoured to reform and integrate Russian society, to fit it for its role as European great-power. The main priority of communities, for their part, was survival in extremely

adverse geopolitical and climatic conditions, which required intense conservatism, the preservation of practices which had worked well in the past.
This conservatism meant that the state's reforming efforts tended always
to fetch up against uncomprehending – perhaps deliberately uncomprehending – resistance. The result has been long periods of stagnation
broken by brief bouts of what Pushkin called 'senseless and merciless
popular rebellion'.[5]

In *Russia: people and empire* I advanced the proposition that the failure
to build institutional or cultural bridges between *gosudarstvo* and *zemlia*
meant that Russia never became a nation, either in the civic or even in the
ethnic sense, certainly not before 1917. I now want to extend the same
hypothesis into the Soviet period, and ask whether Soviet rule did anything
to narrow that gap, and hence – without intending it – to prepare the way
for the Russian Federation to become a nation-state.

Such links as have existed historically between state and local community were essentially patron–client relationships. In Imperial Russia, this
usually meant the power of the landlord, or where nobility and serfdom
were weak, of the *voevoda*, the *gubernator*. These were the men responsible for ensuring that taxes were collected and soldiers recruited, but also
that local communities were kept above the poverty line, a responsibility
which admittedly they discharged imperfectly.[6]

The Soviet state made a serious attempt to combine state and local
communities in integrated structures through the hierarchy of soviets. The
very name of the new state derived from local communities, urban and
rural, in their revolutionary form of 1905 and 1917. But even before Civil
War broke out it was already proving impossible to administer a modern
society by means of the informal and locally-based procedures of the
soviets. The Civil War merely confirmed this impossibility.

Instead, a new type of intermediary appeared between state and community. That, of course, was the party, which itself embodied the dual
principle of centralization and sensitivity to local opinion. At least in
theory. Robert Service has shown how in practice the pressures to put
all the weight on centralization proved irresistible. The crisis of 1920–1
and the Tenth Party Congress completed the process. The party became a
tightly centralized and disciplined institution, and in the process it generated its own patron–client network, a much more systematic one than had
ever existed under the tsars, the so-called *nomenklatura* system. This was
the source of Stalin's unprecedented power and the conveyor by which he
enforced his rule.[7]

It was also a development of enormous significance in the Russian
historical process, for it replaced the informal and often haphazard processes which had previously governed patron–client relations by a meticu-
lously regulated system which operated on the basis of regular reports on
personnel and the keeping of detailed and systematic files. In one sense,
such a system contradicts the essence of patron–client networks, which

tend to be informal and to operate outside society's official norms.[8] But then, the *nomenklatura* system was never officially admitted to be the basis of the Soviet social structure, and its operations were kept secret. Besides, as Ernest Gellner has pointed out, patronage tends to become pervasive where the state is the main employer, where it lacks the means to fulfil all its promises to its population, where it operates an idiom unfamiliar or incomprehensible to most of the people or where it proposes some un-realizable 'overarching national ideal which should command general loyalty'.[9]

In brief, the Soviet Union replicated, though in a new form, the essential structures of the old Russian state. In other respects, too, the Soviet Union was a distinctively Russian project. One might even call internationalist millenarianism a Russian speciality. The idea of Moscow as the 'Third Rome' or the 'Second Jerusalem' had implied that Rus' was the centre of a universal Christian realm which would either absorb all Christendom or else would herald the apocalypse and the second coming of Christ. This idea, not much exploited by Russian officials and diplomats, was a power-ful current in the Church and among Orthodox believers, especially, I have argued elsewhere, among the Old Believers. Russian socialism, from Bakunin onwards, may be said to have tapped this vein of popular eschatology, combining social protest with a mission to liberate the world.[10] When the Soviet Union became the fortress of international socialism, it was logical for Karl Radek to proclaim that 'The workers of the whole world should now become Russian patriots'.[11]

The ideal of socio-economic egalitarianism was also a distinctively Russian one. The mutual dependence forced on local communities by geography and climate had over the centuries become a habit and had generated a mentality in which conspicuous degrees of either wealth or poverty were viewed with disapproval. Egalitarianism had been reinforced within the village community by the widespread custom of periodic redis-tribution of strips of land and within the *artel* by the practice of distribut-ing profits by agreement among the members. However, only the Soviet state made this practice into an ideal – and an ideal it remained in many ways even after Stalin officially repudiated it in 1931. It continued, for example, to be embodied in the social welfare system, which, as surveys have shown, remained to the end an aspect of the Soviet Union that most of its population valued.[12]

There are simpler and more obvious senses, too, in which the Soviet Union embodied Russian patriotism. It was more or less coextensive with the old Russian Empire, most of its rulers (especially after the mid-1930s) were Russian, Russian was its principal language and the language of command in the armed forces, and Russian was the culture which was used to integrate its peoples, even though primary schools in non-Russian areas were using other languages for tuition. In the course of the five-year plans Russian specialists, technicians and manual workers resettled in many non-Russian areas: they were not representatives of a master race, but still they were a reminder that the Union was Russian-dominated.

In one sense this Soviet Russian patriotism was analogous to what the flamboyant newspaper editor Mikhail Katkov had endeavoured to inculcate in the 1870s and 1880s. He had regarded Russia as a kind of supernation, chosen by history to assimilate and bring to fruition the nationhood of others, on condition that they kept that nationhood purely linguistic and cultural, acknowledging the Russians' right to rule over them and to impose statehood on them.[13] One might argue that the communists, having at their disposal a pliant mass media and education system, succeeded where Katkov had failed, giving the Yakuts, the Bashkirs and arguably even the Ukrainians a national identity subsumed in Soviet–Russian statehood.

In some ways, however, the new Soviet Russian patriotism was distinct from what Katkov had preached. It was more explicitly millenarian, and this millenarianism was reified in the Five-Year Plans, in the drive to industrialize and urbanize, to harness working-class idealism in order to make Russia a society at least equal in material wealth and cultural sophistication to the most advanced European and North American models. At the same time it was no less military: the Soviet armed forces played a crucial role in socializing young men from the countryside, bringing them together with recruits of different social and ethnic backgrounds and inculcating in them a multiethnic Soviet patriotism. The Red Army was better able to do this than the tsarist army, since it called up all nationalities, including Muslims, and offered far better promotion prospects to recruits from a humble social background.[14]

This mixture of military and industrial patriotism was what moved many to overlook or forgive Stalin's excesses in the 1930s, such as for example the young Konstantin Simonov:

> Thoughts of the Red Army and the five-year plan were welded into one by the fact of capitalist encirclement: if we could not build everything we had decided to, then we would be defenceless, we would not be able to fight and would go under if anyone attacked us – that could not be doubted.[15]

The Second World War – or the Great Fatherland War – enormously heightened that Soviet Russian patriotism and generated the moral consciousness which formed the principal source of legitimacy for the Soviet Union for two further generations. This was patriotism tempered and chastened by the terrible experience of actual war. For one thing, the generation which fought at the front discovered that the war was not at all of the type which had been anticipated in the military doctrine of the pre-war state. It proved impossible in practice to conduct an 'offensive war with little bloodshed'. Instead the war was defensive, and with enormous bloodshed. It had also turned out not to be a class war, but rather a national one, conducted not to spread revolution throughout Europe, but to defend the homeland. The enemy was not so much the imperialist as the German.[16]

Pride in the Soviet Union could be felt even by those who were not enthusiastic about the way Stalin, or at least the *nomenklatura* bosses, exercised power. Thus Viacheslav Kondrat'ev, whose anti-Stalinist war novels were popular in the 1960s and 1970s, said in 1991

> Veterans and the whole people felt insulted and cheated that the Victory won with such huge bloodshed did not bring the country what we dreamed of at the front, and that the defeated peoples lived a hundred times better than us. But all the same, we had defended our *gosudarstvennost'*, for good or ill, and that meant we had fought and won something meaningful.

In September 1993 Kondrat'ev committed suicide, perhaps because he felt that what had been defended at such cost had once again been surrendered.[17]

Victory in the war provided the psychological basis for the creation of a Soviet nation, on the basis of a multi-ethnic *rossiiskii* culture, but no such nation emerged. Why not? Firstly, because some nations were never properly integrated into that culture, and remained sceptical or even downright hostile to Russian domination. These included the three Baltic nations incorporated in 1940, the west Ukrainians, who had never been part of Russia before 1939, perhaps the Moldavians, and certainly a number of the north Caucasian nationalities, especially those whom Stalin deported in 1944. Last, the Georgians were probably only reconciled to the Soviet Union so long as their own 'local boy made good', Stalin, was in charge of it.

This is quite a large number of nationalities, and their festering discontent played a large part in the ultimate collapse of the Soviet Union. But in numerical terms, they formed together only a small proportion of the Soviet population, and they certainly did not set the tone after the Second World War. No; the main reason why no Soviet nation took shape, it seems to me, was that the *nomenklatura* bosses clung to their own version of the authoritarian and tightly controlled patronage system, which left no room for the creation of the civic institutions appropriate to a nation. Soldiers returning from the front, full of the idealism of victory, found that there was no obvious place for them in post-war society, where the bosses treated them as subjects or at best as dependent clients.[18] Khrushchev attempted to shake up this system, but largely failed, and its tenacity formed the basic reason for the failure of the Gorbachëv reform experiment.

The Soviet system failed, then, to generate a civic culture. But in the ethnic sense, the rift between elites and masses which had existed in tsarist times, right up to the revolution of 1917 – and acting as a fundamental cause of that revolution – was substantially healed in the Soviet period.

For example, during the Soviet period the Russian language became more uniform in its usage. A variety of usages which had been non-standard (regional or associated with a lower social class) were assimilated into the norm as peasants flooded into the towns to do military service or an industrial job. Army barracks, building sites, communal apartments and labour camps acted as a kind of currency exchange for the language, requiring people to adjust to and eventually to adopt different linguistic registers, which in a more stable society they would scarcely have encountered in their ordinary life. These tendencies in the end affected even the most conservative sector of the language – published *bettes lettres*. I remember as a student in 1963 trying to read the recently published sensation, Aleksandr Solzhenitsyn's *A day in the life of Ivan Denisovich*. I was proud of my understanding of Pushkin and Chekhov, but to my surprise I found the new work almost completely baffling. Its Russian had been so heavily filtered through army, kolkhoz and labour camp that much of it was unrecognizable to me: it might have been written in Bulgarian or Ukrainian. That was a measure of the transformation which had taken place in literary usage (though admittedly Solzhenitsyn was a pioneer in assimilating and utilizing demotic Russian). But a little later, when I studied at Moscow University, I found that my student contemporaries there could understand Solzhenitsyn without difficulty. Popular speech, in all its diversity, had become a literary norm.[19]

Before the revolution, even where festivals had existed which were common to different social classes, for example Christmas, *maslenitsa* (Shrovetide) or Easter, they were usually celebrated in very different ways in gentry and peasant households. After the revolution, however, and especially after the Second World War, a common system of festivals and public holidays was established, commemorating the great events of international socialism, the revolution and the victory over Germany. These were atheist festivals and so took a long time to be generally accepted, especially in the countryside. But eventually, particularly after the common effort in the world war, they spanned all social classes and, perhaps even more importantly, all ethnic groups, even where in addition religious festivals were clandestinely celebrated.[20]

Alongside the festivals a new all-class popular culture came into being, as Richard Stites has shown, rather as in the West from the 1920s onwards, but with somewhat greater authoritative input from state and party. People of all social origins and ethnic groups sang the same songs, heard the same radio broadcasts, watched the same films, the same *estrada* (variety theatre) shows and later the same television programmes. Alongside them and operating on the same cultural wavelength, the official socialist realist culture was deliberately monochrome, that is, it did not distinguish between different kinds of audience to anything like the same extent as a commercial culture has to do. During and after the 1960s a new element entered this medley with the guitar song, adapted from folk music, and from criminal and labour camp songs for tape-recorder, first of all in elegiac mode, by Bulat Okudzhava, later with mordant satire by Alexsandr Galich and Vladimir Vysotskii.[21]

More brutally, the Soviet state dismantled cultural barriers in other ways too: by destroying the segregated peasant community and with it much of the old popular culture, along with the institutions which sustained it – the *mir*, the Church. It might be said that Stalin raised up the *rossiiskii* (imperial Russianness) and destroyed the *russkii* (ethnic Russianness). As a result, Russians have today a more or less unified culture, though one which still has about it the whiff of scorched earth. Without an accompanying civic culture it can go only a certain way towards giving them the feeling of belonging to one nation.

Why, then, did the Soviet Union break up? The answer is partly nationalism, but only partly. After Stalin's death the Russian-centred (*rossiiskii*) internationalism of the Soviet project began to unravel. *Korenizatsiia* got stuck halfway on the road to proletarian internationalism: the second stage, when national differences should have begun to fade, never took place. Once the threat of Stalin's terror was removed, indigenous cadres began gradually and unostentatiously to build little embryo nations in the non-Russian republics, assisted by the patron–client networks which they now entirely controlled. By this stage there were only feeble countervailing forces to restrain them. Russians living among them started to feel increasingly out of place in what they had thought of as their own homeland, denied housing, jobs or education in competition with locals. Some Russians even began to leave, especially in the Central Asian republics. The number of Soviet citizens speaking Russian as their main language began to fall off, the number of mixed marriages declined and the incidence of ethnic conflicts within the Soviet army increased.[22]

National dissent made its appearance, directed against the Soviet state and Soviet communist party, which were now seen as imperial exploiters, operating in a new way, but not in principle different from the old Russian state. This was true even of Russians who, underground and discreetly in the official media too, began to assert a Russian (*russkii*) identity distinct from and sometimes opposed to the Soviet one. The fashion for 'village prose' bore witness to a nostalgia for traditional Russian values implicitly at odds with the official ethos of internationalism and modernization.[23]

There were, then, already definite signs long before the 1980s that all was not well with the Soviet multinational state, but they fell far short of presaging the disintegration of the Soviet Union. As late as 1987 a sensible and level-headed scholarly account of the national problem concluded that the non-Russians would *not* rebel against the Soviet state and that therefore it was likely to remain stable.[24]

No; the main reason for the way the Soviet Union disintegrated was, as I suggested earlier, the practical working of the *nomenklatura* patron–client system. By the later decades of the USSR this system was actually working in such a way as to reinforce ethnic particularism rather than to weaken it.

Brezhnev's watchword, 'stability of cadres', gave *carte blanche* to local *nomenklatura* bosses to 'cultivate their own garden', to give absolute priority to the interests of their own patron–client networks and to advance their cause against rival networks in other parts of the Union.

Mikhail Gorbachëv, after his country had fallen apart under him, asked the Minister for Nationalities of the Russian Federation, Valerii Tishkov, what he should have done about the national question. Tishkov replied that he should have allowed republican party bosses to have personal jets for business flights. This was a perfectly serious response. Tishkov had recently escorted Mircea Snegur, President of the Moldavian Republic, from the airport to the special residence reserved for heads of state visiting Moscow. Snegur had said to him: 'Before, we were not even allowed inside these gates. Now we are treated like real people'.[25]

In other words, the collapse of the Soviet Union was caused, in my view, mainly by the struggle for material and symbolic goods within the intensely hierarchical *nomenklatura* patronage system – a struggle which Gorbachëv's liberalizing reforms had released into the open. Today, I think the main question about the fate of the Russian Federation is whether it is to remain a neo-*nomenklatura* fiefdom, fought over by rival clannish networks, many of which have survived the end of the USSR and which now control so much of the country's industry, commerce, finance and mass media, or whether Russians can establish the civic as well as the ethnic fabric of a modern nation.

Notes

1 V. Tishkov, *Ethnicity, nationalism and conflict in and after the Soviet Union: the mind aflame* (London, 1997), pp. 15–21 and ch. 2.
2 Y. Slezkine, 'The USSR as communal apartment, or how a socialist state promoted ethnic particularism', *Slavic Review*, 53 (1994), pp. 414–52.
3 Y. Slezkine, 'The USSR as communal apartment'.
4 G. Hosking, *Russia: people and empire, 1552–1917* (London, 1997).
5 This interpretation rests partly on the work of Aleksandr Akhiezer, as presented in his *Sotsial 'no-kul' turnye problemy razvitiia Rossii: filosofskii aspekt* (Moscow, 1992); idem, *Dumy o Rossii: ot proshlogo k budushchemu* (Moscow, 1994); idem, 'Rossiia kak bol'shoe obshchestvo', *Voprosy filosofii*, no. 1 (1993), pp. 3–19. Akhiezer's periodization of Russian history is unconvincing, but his basic approach is very fruitful. There is a useful exposition and criticism of his work in V.G. Khoros, 'V poiskakh kliucha k proshlomu i budushchemu', *Voprosy filosofii*, no. 5 (1993), pp. 99–110.
6 D. Moon, 'Reassessing Russian serfdom', *European History Quarterly*, 26 (1996), pp. 483–526; M.N. Afanas'ev, *Klientelizm i rossiiskaia gosudarstvennost'* (Moscow, 1997), part 2.
7 R. Service, *The Bolshevik Party in revolution: a study in organisational change, 1917–1923*, (London, 1979); on the origins of the *nomenklatura* system, see T.H. Rigby and B. Harasymiw (eds), *Leadership selection and patron–client relations in the USSR and Yugoslavia* (London, 1983).

8 For a summary of the general characteristics of patron–client relationships, see S.N. Eisenstadt and L. Roniger, *Patrons, clients and friends: interpersonal relationships and the structure of trust in society* (Cambridge, 1984), pp. 48–9.

9 E. Gellner, 'Patrons and clients', in E. Gellner and J. Waterbury, eds *Patrons and clients in Mediterranean Societies* (London, 1977), p. 4.

10 G. Hosking, *Russia: people and empire*, pp. 68–74 and part 4, ch. 2.

11 G. Hosking, *History of the Soviet Union*, 3rd edn (London, 1992), p. 101.

12 See, for example, A. Inkeles and R. Bauer, *The Soviet citizen: daily life in a totalitarian society* (New York, 1968), pp. 233–42: the surveys reported here were carried out among émigrés, whom one would expect to be less favourable than average towards the Soviet system.

13 G. Hosking, *Russia: people and empire*, pp. 374–6.

14 See M. von Hagen, *Soldiers in the proletarian dictatorship: the Red Army and the Soviet socialist state, 1917–1930* (Ithaca, NY, 1990), especially pp. 288–325.

15 K. Simonov, 'Glazami cheloveka moego pokoleniia: razmyshleniia o I.V. Staline', *Znamia*, no. 3 (1988), p. 18.

16 E.S. Seniavskaia, *1941–1945 – Frontovoe Pokolenie: istoriko-psikhologicheskoe issledovanie*, (Moscow, 1995), pp. 71–93.

17 Seniavskaia, *1941–1945*, pp. 165–6; quote from 'Kakaia zhe ona, pravda o voine?' *Pravda*, 20 June 1991; *gosudarstvennost'* might be translated here both in the sense of 'state structure' and 'great power'.

18 Seniavskaia, *1941–1945*, pp. 161–8; E.Iu. Zubkova, *Obshchestvo i reformy, 1945–1964* (Moscow, 1993), ch. 1.

19 B. Comrie, G. Stone and M. Polinsky, *The Russian language in the twentieth century*, 2nd, revised edn (Oxford, 1996), especially pp. 1–10.

20 C. Lane, *Rites of rulers: ritual in industrial society – the Soviet case* (Cambridge, 1981); S. Fitzpatrick, *Stalin's peasants: resistance and survival in the Russian village after collectivization* (New York, 1994), pp. 204–14, 268–72; *Russkie: etno-sotsiologicheskie ocherki* (Moscow, 1992), pp. 312–35.

21 R. Stites, *Russian popular culture: entertainment and society since 1900* (Cambridge, 1992); G. Stanton Smith, *Songs to seven strings: Russian guitar poetry and Soviet 'mass song'*, (Bloomington, IN, 1984); on the socially eclectic nature of socialist realist literature, the forthcoming doctoral thesis by S. Lovell, 'The Russian reading revolution: society and the printed word, 1986–1995', University of London, 1998, will be informative.

22 Hosking, *History of the Soviet Union*, ch. 14.

23 K. Parthé, *Russian village prose: the radiant past* (Princeton, NJ, 1992).

24 A.J. Motyl, *Will the Non-Russians rebel? State, ethnicity and stability in the USSR* (Ithaca, NY, 1987).

25 Tishkov, *Ethnicity, nationalism and conflict*, pp. 44–5.

Index